The Future of EMU

The Future of EMU

Edited by

Leila Simona Talani

First published 2009 by
PALGRAVE MACMILLAN

Palgrave Macmillan in the UK is an imprint of Macmillan Publishers
Limited, registered in England, company number 785998, of Houndmills,
Basingstoke, Hampshire RG21 6XS.

Palgrave Macmillan in the US is a division of St Martin's Press LLC,
175 Fifth Avenue, New York, NY 10010.

Palgrave Macmillan is the global academic imprint of the above
companies and has companies and representatives throughout the world.

Palgrave® and Macmillan® are registered trademarks in the
United States, the United Kingdom, Europe and other countries.

ISBN-13: 978–0–230–21841–3   hardback
ISBN-10: 0–230–21841–5   hardback

This book is printed on paper suitable for recycling and made from
fully managed and sustained forest sources. Logging, pulping and
manufacturing processes are expected to conform to the
environmental regulations of the country of origin.

A catalogue record for this book is available from the British Library.

Library of Congress Cataloging-in-Publication Data
The future of EMU / edited by Leila Simona Talani.
      p. cm.
Includes bibliographical references and index.
ISBN 978-0-230-21841-3
1. Economic and Monetary Union.   2. European Union.   3. Euro area.
4. Monetary unions—Europe.   5. Europe—Economic integration. I.
Talani, Leila Simona.
  HC241.F88 2009
  332.4'94—dc22   2008039179

10   9   8   7   6   5   4   3   2   1
18 17 16 15 14 13 12 11 10 09

Printed and bound in Great Britain by
CPI Antony Rowe, Chippenham and Eastbourne

Al piccolo Gabriellino

Contents

List of Figures

List of Tables

List of Contributors

Michael Artis is Director of the Manchester Regional Economics Centre, Institute for Political and Economic Governance, University of Manchester, UK

Stefan Collignon is Professor of Political Economy at Sant'Anna School of Advanced Studies, Pisa and Chairman of the Scientific Committee of the Centro Europa Ricerche (CER), Rome

Paul De Grauwe is Professor of International Monetary Economics at the Katholieke Universiteit Leuven, Faculty of Economics and Applied Economics and Research Fellow at the Centre for Economic Policy Research, London

Giorgio Fazio is Assistant Professor in Economics at the DSEAF, University of Palermo

Erik Jones is Resident Professor of European Studies at the Johns Hopkins Bologna Center

Leila Simona Talani is Assistant Professor in Political Sciences, University of Bath and Research Associate at the London School of Economics

Francisco Torres is Professor and Head of Research at IEE, Catholic University, Lisbon. He also co-ordinates the European Studies programme of the Portuguese National Institute for Public Administration

Antimo Verde is Professor of International Economics at the Università degli Studi della Tuscia, Viterbo

Preface

This book is the outcome of a workshop on the future of EMU, organized by the editor at the London School of Economics on 12 October 2007 and financed by the British Academy.

The book represents a unique opportunity to gather the opinions of the most established experts on EMU from different academic disciplines and from different academic traditions debating over the future of the major economic endeavour of the process of European integration. Leading economists are confronted with leading political scientists in an effort to produce an overarching view of the future of EMU and to propose solutions to the problems they envisage. The book therefore provides an interdisciplinary discussion on a subject whose importance can hardly be overestimated.

Although the book is based on the original contributions of the scholars who participated in the workshop, the idea is to stimulate discussion about the future of EMU from a policy-oriented as well as an interdisciplinary perspective. To this aim the book will try to assess the impact of EMU on various EU policy areas, from the future of trade policy to the integration of business cycles, and from the impact of EMU on fiscal policy and political union to its impact on the labour markets.

The structure of the book as well as the content of the chapters reflects this objective, and this serves also a didactic purpose. Indeed, although based on original research, the book may easily be used as a well-informed handbook on the consequences of the establishment and working of EMU for the different EU policy integration areas, as well as on the future of the EU process as a whole.

The editor wishes to thank the British Academy for funding the workshop 'The future of EMU', which took place at the European Institute of the London School of Economics on 12 October 2007.

Introduction

Leila Simona Talani

No topic in European integration theory has raised so many questions and provoked such a flourishing academic and intellectual debate as the one concerning European monetary integration. The establishment of a European currency union with the adoption of the euro as the single currency for millions of EU citizens is arguably the single most important accomplishment of the European Union. The European Monetary Union (EMU) has massive economic, political and social consequences for the European and international political economy.

This book does not attempt a comprehensive historical account of the process leading to EMU, of its institutional setting and organization, its economic characteristics and socio-political implications. The aim of this book is more modest, although theoretically challenging. It seeks to identify the underlying factors that made it possible to agree on such a complicated and controversial matter, to explain why EMU occurred within a particular time and institutional frame, and to identify the winners and losers that resulted from EMU with an eye to distributional politics and socio-economic interest groups. Above all the book will try to assess the future of EMU in the context of the process of European integration. The main question the book seeks to answer is whether EMU can lead to the creation of the European supranational community or will produce the disruption of the EU project.

Only recently have scholars tended to focus on the disruptive potential of EMU, especially in the lack of political union. However, no existing contribution addresses directly the issue of the future of EMU by analysing its impact on a variety of EU policies. Some authors focus mainly on the consequences of the lack of political union for the legitimacy of the EMU and EU integration project. De Grauwe (2006), for example, highlights the importance of a political union to reduce the impact of asymmetric shocks on the public's assessment of EMU. From this point of view the credibility of the member states' commitments to EMU is higher the closer EMU is to an optimal currency area (OCA). OCA theory says that if the benefits of the monetary union exceed the costs, member countries have no incentive to leave the union. They form an optimal currency area. Or put differently, they are in a Nash equilibrium, and the monetary union is sustainable. Political union and the adoption of a common fiscal policy increase the benefits of a currency union. Moreover, by increasing fiscal support to countries in a business cycle downturn, a single budgetary policy could ease the support for EMU and facilitate the legitimacy and implementation of structural reforms. These are necessary as flexibility is another essential dimension of an OCA. In the absence of political and fiscal union, De Grauwe suggests that the credibility of the member states' commitment to EMU is reduced and the chances are that the project will collapse, producing a disruptive impact on the whole European integration process.

Another group of scholars has focused on how structural reforms have already produced a number of political struggles which have been considered in the literature as a natural consequence of the lack of legitimacy of the EMU project and as having potential disruptive consequences for the desire of the member states to keep adhering to a currency union.

For example, David McKay (2002) addresses the issue of the impact of EMU and the lack of fiscal co-ordination on the behaviour of domestic political actors. In particular, McKay identifies three dimensions of EU fiscal policy: fiscal federalism, fiscal co-ordination through the implementation of the Stability and Growth Pact (SGP) and fiscal harmonization. For each of these dimensions, the author makes hypotheses relating to the effects of fiscal policy on domestic politics. Leaving aside the questions relating to fiscal federalism and fiscal harmonization, which are outside the scope of this contribution, it is worth recalling the implications of the EMU and the SGP on the domestic structure. One obvious consequence, often emphasized in the literature (Crouch 2002; McKay 2002; Talani 2004), is that budgetary constraints would imply a reform of the domestic labour market structure, activating socio-economic domestic actors such as the trade unions and the employers' organizations. The rationale, in its simplified form, is that in the absence of other tools to react to asymmetric shocks, euro-zone member states would have to revert to labour market flexibility to solve their economic imbalances (Talani 2004). What is relevant for McKay, however, is what kind of effect the structural reforms brought about by the SGP will have on the electorate once it realizes that labour market practices and social benefits taken for granted are being removed as a consequence of the implementation of this particular form of EMU. While some political scientists address this issue in terms of legitimization crisis (Weale 1996; Verdun and Christensen 2000), McKay is interested in how single countries will react to these developments. From his point of view, reactions will be different in different countries, and may well produce, in times of recession, a breach of the fiscal rules adopted through the SGP. Indeed this prediction is in line with those of many economists, who have forecasted that the SGP will not hold in many circumstances (Eijffinger and de Haan 2000: 92–3). And indeed, this is exactly what happened with the crisis of the SGP in November 2003. What McKay failed to realize, however, is that this did not have any major effect on the euro, the European Central Bank (ECB) or the EMU project. His idea was that 'Unchallenged fiscal recidivism on the part of some members would damage the euro on the foreign exchanges, and, via imported inflation, might undermine the whole project' (McKay 2002: 84).

But this is precisely what did not happen. How might this be explained?

Crouch (2002) analysed how the socio-economic sectors have pursued their quest for competitiveness by first relying on the devaluation of the euro. In Crouch's opinion, however, the euro-devaluation strategy could not be sustained for very long, and would be substituted in the medium term by social pacts and labour market reforms which, in turn, would have to be supported by the social partners. Indeed, as Dyson points out (2002: 182), Shroeder, his economic adviser Klaus Gretshmann Eichel, economics minister Werner Muller and labour and social affairs minister Walter Riester all agreed that the way forward for Germany to improve its competitiveness was 'managed capitalism'. Managed capitalism revolved around co-operation, co-ordination in wage bargaining, dialogue with the social partners and consensus in managing supply-side reforms. Consensus was indeed the main principle of managed capitalism and was deeply entrenched in both the political and economic German systems (Dyson 2002). By the same token, France's recipe to combat the loss of competitiveness resulting from globalization implied a short-term reliance on devaluation and a medium-term consensus by the social partners on pension reform (Crouch 2002). It is true that, since Mitterand's decision in 1983 to keep the franc in the Exchange Rate Mechanism (ERM), the process of European monetary integration had been seen as a tool to reinforce domestic economic reform. However, particularly after German reunification, the constraints of EMU were increasingly blamed for the French economic crisis (Howarth 2002).

Indeed, the substantial decline of the euro in relation to the dollar and the yen suited French preferences. Throughout the 1990s the French government had argued that European currencies were overvalued in relation to the dollar (Howarth 2002). In both Germany and France, consensus over structural reform, given the impossibility of sustaining the short-term strategy of devaluation of the euro, would mean relaxing the adherence to the SGP's budgetary constraints.

Has this reduced the credibility of the EMU project and, therefore, jeopardized the future of EMU? This is a question which is still the subject of lively debate in the literature.

The originality of this book lies precisely in the fact that it addresses this question from an interdisciplinary perspective, summarizing the debate in a systematic way. The first three chapters of the book are explicitly devoted to answering the general question at the heart of the book: What is the future of EMU?

In Chapter 1 De Grauwe argues that the long-run success of the euro-zone depends on the continuing process of political unification. Such political unification is needed to reduce the scope for asymmetric shocks and to embed the euro-zone in a wider system of political ties that are needed to deal with the divergent economic movements within the euro-zone. In addition, political union is necessary to overcome the flaws in the governance of the euro-zone. The major flaw is that while national politicians continue to take political responsibility for unfavourable economic developments, key instruments to deal with these have been transferred to European institutions that bear no political responsibility for their decisions.

The absence of a 'deep' variable, that is to say a common sense of purpose in the European Union today, makes it unlikely that significant progress in political unification can be made. This will continue to make the euro-zone a fragile regime.

According to Jones in Chapter 2, the asymmetric constitution of European macroeconomic governance is evident and creates pathologies. Whereas monetary policy is in the hands of European institutions, fiscal policy remains firmly under the control of national authorities. This is not an optimal arrangement and some degree of fiscal policy co-ordination would be advisable.

However, quite apart from the fact that this is neither easy nor in the short-term interest of member states, according to Jones too much fiscal co-ordination is not a good idea. Indeed, the level of flexibility that is guaranteed by the current state of affairs could prove essential on many occasions.

Chapter 3, by Torres, re-addresses the rationale behind the building-up of EMU and looks at the issue of its sustainability in the long run. In doing so, it examines both the economic and the political/institutional dimensions and associated conditions (broader optimal currency area criteria).

Moreover, it attempts to use both dimensions in order to shed light on which political economy contributions (assumptions, hypotheses, predictions) have been more or less helpful in explaining EMU and on what we have learned from EMU. Looking back at the discussions about the need and/or desirability of EMU, one rarely sees an integrated approach in terms of both economic and political/institutional criteria. In general, the political desirability of EMU was taken as exogenous to its economic viability and European political integration has not been analysed in terms of its impact on the sustainability of EMU. This chapter tries to do exactly this by devising a framework of analysis where both economic and political preferences concur to determine a sustainable currency area (SCA).

In the following three chapters the question of the impact of EMU on the EU integration project is related to more specific policy dimensions. Chapter 4, by Artis, deals with business cycle integration in the euro-zone and asks whether the introduction of the euro has produced an Europeanization of the business cycle. It suggests that the European grouping is not a very distinctive one. 'Globalization' may be overwhelming 'Europeanization'. To demonstrate this Artis derives deviation cycles for OECD countries and examines their synchronization through cross-correlations and the application of clustering techniques.

Dividing the whole period (1970–2003) into three sub-samples allows an assessment of changes in business cycle affiliation over time. The UK, for example, appears to move from a US association to a European one. The chapter also reports the results of applying a non-parametric procedure to test for business cycle association.

In Chapter 5, Fazio assesses the impact of EMU on the Euro-Mediterranean integration process. In 1995 the Barcelona Conference identified greater trade integration as the means to promote 'peace and shared prosperity' and 'sustainable and balanced economic and social development' in the Euro-Mediterranean area. The establishment of a free trade area in the region by 2010 was considered by the Conference participants as a crucial step in this direction. Yet, the patterns of trade in the Euro-Mediterranean area have received little attention in the literature. The main objective of this chapter is to investigate the nature and the extent of trade integration between the countries that will form the free trade area and assess the impact of the introduction of the euro for trade in the region. In particular, the author uses a gravity model specification to identify the presence of potential trade blocs both between countries within the euro area and between euro countries and third-Mediterranean countries and monitor their evolution over time before and after the introduction of the common European currency.

In Chapter 6, Verde focuses on the impact of EMU on EU integration patterns and assesses whether it could lead to a multi-speed union model. Starting from the assessment of the inadequacy of the OCA theory to cope with the problems of a monetary union which is not a political one, the author devises an alternative conceptual scheme in order to identify the decision-making process urging member states either to join a monetary union or to leave it, focusing on their objectives and policies in reaching their decisions. At the same time, the model suggested borrows from the OCA theory the traditional criteria and effects of the single currency, capable of affecting policies effectiveness and macroeconomic results.

Then the model is used to simulate the event of a two-speed EMU. The results suggest that EU enlargement to 27 implies for the time being:

- higher economic as well as social costs;
- a lower level of economic welfare for the 'old' member states;
- a delay in the achievement of European political union because of the enlargement-related losses in terms of common purpose and ownership after the accession of the new Eastern European countries.

This paves the way for a two-speed union unless the old states close the gap between costs and benefits with their solidarity.

The last two chapters address the hot question of European competitiveness as affected by the adoption of a single currency. In Chapter 7 Talani studies, from a historical perspective, all the phases of the quest for competitiveness of the European member states and their leading socio-economic sectors. The chapter starts by evaluating the first phase in the quest for competitiveness represented by monetary policy and the ECB's exchange rate policy of 'benign neglect' vis-à-vis the devaluation of the exchange rate and the overshooting of monetary targets. In the second phase from 2002 onwards, given the unlikelihood that the ECB could reverse or even slow down the depreciation of the dollar, the imperative of competitiveness produced a new focus on structural reforms and the flexibility of the labour markets. The chapter highlights the relation between EMU, unemployment and structural reforms and their importance for the leading European socio-economic sectors. Finally this contribution stresses how the most powerful member states, namely Germany and France, sought to obtain a relaxation of the macroeconomic policy framework, much needed by their economic domestic actors, by loosening the grip of the SGP.

Chapter 8, by Collignon, asks why Europe is not becoming the most dynamic economy in the world. Due to collective action problems, the euro-zone is stuck in a sub-optimal macro-policy mix of too expansionary fiscal policy and too restrictive monetary policy. Although the Lisbon Strategy pays lip service to macroeconomic policy co-ordination, no mechanisms, institutions or effective rules have been established in order to overcome collective action problems. Empirically, this failure is demonstrated by comparing the euro-zone policy mix with the US policy mix and attributing it to the low investment performance which resulted in low average GDP growth and low average productivity growth – contrary to the aims of the Lisbon Strategy to make the EU the world's most dynamic economy.

The chapter also argues that in order to overcome these difficulties, a proper government for the European Union is needed. More delegation to the European level is only legitimate if European citizens can exert their democratic rights. This brings us back to the question of the future of EMU which, in turn, is the subject of the concluding remarks of this book.

References

Crouch, C. (2002), 'The Euro, and labour markets and wage policies', in K. Dyson (ed.), *European States and the Euro*, Oxford: Oxford University Press.

De Grauwe, P. (2006), 'What have we learnt about monetary integration since the Maastricht Treaty?' Paper prepared for the Special Issue of the *Journal of Common Market Studies*, 'The theory and practice of economic governance in EMU revisited: What have we learnt?', January, Guest Editor, Waltraud Schelkle.

Dyson, K. (2002), 'Germany and the Euro: redefining EMU, handling paradox and managing uncertainty and contingency', in K. Dyson (ed.), *European States and the Euro*, Oxford: Oxford University Press.

Eijffinger, S. and de Haan, J. (2000), *European Monetary and Fiscal Policy*, Oxford: Oxford University Press.

Howarth, D. (2002), 'The French state in the euro-zone: modernization and legitimizing dirigisme', in K. Dyson (ed.), *European States and the Euro*, Oxford: Oxford University Press.

McKay, D. (2002), 'The political economy of fiscal policy under monetary union', in K. Dyson (ed.), *European States and the Euro*, Oxford: Oxford University Press.

Rhodes, M. (2002), 'Why EMU is, or may be, good for European welfare states', in K. Dyson (ed.), *European States and the Euro*, Oxford: Oxford University Press.

Talani, L. (2004), *European Political Economy: Political Science Perspectives*, Aldershot: Ashgate.

Verdun, A. and Christensen, T. (2000), 'Policies, institutions and the euro: dilemmas of legitimacy', in C. Crouch (ed.), *After the Euro: Shaping Institutions for Governance in the Wake of European Monetary Union*, Oxford: Oxford University Press.

Weale, A. (1996), 'Democratic legitimacy and the constitution of Europe', in R. Bellamy, V. Bufacchi and D. Castoglione (eds), *Democracy and Constitutional Culture in the Union of Europe*, London: Lothian Foundation Press.

1
Some Thoughts on Monetary and Political Union

Paul De Grauwe[1]

1 Introduction

Recent political developments in Europe, in particular the rejection of the European Constitution in France and in the Netherlands in 2005, are leading to soul searching about the future of the European Union. There can be little doubt that these developments signal distrust towards further political integration in Europe.

The risk that the process towards political union will be halted or even reversed has triggered a new debate about the link between political and monetary union. Two schools of thought have emerged. According to one school monetary union cannot survive in the long run without a strong political union among the member states. This school of thought seems to have history on its side. Monetary unions that were not embedded in a strong political union have not survived.

According to the second school of thought the present degree of political unification reached in the EU is sufficient to guarantee the long-run survival of the monetary union. In this view, the euro-zone can survive even if the EU does not become a federal state like the United States of America.

The debate between these two views about the link between political and monetary union is made difficult by a lack of clarity about the meaning of political union. While a monetary union can easily be defined, that is to say it is a union between countries that use the same currency which is managed by one common central bank, such a neat definition is not easily found for the concept of political union. There are many dimensions and many gradations of political union. In contrast to monetary union, a political union is not a black and white affair that allows us to say when exactly the political union has been reached.

In this chapter we analyse the link between political and monetary union. We start by clarifying the concept of political union, and then we go on to analyse what kind of political union is necessary to sustain the monetary union in the long run.

2   The many dimensions of a political union

A political union has many dimensions.[2] Let us distinguish between an institutional and a functional dimension.

At the institutional level one can analyse the nature of the institutions that govern the union. There can be little doubt that the European Union has now developed a whole set of institutions to which the member states have delegated part of their national sovereignty. There is an executive branch consisting of the Commission and the Council. There is a legislative branch consisting of the Council and the European Parliament, and there is a judicial branch, the Court of Justice. Apart from the peculiar role of the Council as an institution with both a legislative and executive responsibility, the European Union has all the institutions of a modern democracy, capable of taking decisions that have a direct impact at the national level. In this sense there is already a significant degree of political union within the EU. The question we will have to discuss is whether the existing level of political union is sufficient to sustain the monetary union.

At the functional level one can ask the question about the areas in which the member states have transferred their sovereignty to the European institutions. Here we have a very diverse picture. In some areas, the transfer has been significant. In agriculture, competition policy and external trade policy there is a substantial transfer of sovereignty.

In other areas there has been very little transfer. The most prominent (economic and social) areas where the member states have maintained the whole or close to the whole of their sovereignty are taxation, social security and wage policies, to name the most obvious ones. There are other areas where the transfer of sovereignty has been very limited, for example defence and foreign policies (Alesina et al. 2001; Alesina and Spolaore 2003).

Thus it appears that the transfer of sovereignty has proceeded in a very unequal way in the European Union, some areas being characterized by almost complete transfer of sovereignty and others by only very limited transfers.

The question that arises is what areas are important for a monetary union. Do we need a transfer of sovereignty in all these areas so that the

European institutions become the embodiment of a true 'superstate', or can this transfer be selective? If the latter is the case, what principles should be followed to allocate responsibilities between the union and the member states? In order to answer these questions we turn to the theory of optimum currency areas.

3   The theory of optimum currency areas and political union

There is a fundamental difference between the monetary union of the US states and that of the European Monetary Union. The US federal government has a monopoly on the use of coercive power within the union, and will surely prevent any state from seceding from the monetary union. The contrast with the member states of the euro-zone is a very big one. There is no supranational institution in the EU that can prevent a member state of the euro-zone from seceding. Thus, for the euro-zone to survive the member states must continue to perceive their membership of the zone to be in their national interest. If that is no longer the case, the temptation to secede will exist and at some point this temptation will lead to secession.

The theory of optimum currency areas (OCAs) determines the conditions countries should satisfy to make a monetary union attractive, that is to say, to ensure that the benefits of the monetary union exceed its costs. This theory has been used most often to analyse whether countries should join a monetary union. It can also be used to study the conditions in which existing members of a monetary union will want to leave the union.

In its most general formulation the OCA theory says that if the benefits of the monetary union exceed the costs, member countries have no incentive to leave the union. They form an optimum currency area. Or put differently, they are in a Nash equilibrium, and the monetary union is sustainable.

The conditions that are needed to guarantee sustainability are well known from the literature on optimum currency areas (McKinnon 1963; Kenen 1969). They can be summarized by three concepts:

- Symmetry (of shocks)
- Flexibility
- Integration

Countries in a monetary union should experience macroeconomic shocks that are sufficiently symmetric with those experienced in the rest

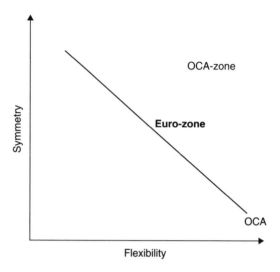

Figure 1.1   Symmetry and flexibility as OCA criteria

of the union (*symmetry*). These countries should have sufficient *flexibility* in the labour markets to be able to adjust to asymmetric shocks once they are in the union. Finally they should have a sufficient degree of trade *integration* with the members of the union so as to generate benefits from using the same currency. This theory is presented graphically in Figures 1.1 and 1.2.

Figure 1.1 presents the minimal combinations of *symmetry* and *flexibility* that are needed to form an optimum currency area by the downward sloping OCA-line. Points on the OCA-line define combinations of symmetry and flexibility for which the costs and the benefits of a monetary union just balance. It is negatively sloped because a declining degree of symmetry (which raises the costs) necessitates an increasing flexibility. To the right of the OCA-line the degree of flexibility is sufficiently large given the degree of symmetry to ensure that the benefits of the union exceed the costs. To the left of the OCA-line there is insufficient flexibility for any given level of symmetry.

Figure 1.2 presents the minimal combinations of *symmetry* and *integration* that are needed to form an optimum currency area. The OCA-line represents the combinations of symmetry and integration among groups of countries for which the cost and benefits of a monetary union just balance. It is downward sloping for the following reason. A decline in symmetry raises the costs of a monetary union. These costs are mainly

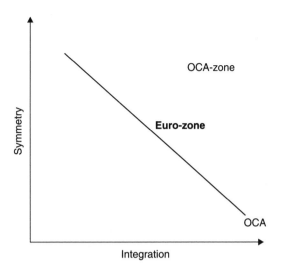

Figure 1.2 Symmetry and integration as OCA criteria

macroeconomic in nature. Integration is a source of benefits from a monetary union, that is to say the greater the degree of integration the more the member countries benefit from the efficiency gains of a monetary union. Thus, the additional (macroeconomic) costs produced by less symmetry can be compensated by the additional (microeconomic) benefits produced by more integration. Points to the right of the OCA-line represent groupings of countries for which the benefits of a monetary union exceed its costs.

We have put the present euro-zone within the OCA zone, but close to the border line, taking the view that the euro-zone may be an optimum currency area, without, however, being really sure of this. The euro-zone may also be on the left hand side of the OCA-line. This implies that we are not really sure whether it is sustainable in the long run. As a result, there may be scope for improving the sustainability of the euro-zone.

4   How does political integration affect the optimality of a monetary union?

We take the view that the degree of political integration affects the optimality of a monetary union in several ways. First, political union makes it possible to centralize a significant part of national budgets at the level of the union. This makes it possible to organize systems of automatic fiscal transfers that provide some insurance against asymmetric shocks. Thus when one member country is hit by a negative economic shock, the centralized union budget will automatically transfer income from the member states that experience good economic conditions to the member state experiencing a negative shock. As a result, this member state will perceive the adherence to the union to be less costly than in the absence of the fiscal transfer.

Second, a political union reduces the risk of asymmetric shocks that have a political origin. Let us give some examples relevant for the euro-zone. Today spending and taxation in the euro-zone remain in the hands of national governments and parliaments. As a result, unilateral decisions to lower (or to increase) tax rates create an asymmetric shock. Similarly, social security and wage policies are decided at the national level. Again this creates the scope for asymmetric shocks in the euro-zone, such as in the case of France when it decided alone to lower the working week to 35 hours. Or take the case of Germany which, by applying tough wage moderation since 1999, dramatically improved its competitive position within the euro-zone at the expense of other countries, for example Italy (see section 5 where we elaborate on this). From the preceding it follows that political unification reduces the scope for such asymmetric shocks.

One can represent the effect of political unification in two ways (see Figure 1.3). First, the existence of a centralized budget makes it possible to alleviate the plight of countries hit by a negative shock. Thus the cost of the union declines for any given level of asymmetry. This has the effect of shifting the OCA-lines downward in Figures 1.1 and 1.2.[3] Second, political union reduces the degree of asymmetry, thereby shifting the euro-zone upwards. As a result of these two shifts, political unification increases the long-term sustainability of monetary unions.[4]

From this brief survey of the OCA theory we conclude that in order to enhance the sustainability of a monetary union it is important to have a central budget that can be used as a redistributive device between the member states and also to have some form of co-ordination of those areas of national economic policies that can generate macroeconomic shocks. The reason why this co-ordination is important is that these macro-economic shocks spill over into the monetary union. For example, the decline in the working time in France was equivalent to a negative supply shock in France. This affected aggregate output in the euro-zone and thus the conduct of monetary policies by the ECB. This in turn influences all the other member states of the euro-zone.

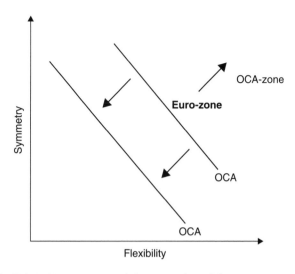

Figure 1.3 Political integration and the optimality of the euro-zone

A central budget is important as a redistributive device. It also matters as a stabilizing instrument (Musgrave 1959). The absence of a central budget in the euro-zone implies that no budgetary policy aimed at stabilizing the business cycle in the union is available. The question that arises here is how important this is. In Figure 1.4 we show the contrast between the US and the euro-zone since 1999. We observe that the US allowed its budget deficit to increase significantly as a response to the recession of 2001. There is no central budget in the euro-zone but the aggregate of the national budget balances could work in a similar stabilizing way. The evidence of Figure 1.4, however, shows that this aggregate did not respond to the worsening economic conditions in the euro-zone from 2002 on. Thus there is an absence of a system-wide budgetary policy in the euro-zone capable of performing a stabilizing role at the level of the euro-zone.

5 Asymmetric shocks and lack of political union

One of the surprises of the functioning of the euro-zone has been the extent to which the competitive positions of the euro-zone countries have diverged. We show the real effective exchange rates in the euro-zone (based on unit labour costs) since 1998 in Figure 1.5. The striking fact is the extent to which the relative unit labour costs have tended to diverge. As a result of these trends, some countries (Portugal, Netherlands, Spain

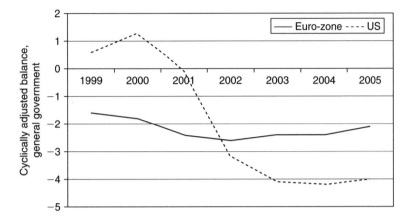

Figure 1.4   Cyclically adjusted budget balance in the euro-zone and the US
Source: European Commission.

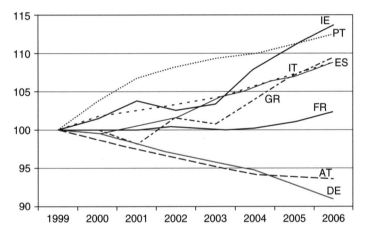

Figure 1.5   Intra-euro area real effective exchange rates (based on unit labour cost (ULC))
Source: European Commission (2004).

and Italy) have lost a significant amount of price and wage competitiveness. Others, like Germany and Austria, have gained a significant amount of price and wage competitiveness.[5]

There can be no doubt that part of these divergent developments in prices and wages are the result of divergent national wage policies. Since 1999, Germany has followed a tight policy of wage moderation. We show

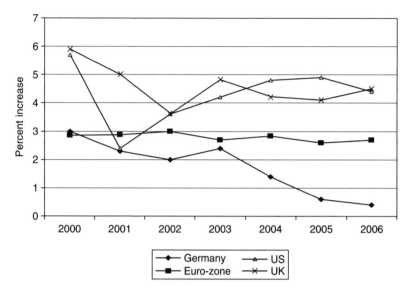

Figure 1.6 Nominal wage increases in %
Source: European Commission.

some evidence for this in Figure 1.6. This presents the yearly nominal wage increases in Germany and in the rest of the euro-zone (excluding Germany). We observe the strong decline of nominal wage increases in Germany. The rest of the euro-zone maintained more or less constant wage increases around 3 per cent per year. Thus, each year Germany tended to improve its competitive position vis-à-vis the rest of the euro-zone. The contrast between Germany on the one hand, and the UK and the US on the other, is even stronger. The latter allowed their wages to increase by 4 or 5 per cent per year.

This German policy of wage moderation has not been without consequences for the other euro-zone countries which have seen their competitive positions deteriorate thanks to these German wage policies. Thus the latter have worked as 'beggar-thy-neighbour' policies forcing other countries in turn to also institute drastic policies of wage moderation. In this sense the lack of political union is responsible for a co-ordination failure and the emergence of a major asymmetric shock that will have to be corrected.

The correction mechanism is likely to be painful. Other countries will be forced to intensify their policies of wage moderation, inducing the former again to restrict wage increases. All this is adding to deflationary tendencies characterized by low growth in consumption and investment and by increasing unemployment.

The divergent movements of competitive positions within the euro-zone are not only the result of German wage policies but also of the different speeds in the structural reform process in the member countries. The process of structural reforms (labour market reforms, liberalization of output markets) has remained a strictly national affair. Some countries, for example the Netherlands and Spain, have gone some way in deregulating employment protection systems, while other countries, for example France and Italy, have a long way to go. These divergent movements have much to do with differences in national political systems. They generate a potential for divergent movements in employment and output (asymmetric shocks) within the euro-zone which will necessitate adjustments in the future. As these are likely to be painful, they are bound to lead to tensions in a monetary union.

6 Criticism of the traditional OCA theory

The previous analysis is based on the traditional OCA theory that started with Mundell (1961). The theory is not without its critics. The most important one is probably Mundell himself. He formulated an alternative theory in his 1973 article 'Uncommon arguments for common currencies'. Let us call the Mundell of this alternative view on monetary unions Mundell II in contrast to Mundell I which laid the foundation of the traditional OCA theory.

There are two major insights in Mundell II that are important for our discussion here. First Mundell II argues that the provision of private insurance against asymmetric shocks is made easier inside a monetary union than outside it. In a monetary union risk premia associated with the existence of different currencies disappear. As a result, member countries of a monetary union that are hit by a negative shock will find it easier to borrow in the capital markets of the union and therefore it will be easier for them to smooth consumption. If these countries stay outside the union, the existence of a risk premium associated with the existence of a national currency creates an obstacle for them to borrow in outside financial markets.

A second insight provided by Mundell II is that the exchange rate cannot be seen as an instrument that can be used to stabilize the economy following an asymmetric shock. Quite often, the exchange rate becomes a source of asymmetric disturbances especially in a world of high capital mobility, which is often gripped by speculative dynamics. Thus, while in Mundell I the exchange rate is seen as an insurance policy to be used in the event of an asymmetric shock, in Mundell II holding such an insurance policy triggers speculative turmoil and macroeconomic volatility.

This criticism is quite important in the context of our discussion on political union. If financial markets in a monetary union provide for insurance against asymmetric shocks, the need to do this by political means, that is to say by integrating national budgets, becomes weaker. So does the need for a political union. In this view of the world, financial market integration substitutes for political integration.

In addition, if the exchange rate instrument cannot be relied upon to deal with asymmetric shocks, the cost of abandoning it is reduced, and so is the cost of joining a monetary union. This also has the effect of reducing the need for political union. Indeed, our argument for political union has been that it is a way to reduce the costs of a monetary union. As the latter are reduced, so is the need for political unification. Translated in the framework of Figure 1.3, the world of Mundell II is one where the OCA-line is close to the origin. As a result, the present euro-zone is likely to be safely embedded in a large OCA-zone.

So, it appears at first sight that in the Mundell II world monetary unions can be sustained more easily without having to take the difficult steps of political unification. This is quite a comfortable thought for the euro-zone member countries who find it difficult to move forward into a political union. It will therefore be no surprise that the Mundell II analysis has become the favoured official frame of thinking about the subject.

7   Comparing the two views

What should one think of these two strongly opposing views? At the outset it may be interesting to focus on the underlying economic paradigms of these two views.

Let us start with Mundell II. This view is very much embedded in what is now called the 'New Classical Synthesis' (NCS) which is a blend of monetarism and 'real business cycle' theory.[6] In the NCS view of the world, the central bank cannot do much to stabilize the economy. The sources of economic cycles are shocks in technology (supply-side shocks) and changes in preferences (unemployment being mainly the result of workers taking more leisure). There is very little the central bank can do about these movements. If it tries too hard to 'fine-tune' the economy it will end up with more inflation. Thus the best thing a central bank can do is to stabilize the price level. This will have the incidental effect of producing the best possible outcome in terms of stability of the economic cycle. In addition, a macroeconomic policy based on the objective of price stability is the best thing the central bank can do to promote growth. As Lucas has stressed, the central bank's contribution to economic growth by maintaining price stability is immensely more important than an ephemeral success in reducing business cycle movements.

It will come as no surprise that if one adheres to this view the present institutional setup in the euro-zone is the best of all possible worlds: a central bank that cares about price stability and in so doing makes the best possible contribution to maintaining macroeconomic stability and to fostering economic growth, and national governments that keep budgetary discipline and do their utmost to introduce market flexibility. In such a world the productivity-driven shocks can best be dealt with by governments keeping budgets in balance. Furthermore, in such a world the need to have an active budgetary policy at the euro-zone level does not exist.[7]

The theoretical underpinnings of Mundell I are very different and are deeply rooted in Keynesian and neo-Keynesian ideas. In this view, economies are characterized by many rigidities. As a result, macroeconomic shocks can lead a country into divergent paths. This is a world with multiple equilibria, some good, others bad. It is also a world where not all shocks in the economy originate from the supply side but where some find their origin in the demand side. 'Animal spirits', that is to say waves of optimism and pessimism, capture consumers and investors. These waves have a strong element of self-fulfilling prophecy. When pessimism prevails, consumers and investors alike hold back their spending, thereby reducing output and income, and validating their pessimism. Similarly, when optimism prevails, consumers and investors will spend a lot, thereby increasing output and income, and validating their optimism.

The corollary of this effect is the well-known savings paradox. When pessimism prevails and consumers attempt to save more, the ensuing decline in income will prevent them from increasing their savings ex post. These phenomena were analysed by Keynes long ago, and have been consigned to the archives of economic history. Yet these ideas remain powerful, and have important influences on the optimal design of the monetary union.

In the logic of these Keynesian ideas, a monetary union needs a central budgetary authority capable of offsetting the desire of consumers gripped by pessimism to increase their savings, by 'dis-saving' of the central government. In addition, to the extent that there are asymmetric developments in demand at the national level, the existence of an automatic redistributive mechanism through a centralized budget can be a powerful stabilizing force. Finally, in this view the responsibility of a central bank extends beyond price stability (even if this remains its primary objective). There are movements in demand that cannot be stabilized by only caring about price stability.

From the preceding analysis it appears that the present governance of the euro-zone has been devised based on the assumption that the world is one which fits the 'New Classical Synthesis'. If the latter theory is indeed the correct view of the world, there is little need to move on with political integration in the euro-zone, and the present political governance of the euro-zone is perfectly adapted to the world in which we live.

8   A preliminary evaluation

It is not easy to evaluate these radically different views. In this section I provide some preliminary observations. Let us start with the Mundell I view and its implications for the need of more political union. The central point here is that budgetary centralization is seen as a critical step to be taken to sustain the monetary union. The major weakness of this conclusion is that it underestimates the importance of moral hazard. The experience of many countries in which the government budget is centralized is that it creates large transfers in one direction, for example from the north to the south in Italy and Belgium, or from the west to the east in Germany. These transfers persist for decades. The main reason is that they give incentives to whole regions not to adjust to shocks.

In countries like Germany and Italy there is a 'deep variable', that is to say a strong national sense of common purpose and an intense feeling of belonging to the same nation,[8] that allows these transfers to persist without blowing the country apart. It is not clear whether this deep variable exists in Belgium. It seems quite clear to me that it does not exist at the EU level. As a result, a budgetary union that leads to similar one-way flows would not be sustainable and would create strong disintegrating pressures.

The Mundell II view also suffers from weaknesses. First, the view that, in the absence of a budgetary union, private financial markets can provide for insurance against asymmetric shocks is overly optimistic. True, there have been empirical studies for the US suggesting that this private insurance is of equal if not more importance than the public insurance provided by the federal budget. This conclusion, however, overlooks the fact that the insurance provided by the markets is only supplied to those who hold sufficiently high stocks of assets. Since wealth is much less equally distributed than income, this private provision of insurance will overwhelmingly favour the wealthy while keeping the poor relatively uninsured.

A second flaw of the Mundell II view, especially as it is embedded in the NCS paradigm, is that it brushes aside the possibility that countries get caught in a 'bad equilibrium' following a negative shock without adequate instruments to pull the economy out of such an equilibrium. That is when the exchange rate sometimes can be seen as an instrument of last resort allowing for a shock therapy that (together with other policy instruments) can pull the country into a better equilibrium. There are plenty of historical examples showing the power of such a shock therapy (Belgium and Denmark in 1982, Finland in the early 1990s, Argentina in 2002). The absence of such an instrument for member countries in a monetary union remains a major risk for the survival of such a union, in the absence of the deep variable we talked about earlier. This conclusion is reinforced by the fact that the absence of a political union continues to pull the member countries of the euro-zone in different directions.

9   The institutional weakness of the present euro-zone governance

The present institutional design of the euro-zone is weak. This weakness manifests itself both at the level of fiscal policies and at the level of monetary policies.

The Stability and Growth Pact (SGP) is seen as the cornerstone of the governance of fiscal policies in the euro-zone. As argued earlier, the proponents of this view see the SGP as the necessary fiscal framework providing long-run sustainability of national fiscal policies. In so doing, the SGP makes a stability-oriented monetary policy of the ECB possible while at the same time providing sufficient flexibility for national budgetary authorities to accommodate for asymmetric shocks.

The SGP, however, is built on a weak institutional foundation. The reason is the following. As argued earlier, spending and taxation are still very much the responsibility of national governments and parliaments. That is also the level at which democratic legitimacy is vested. As a result, these spending and taxation decisions are backed by an elaborate process that is deeply embedded in national democratic institutions.

The SGP now imposes top-down an extensive control and sanctioning system on the net effect (budget deficit) of this democratic decision-making process by institutions that are perceived to lack the same democratic legitimacy. Lawyers will undoubtedly object that the SGP is the result of a treaty that has been ratified by the same democratic institutions, the national parliaments, so that it has the same legitimacy as the national parliaments. This is undoubtedly true from a legal point of view. It is not from a political point of view.

When the Commission starts an excessive deficit procedure which aims at forcing national governments to cut spending and/or increase taxes, it bears no political responsibility for these decisions. In fact, the national governments do. When these follow up on the Commission's procedure and cut spending and raise taxes they are the ones who will be judged by their national electorates, and who face the threat of being punished by the voters at home. In contrast, the European Commission at no time faces the prospect of being voted away. Thus from a political point of view, the European Commission, which initiates the control and sanctioning procedure of the SGP, lacks democratic legitimacy, because there is no mechanism to make the Commission accountable before an electorate for its actions.

This lack of accountability of the Commission makes the SGP unsustainable. Each time a conflict arises between the Commission and the national governments, the former is bound to lose. This is what happened in November 2003 when France and Germany disregarded the SGP (Talani and Casey 2008). It will happen again when conflicts arise between the Commission and the national governments. Thus, it can be concluded that the SGP is a fragile institutional construction that is unlikely to lead to its objective.

This problem will continue to exist as long as the nation-states maintain their sovereignty over spending and taxation, and as long as those who decide about spending and taxation are made accountable for decisions before a national electorate.

A similar institutional weakness exists at the level of monetary policies. The Maastricht Treaty has defined the objectives of the ECB. The primary objective is price stability. The Treaty, however, adds that if price stability is not at risk, the ECB should pursue other objectives, in particular, sustaining economic activity.

The ECB has filled out the fine print of its mandate by essentially dropping the requirement that it should pursue objectives other than price stability. It has done so using the monetarist-real-business-cycle theory and claiming that by focusing on price stability it automatically guarantees that the other objectives mandated in the Treaty are fulfilled.

In addition, the ECB has given a practical content to the objective of price stability by defining this as a rate of inflation below (but close to) 2 per cent. Without asking permission, the ECB has absolved itself from any responsibility for unemployment. It has relegated this responsibility to the national governments. It has done this using the wisdom of an academic theory, the empirical evidence for which is still being debated. As a result the rest of society is not convinced and will not easily accept the attempt of the ECB to extricate itself from any responsibility for unemployment.

In addition, by relegating the responsibility of unemployment to the national governments it creates a political problem that is similar to the problem identified with the SGP. If national politicians have to bear the sole responsibility for unemployment, it is only natural that they will want to use all available instruments to fight it. The claim that all they have to do is to introduce 'structural reforms' (whatever that means) will not solve the problem because there is more to unemployment than the structural component. The lack of will by European institutions to use monetary and budgetary instruments to fight the cyclical component of unemployment will lead national politicians to the temptation to take back these instruments at the domestic level because these politicians will be made accountable before national electorates when they fail to lower unemployment. One cannot maintain a political system where national politicians are made fully responsible for unemployment while key instruments to deal with this problem have been taken away from them, and are held by those who do not want to be made accountable for this problem.

The conclusion is that either one gives those who are bearing the burden of political accountability for unemployment the full panoply of economic instruments, or one transfers at least part of the political accountability for this problem to European institutions, including the ECB.

10   Conclusion: the need for further political integration

In the preceding sections we have argued that there is a problem of governance in the euro-system. We identified three problems. First, important instruments of macroeconomic policy (monetary policy and the management of the government debt and deficits) have been transferred to European institutions. However, the political accountability for the results of the decisions taken in these fields is still vested with national governments. This creates a tension that is bound to be won by national governments.

Second, the euro-zone lacks a system of redistribution that will compensate those who are hit by a negative shock. These negative shocks, quite surprisingly, have remained large within the euro-zone. One cannot simply tell those countries faced by such a shock that they should solve the problem on their own. A redistributive system is essential to create an 'allegiance' to the union, which in turn is important to maintain its sustainability.

Finally, the fact that large areas of economic policies remain in the hands of national governments creates asymmetric shocks that undermine the sustainability of the monetary union. In particular, the use of uncoordinated national wage policies leads to divergent trends in the competitive positions of the member countries of the euro-zone. This in turn leads to a vicious circle in which each country tries to recover its competitive position by wage cuts, leading to a deflationary spiral. It is not only wage policies that have remained in the hands of national governments: all social policies together with the structural reform processes are national affairs. These create a potential for structural divergences between member states leading to diverging trends in output and employment.

These three problems call for further steps towards political union. Without a political union the euro-zone is at risk. The previous analysis allows us to describe how such a political union should look.

A first element of such a political union is a certain degree of budgetary union, giving some discretionary power to spend and to tax to a European executive, backed by full democratic accountability of those who are given the authority to do so. This will allow setting up an insurance system against asymmetric shocks in the euro-zone. This can take many forms, and several proposals have already been made (Mélitz and Vori 1993; Von Hagen and Hammond 1995). The transfer of budgetary power does not have to be spectacular as was shown by those authors. In fact we have argued that it should not be too large. Large centralized budgets create large problems of moral hazard that in the end undermine the sustainability of the union. Nevertheless, it will require a European budget that increases significantly relative to its present level of about 1 per cent of GDP.

Second, an increased institutionalized co-ordination of a number of economic policy instruments that have macroeconomic consequences will be necessary. We have mentioned social policies (including structural reform policies) and wage formation. The need to co-ordinate does not imply that these areas should be fully centralized. Rather it means that spill-over effects of decisions in these areas into the monetary union should be internalized. Thus, decisions like cutting the working week in France, which have obvious implications for the euro-zone as a whole, should be a matter of common concern, and should not be allowed to be decided by individual countries without consultation with others. Similarly, national wage policies will have to be co-ordinated in order to avoid asymmetric developments in competitive positions of the member countries.

Third, accountability of the European institutions that today take major decisions at the macroeconomic level will have to be improved significantly. This includes the ECB, an institution that singularly has managed to escape any serious degree of accountability. Improving accountability of the ECB also implies that the definition of the objectives of monetary policy should not be left to the sole judgement of the ECB, as it is today. The definition of the objectives of the central bank belongs to the political sphere. It is not just a technical problem that the ECB alone should decide. It also follows that the independence of the ECB should be restricted to instrument independence, in much the same way as this is done today in major countries in the world, such as the UK, the US and other industrialized countries. This means that once the objectives have been defined by accountable politicians, the central bank should be left free to pursue a policy that leads to these objectives.

We have no illusions, however, about the feasibility of significant steps towards a political union. The 'deep variable' that is necessary to maintain social and political cohesion is absent at the European level. It is this absence that makes progress towards political union so difficult in Europe. The lack of a deep variable also explains why Europe started with monetary union. The latter can be considered to be the easy part on the road to political union. But at the same time it puts the whole process at risk. Without a sense of common purpose it is very doubtful that further progress towards political union will be made. And as we have argued, without these steps towards political union the monetary union will remain a fragile construction.

Notes

1. Previous versions of this chapter were presented during seminars at Sciences Po, Paris, at the London School of Economics, at the Universities of Genoa, Macerata and Siena, at the European University Institute, Florence and at CESifo, Munich. I am grateful to Helge Berger, Elisabetta Croci Angelini, Francesco Farina, Marc Flandreau, Franco Praussello, Francesco Saraceno, Waltraud Schelkle, An Sibert, Cezary Wójcik, Patrizio Tirelli and Frédéric Zumer for comments and criticism.

2. It is not the intention here to develop a fully-fledged theory of political unions. We only want to highlight those features that are important for the debate about the link between political and monetary union. For a profound analysis, see the well-known textbook of Wallace and Wallace (2000).
3. It is important that these transfers be reversible to maintain their insurance character. If these transfers attain a permanent one-way character they are likely to become unpopular in the 'donator' country, leading to a perception of a high cost of the monetary union. This calls for the use of transfers only to alleviate the effects of temporary asymmetric shocks (business cycle movements) or, in the case of permanent asymmetric shocks, to make these transfers temporary, allowing receiving countries to spread the adjustment cost over a longer time.
4. A similar analysis can be done using the symmetry-integration space of Figure 1.2.
5. It could be argued that these trends may also be the result of different initial levels of per capita income so that they reflect a catch-up process (Balassa-Samuelson effect). Since the real effective exchange rates shown here are based on unit labour costs they take into account differences in productivity growth.
6. I am lumping together monetarist and business cycle theories. This does not mean that they may not be very different in some respects. For example, monetarists recognize that monetary policies can be important sources of business cycle developments, while real business cycle theorists tend to dismiss this view.
7. It will also not come as a surprise to those who have studied economic history that these were also the views that prevailed prior to the Great Depression.
8. See Baldwin and Wyplosz (2006) on this issue.

References

Alesina, A., Angeloni, I. and Etro, F. (2001), *The Political Economy of Unions*, NBER Working Paper, Cambridge, MA.

Alesina, A. and Spolaore, E. (2003), *The Size of Nations*, Cambridge, MA: MIT Press.

Baldwin, R. and Wyplosz, C. (2006), *The Economics of European Integration*, 2nd edition, Maidenhead: McGraw-Hill

European Commission (2004), *EMU after Five Years*, European Economy, Special Report 1/2004.

Kenen, P. B. (1969), 'The optimum currency area: an eclectic view', in R. Mundell and A. Swoboda (eds), *Monetary Problems of the International Economy*, Chicago: University of Chicago Press.

McKinnon, R. (1963), 'Optimum currency areas', *American Economic Review*, 52: 712–25.

Mélitz, J. and Vori, S. (1993), 'National insurance against unevenly distributed shocks in a European monetary union', *Recherches Economiques de Louvain*, 59: 1–2.

Mundell, R. (1961), 'A theory of optimum currency areas', *American Economic Review*, 51: 657–65.

Mundell, R. (1973), 'Uncommon arguments for common currencies', in H. Johnson and A. Swoboda (eds.), *The Economics of Common Currencies*, London: Allen & Unwin, pp. 114–32.

Musgrave, R. (1959), *The Theory of Public Finance*, New York: McGraw-Hill.

Talani, L. S. and Casey, B. (2008), *Between Growth and Stability: the Demise and Reform of the Stability and Growth Pact*, Cheltenham: Edward Elgar.

Von Hagen, J. (1996), *Währungsunion, Fiskalunion, Politische Union*, mimeo, Universität Mannheim, May.

Von Hagen, J. and Hammond, G. (1995), 'Regional insurance against asymmetric shocks', CEPR Discussion Paper, no. 1170.

Wallace, H. and Wallace, W. (2000), *Policy-Making in the European Union*, Oxford: Oxford University Press.

2
European Fiscal Policy Co-ordination and the Persistent Myth of Stabilization

Erik Jones

1 Introduction

The asymmetric constitution of European macroeconomic governance is well known. Monetary policy is made at the European level, while fiscal policy remains the purview of the member states. The pathologies this creates are also well known. Macroeconomic policy is uncoordinated at the European level and fiscal policy is uncoordinated across the member states. The result is almost universally regarded as sub-optimal (Tsoukalis 2005: 161). Better co-ordination of monetary and fiscal policy at the European level could improve aggregate demand management for those countries that have adopted the euro taken as a group (the euro-zone). Better co-ordination of national fiscal policies could also enhance predictability (and reduce negative externalities) in a context of high interdependence and so improve national achievement of national objectives with national fiscal instruments. Alas, the prospects for better co-ordination are slim.

The prospects for a first-best alternative – the creation of common European fiscal institutions – are even slimmer. Despite repeated calls (particularly in France) for the creation of a fiscal counterpart to the European Central Bank (ECB), the willingness of the member states to transfer significant tax authority to the European Union is virtually non-existent. Even more modest proposals to create thin fiscal institutions designed to stabilize income performance across member states have little support (Tsoukalis 2005: 155). Moreover, the stakes are high. As De Grauwe (2006: 728) explains: 'It is difficult to conceive how a union can be politically sustainable if each time a country of the union gets into trouble because of asymmetric developments, it is told by the other members that it is entirely its own fault and that it should not count on any help. Such a union will not last.'

Of course, this two-paragraph summary of the conventional wisdom hinges on the phrase: almost universally regarded. There are policy-makers and economists who do not support such a grim view of European macroeconomic governance. Most of them live and work in Brussels and Frankfurt. That geographic location is a disadvantage, if only because it suggests a strong, institutional self-interest in perpetuating (or at least justifying) the status quo. Attempts to unite these voices in a 'Brussels-Frankfurt consensus' in loose parallel with the old 'Washington consensus' only make matters worse (De Grauwe 2006: 724–7; Tamborini 2006). There is nothing more disconcerting than the threat of ideological condominium.

Institutional and ideological influences are not as important as they might seem at first glance. Seen from Bologna, there are good reasons to doubt the mainstream critique of European macroeconomic governance. Probably the most important is the bias in the conventional wisdom against diversity, asymmetry, inequality and difference. A close second is the weak scrutiny of realistic alternatives. It may be possible to make macroeconomic governance better in Europe, but the reverse is also true. We should be sure that what we have is broken before we try to fix it.

The purpose of this chapter is to present an alternative view. It is not a comprehensive argument. Rather it is a piecemeal attack on three of the building blocks in the conventional wisdom. Specifically, I am interested in examining the relationship between stabilization and adjustment; the prospects for fiscal stabilization; and the idea of international fiscal stabilization – by which I mean the timely transfer of fiscal resources to offset asymmetric economic performance across national economies within a common currency area like the euro-zone. My contention is that if we took a different view on these issues, we would find it hard to sustain the conventional wisdom and easy to see how suggestions for closer macroeconomic and fiscal policy co-ordination are likely to make matters worse.

2   Stabilization and adjustment

At its heart, the economic debate about national currencies, common currencies, and optimum currency areas hinges on the problem of shocks and adjustment. The trick is to make sure that unemployment levels do not rise (or endure) every time something bad happens and the national economy suffers from an adverse shock. This debate assumes that price (and wage) adjustments are neither smooth nor automatic. If prices and wages adjusted smoothly and automatically in response to economic

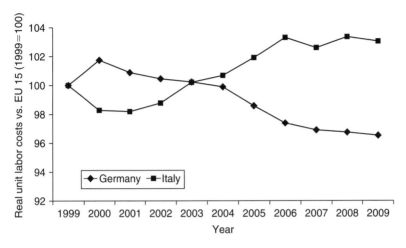

Figure 2.1   Italian and German competitiveness after 1999
Source: AMECO database, European Commission.

shocks, there would be little or no debate about optimum currency areas because there would be no connection between money and unemployment. As it is, prices do not adjust automatically or smoothly. Consider the case of Italy versus Germany. When Italy joined the single currency it had to adapt to German norms for price inflation. Failure to do so quickly would cause a shock, as Italy lost ground in terms of labour-cost competitiveness relative to other countries across the single currency as a form of irrevocably fixed exchange rates. The results can be seen in Figure 2.1, which shows the movement of Italian and German real unit labour costs relative to fifteen EU member states since 1999. Absent the possibility of changing relative prices by moving the exchange rate, Italian adjustments are more likely to take place in terms of quantities than in terms of prices – and the adjustments we are most concerned about are measured in terms of the quantity of labour, meaning increased unemployment. Small wonder, then, that some economists question whether the euro-zone may crack (Tilford 2006; Chapter 1, this volume).

National currencies and exchange rates enter into the debate about shocks and adjustment in two ways: through relative prices; and through macroeconomic policy instruments. The relative price mechanism is the easiest to explain. If, for example, foreign demand declines for a country's major exports, then a depreciation of the currency could stimulate foreign demand and switch domestic spending by changing the relative price of foreign and domestic goods. In other words, the flexibility of exchange rates can replace the rigidity of domestic prices (Chapter 7). The role of macroeconomic policy flexibility is a bit more complicated. If foreign demand declines for a country's major exports, then a timely reduction in domestic interest rates could stimulate investment and consumption to compensate for the decline in output. The problem is that such a monetary policy change is not possible under conditions of fixed exchange rates and international capital mobility. Any reduction in relative nominal interest rates will spark capital movements out of the country to take advantage of higher yields elsewhere, drawing down the foreign exchange reserves of the central bank and ultimately (if not immediately) bringing down the exchange rate peg as well. In a fully-fledged monetary union there is no recourse to national monetary policy at all – because interest rates are set at union level. Either way, domestic monetary autonomy and the demand stabilization that it promises are lost as a result.

These features of national currencies – relative price flexibility and macroeconomic policy autonomy – are well known and often described in the literature. The assumptions that underpin them are less prominent. For example, commitment to flexible exchange rates rests on four assumptions:

1. exchange rate determination takes place in the goods market;
2. aggregate trade and industry data reflect conditions for individual firms and markets;
3. bilateral exchange rates move independently;
4. the exchange rate policy choices of other countries are the same as those taken at home.

If exchange rate determination does not take place in the goods market, then exchange rate changes will not move mechanically to mitigate exogenous shocks like a fall in foreign demand. Export demand will fall, but the exchange rate will not depreciate as a result. This is likely to be the case when international capital flows are more important in the balance of payments than international trade flows – as they are today. That explains why countries experience prolonged deviations from balance on their current accounts. And while it may be true that such current account imbalances have to be rectified in the long run, that truism tells us very little about the usefulness of exchange rates in preventing unnecessary unemployment when an adverse shock takes place (Tavlas 1993: 678–9). Hence it is not surprising that economics commentators in policy journals would suggest we need fewer national currencies (Steil 2007).

The assumption about aggregate data and individual firms and markets is a reference to the ecological fallacy. In the context of unemployment and exchange rates, there are many ways that this fallacy can be revealed. To begin with, the value structure of foreign trade may not reflect its employment content. This was the case for Ireland in the early 1990s (Kavanagh et al. 1998: 135). As demand increased for high-value Irish exports to the European continent, the Irish pound appreciated against the British pound and cut into the profitability of high-employment exports from Ireland to the UK. Given the strength of the Irish economy overall, this unemployment in traditional industries proved not to be a problem. Still the point is that exchange rate movements add to rather than mitigate the pressures for adjustment.

A second version of the ecological fallacy is that a given country's predominant exports are not predominant in all export markets and individual exporters are potentially market-specialized as well. Such firm and market specialization is characteristic of trade resulting from scale economies including manufacturing processes and product lines that are distributed across different foreign subsidiaries of the same national firm – a point that has been underscored by Gowa and Mansfield (2004: 779–81). The implication is that a general fall in demand for a particular export will have greater exchange rate implications with some trading partners than with others and that the beneficial effects of any resulting exchange rate movements could be firm-specific as well. Otmar Issing tells the story of his encounter with an Austrian machine tool manufacturer in the early 1990s who claimed he was ruined by Germany's tight monetary policy and Italy's subsequent exit from the exchange rate mechanism (ERM). Of course with the law of large numbers, such anecdotes tend to iron out. Nevertheless, the implication is that such ironing out takes place through movements in the labour market and it is precisely these movements that exchange rates are meant to mitigate if not to prevent.

The assumption about the independence of bilateral exchange rates is a modelling convention. Usually, economists model arguments about exchange rates in terms of two-country dyads: Country A and Country B or, to borrow from Robert Mundell (1973: 116), Capricorn and Cancer. When they generalize from these models, the assumption is that there is no link between any two dyadic pairs. In essence, the exchange rate between the British pound and the euro is independent of the exchange rate between the pound and the dollar. Of course this is obviously not the case. The pound/euro and the pound/dollar are connected via the euro/dollar exchange rate. Nevertheless modelling that

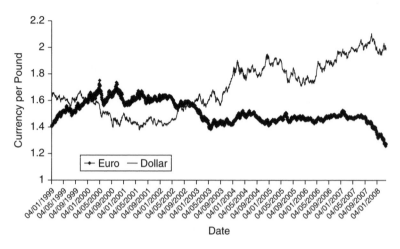

Figure 2.2   Pound exchange rates
Source: Dutch National Bank.

connection presents a significant complexity for the argument about exchange rate stabilization. If the euro/dollar exchange rate moves in response to an exogenous shock, then either the pound/dollar or the pound/euro exchange rate must change as well. Reference to trade-weighted or 'effective' exchange rates does not eliminate this problem. However much they move against either currency, pound exchange rates become the source of the exogenous shock for the British economy, not the response. Figure 2.2 shows how the pound has been whip-sawed by the euro–dollar relationship since the start of the single currency in 1999. These exchange rate movements are the cause of shocks in the British economy, not the response. On 17 May 2007, the *Financial Times* ran an editorial celebrating that exchange rates movements such as these had finally crushed traditional British manufacturing and ushered in a pre-dominantly service-sector economy. It is hard to believe (even if true) that they were not being ironic.

A tighter focus on exchange rate volatility as opposed to changes does not solve the problem of independence either. This point is worth dwelling on because a number of authors have tried to explain dyadic exchange rate volatility either as a function of optimum currency area indicators (Bayoumi and Eichengreen 1997, 1998) or as the 'cost' of monetary integration (Sadeh 2005, 2006a, 2006b). By putting exchange rate volatility – measured as the standard deviation of first-order log changes – on the left-hand side of the equation, they make a strong commitment to the assumption of dyadic exchange rate independence. This is possible, as Bayoumi and Eichengreen (1997: 764; 1998: 202) suggest, because: 'while it is true that changes in bilateral rates are not independent ... the standard deviations of these rates are independent as the covariances can differ across pairs of countries'. They may have a point. Nevertheless, from an algebraic perspective, it is hard to see how the standard deviations of dyadic pairs can be independent when the formula for the covariance of any one exchange rate dyad (euro/pound) can be written exclusively in terms of two others (euro/dollar; pound/dollar). From an empirical perspective, it is relatively easy to demonstrate that the standard deviations of first-order log changes are highly correlated from one set of national currency dyads to the next. Table 2.1 provides the cross correlation in volatility measures among those countries participating in the European Union's exchange rate mechanism (ERM) from 1991 to 1998. With the exception of Italy (and the partial exception of Finland), the correlations are all strong. Indeed, many are very close to 1.

Of course Bayoumi and Eichengreen are right to assert that the covariances can differ. The point is that they do not have to differ and there are good reasons why they would not differ. Where one market and one currency predominate in regional trading arrangements, we should expect any shocks to that market and that currency to propagate outward across the regional exchange rate system as a whole. Such propagation is even more likely when other countries peg their currency values on the regional core. This is why the ERM country dyads are highly correlated and it is where the fourth assumption that other countries' choice of exchange rate policy is the same as the home country comes into play. As Peter Kenen (1969: 53) stresses, it is no use telling the home country to opt for flexible exchange rates while other countries prefer to fix: 'How many times have we to remind our students – and ourselves as well – that an exchange rate is common to two countries, not the exclusive national property of one or the other?'

Further illustration of this problem of foreign country exchange rate preferences can be seen in the current debate about 'global imbalances'. The Chinese government intervenes in currency markets to stabilize the value of the yuan/renminbi against the dollar despite a widening trade surplus with the United States. Meanwhile, the dollar depreciates against the euro although trade relations between the United States and euro-zone economies are relatively close to balance. Another example could be Lithuania. When the Lithuanian government switched its currency peg from the dollar to the euro in February 2002, it switched its pattern of exchange rate volatility from the dollar to the euro as well. Finally, we

Table 2.1 Correlations and currency dyads, 1991–1998

	Dutch	Belgian	German	Greek	Spanish	French	Irish	Italian	Austrian	Portuguese	Finnish
Dutch Guilder	1.00										
Belgian Frank	0.98	1.00									
German Mark	1.00	0.97	1.00								
Greek Drachma	0.93	0.97	0.92	1.00							
Spanish Peseta	0.76	0.83	0.76	0.91	1.00						
French Franc	0.96	0.99	0.96	0.99	0.86	1.00					
Irish Pound	0.88	0.95	0.88	0.98	0.92	0.98	1.00				
Italian Lire	-0.54	-0.47	-0.55	-0.25	0.00	-0.45	-0.21	1.00			
Austrian Schilling	1.00	0.97	1.00	0.92	0.76	0.96	0.88	-0.55	1.00		
Portuguese Escudo	0.88	0.92	0.87	0.96	0.94	0.95	0.96	-0.15	0.87	1.00	
Finnish Maarkka	0.38	0.45	0.37	0.56	0.74	0.52	0.78	-0.03	0.37	0.64	1.00

Note: The dyads are correlated across month-to-month log changes.
Source: Own calculations using data from the Dutch National Bank.

Table 2.2 Day-to-day exchange rate variability, January 1999–October 2007

	Dollar	Euro
US Dollar		0.62
Japanese Yen	0.61	0.71
Bulgarian Lev	0.62	0.04
Polish Zloty	0.67	0.34
Romanian Leu	0.62	0.02
Slovak Koruna	0.62	0.00
Swedish Kroner	0.61	0.06
British Pound	0.37	0.38
Czech Koruna	0.45	0.43
Danish Kroner	0.73	0.43
Estonian Kroner	0.52	0.26
Cypriot Pound	0.69	0.62
Latvian Lat	0.65	0.71
Lithuanian Litas	0.69	0.30
Hungarian Forint	0.64	0.34
Maltese Pound	0.50	0.43
New Turkish Lira	1.56	1.58
Norwegian Kroner	0.64	0.36
Mexican Peso	0.70	0.61
South African Rand	0.64	0.22
Suriname Dollar	0.46	0.65
Dutch Antilles Gilder	0.68	0.63
Aruban Gilder	0.77	0.71
Russian New Ruble	0.00	0.62
Croatian Kuna	0.24	0.60
Swiss Franc	0.97	1.13
Canadian Dollar	0.51	0.77
Islandic Kroner	1.03	1.02
Correlation		**0.55**

Note: Variability is the standard deviation of day-to-day log changes.
Source: Own calculations using data from the Dutch National Bank.

can connect the two stories by looking at the relationship between dollar volatility and euro volatility. The Chinese decision to peg on the dollar has shifted the bulk of any exchange rate turbulence resulting from the US current account deficit onto the euro/dollar relationship. In turn this turbulence has spread outward onto third currencies whose governments choose to peg on either the euro or the dollar. Hence it is possible for country dyads to be correlated even outside of a formal system like the ERM. Table 2.2 provides data for the standard deviation in day-to-day log changes in third country exchange rates against both the euro and the dollar from January 1999 to October 2007. It also includes entries for

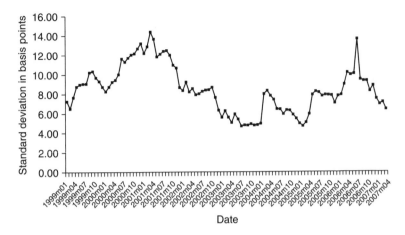

Figure 2.3   Cross-country variability in long-term nominal interest rates, original euro-zone 11 (excluding Greece)
Source: Eurostat.

the dollar against the euro and the euro against the dollar. Omitting the euro and dollar entries, the coefficient of correlation between the two columns is 0.55.

This brings us to the question of monetary policy autonomy. Here the focus of the debate is on the possibility that a common monetary policy will not be right for any given member state – or, as Henrik Enderlein puts it, the problem that the ECB provides a monetary policy for a country that does not exist. The debate hinges on two observations: one concerns nominal interest rate convergence and the other concerns inflation and therefore real-interest rate divergence. The basic picture can be seen in Figures 2.3 and 2.4. Figure 2.3 plots the standard deviation across national long-term nominal interest rates. Figure 2.4 gives the standard deviation across national inflation rates. The first point to note in comparing the figures is the relative magnitudes of y-axes. Measured in basis points, the standard deviation across inflation rates is approximately eight times greater than the standard deviation across long-term nominal interest rates. A second point is that while the two measures are correlated, the coefficient of correlation (0.51) is less than one. Changes in the dispersion of national inflation rates do not translate wholly into changes in the dispersion of national long-term interest rates. As a result, changes in national inflation rates promote changes in national measures for long-term real interest rates.

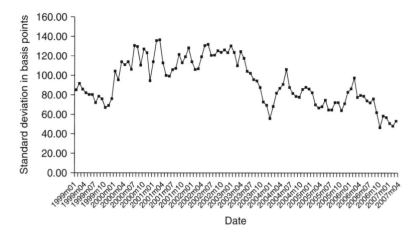

Figure 2.4 Cross-country variability in annualized HICP inflation rates, original euro-zone 11 (excluding Greece)
Source: Eurostat.

These data raise concern that the common monetary policy may have a strong pro-cyclical bias within the member states. Countries with relatively fast growth and high rates of inflation will face low real interest rates while countries with relatively slow growth and low rates of inflation will face high real interest rates. As a consequence, the common monetary policy will slow the pace of borrowing for investment and consumption where it is most needed and raise the pace of borrowing where it is not (Enderlein 2006: 114; Goodhart 2006: 772).

The assumption here is that borrowers and lenders perceive real interest rates differently. Lenders look at interest rates across the euro-zone as a whole. Hence their willingness to enter into national markets or national financial instruments does not depend upon inflation differentials and is instead only a function of relative liquidity and default risk. Because liquidity is high and default risk is low, at least in the sovereign debt market, nominal interest rate differentials across euro-zone countries are small. The widest range recorded in monthly data for long-term nominal interest rates across sovereign borrowers in the euro-zone between January 2001 and May 2006 was just 83 basis points, the tightest was 18, and the average range was 39. Since lenders who ignore national inflation rate differentials are implicitly using a common price deflator, these differences in nominal interest rates measure the difference in real interest rates as well.

This perception of real interest rates is not the same on the other side of credit markets – or so the assumption runs. People who borrow do not use a common measure of inflation to calculate real interest rates. Instead, they deflate nominal interest rates with national price indexes. Hence, for borrowers, the range of experience is much larger. Using the same monthly data, the greatest dispersion in national real interest rates ranged by 357 basis points, the tightest ranged by 223, and the average dispersion was 299 basis points (or roughly 3 per cent). These numbers are very large. Even so, they must be invisible to lenders otherwise it would be hard to explain why anyone would lend money in countries like Ireland (where real interest rates are often negative) instead of Germany or Austria (where they are strongly positive). Given the tightness of nominal interest rate differentials, it is clear that differences in real interest rates deflated by national price indexes do not matter to lenders.

The assumption that lenders and borrowers perceive different real interest rates is not as strange as it sounds. Banks and other financial institutions usually care more about the rate of intermediation – meaning the difference between borrowing costs and lending rates within a fixed risk category – than they care about price-deflated real interest rates per se. This explains why banks continue to lend even when nominal interest rates fall below the rate of inflation and national real interest rates are negative. Likewise it is obvious that firms and other domestic actors would take local inflation rates into account when making their investment decisions. What is less obvious is how domestic actors are using domestic inflation rates in their discounting.

To understand this point it is necessary to consider the microeconomic foundations for the influence of real interest rates on investment. The standard notion is that the real interest rate represents the cost of borrowing or the opportunity cost of forgoing a financial investment in order to purchase plant, equipment or other capital goods. But firms do not base their investment decisions solely on financial cost. Returns are important as well. Hence firms have to come up with business models within which the cost of investment and the cost of doing business are covered by future revenues. In these calculations, real interest rates are important only in terms of opportunity costs in comparing the rate of return from the business model with the alternative of the firm investing in financial instruments. The real or price-deflated cost of borrowing does not enter into business models themselves because the nominal cost of repayment is included along with the other costs of doing business as a whole.

This is where the micro-foundations of the investment function get tricky. For a domestic manufacturer, operating costs are local but revenues are earned both at home and abroad. Labour costs are doubly local because labour does not move (and so cannot be arbitraged) and because trade unions take local rates of inflation into account in wage bargaining. Hence, while local costs may differ significantly from one production site (and one member state) to the next, manufacturing prices can be arbitraged across the monetary union as a whole and so should be roughly the same. In this context, it is reasonable for firms in traded goods industries to use domestic inflation rates to anticipate the rise in local production costs – including, particularly, labour costs – and international inflation rates (in traded goods prices) to calculate future earnings.

The implication is that net nominal returns from a capital investment made in a high-inflation environment will be lower than net nominal returns from the same investment made in a low-inflation environment. This comparison of net nominal returns is important for firms choosing between making similar investments in different parts of the monetary union. Moreover, such firms are unlikely to use different price deflators for different countries because they will compare both possible investments to a single opportunity cost. Like other international lenders, they will calculate relative real returns using a price deflator that applies to the monetary union as a whole. Financial industries may be focused on the rate of intermediation, but both lenders and borrowers are seeing the same real interest rates.

There are two exceptions to this argument: service industries that are not traded internationally and the housing market. Exclusively domestic service industries would be right to focus on national price deflators for discounting both nominal interest rates and returns on investment. Even so, the contribution of such investments to gross fixed capital formation is relatively small and so the pro-cyclical influence of having a common monetary policy via this sector of the economy is small as well. In 2005, for example, gross investment in manufacturing across the EU-25 was five times greater than investment in construction and eight times greater than investment in hotels and restaurants (Eurostat). This is why economists spent little time worrying about local real interest rate differentials within national monetary unions before the single currency came about.

The housing market is a more important exception. First, outside the second-home market, housing is not subject to international arbitrage and so has to be discounted using local rates of inflation. Second, house price increases are often the major motivation behind making a housing investment. Put another way, home ownership is a form of savings (or deferred consumption). When house prices rise against a backdrop of fixed nominal interest rates, the build-up of pressure in the housing market can be intense. The temptation to refinance and use home equity for current consumption can be intense as well. In this sense it is true that the common monetary policy fuels housing booms where they have started and deepens housing busts where they have already set in. Of course these developments in housing costs strengthen the counter-cyclical pattern of firm investment sketched above by raising or lowering the pressure on wages, but that is small consolation to those who find themselves unable to get on the property ladder or caught in a negative equity trap.

The question is whether separate national currencies and national monetary authorities are really the first best solution to address the problem of house-price speculation. The evidence from the United States and Great Britain is not promising. And yet while the question is important, it is also different from the more general consideration of stabilization and adjustment in a monetary union. With respect to stabilization and adjustment, the situation within the single currency is not so different from the state of affairs before the euro was introduced. Before the euro, exchange rates did not insulate countries from shocks because exchange rates are not determined by the trade in goods and services, because firm-level exposure to foreign trade is not the same as national exposure, because exchange rate pairs are influenced by third currencies, and because many countries choose to fix exchange rates even outside the context of a monetary union. A more important change is the loss of autonomy over monetary policy. Even there, however, the effects are modest. Governments have lost some discretion in setting domestic interest rates. But those countries that joined the single currency gave up much of that monetary policy autonomy already when participating in the ERM. The irrevocable fixing of exchange rates eliminated the residual. Under the resulting common monetary policy, monetary conditions are not always the same across the member states and national central banks might opt for different conditions given the choice. Nevertheless, the influence of real interest rate differentials across countries is not as significant as some authors suggest.

3   Fiscal stabilization

National fiscal authorities shoulder the major burden for macroeconomic stabilization in Europe's single currency – just as they did before the single currency was introduced. When countries suffer from an adverse shock, national fiscal authorities must act to mitigate the impact on unemployment. The difference under monetary union is twofold. First, national fiscal authorities are constrained by the formal institutional commitments collected under the Stability and Growth Pact (SGP). Second, national fiscal authorities are empowered by the ease and low cost of sovereign borrowing and by the elimination of the balance of payments constraint.

The structure and influence of the SGP has received extensive coverage in the literature. The failure of the member states to abide by their commitments has received extensive coverage as well. At this point it is clear that the rules function only insofar as the member states agree to comply. This is bad news in terms of fiscal consolidation but it is good news for fiscal stabilization – at least in the short term. Those countries that suffered the worst of the recession of 2001–3 could at least benefit from fiscal stimulus. This can be seen in Figure 2.5, which shows output growth and deficit performance for the euro-zone as a whole. In aggregate terms, as growth declined, fiscal deficits increased. This pattern results from the automatic stabilization provided via taxes and transfers. When income falls, taxes fall as well and when unemployment rises transfers increase. This did not require a positive decision by policymakers to stimulate their economies but it did require a decision not to cut deficits pro-cyclically by restricting expenditure during the economic downturn. The results are better than critics of the SGP expected – more because of the advantages of already having undertaken a significant

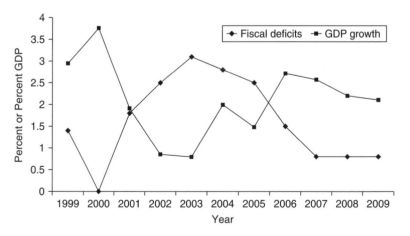

Figure 2.5   Deficits and growth in the euro-zone
Source: AMECO database, European Commission.

debt consolidation in order to join the monetary union than as a result of a repudiation of the Pact. Indeed, there was evidence that fiscal policy had become more effectively counter-cyclical even before the SGP broke down (Galí and Perotti 2003).

The empowering influence of the single currency is less well documented even if widely understood. By lowering borrowing costs across the euro-zone as a whole, and in traditionally high inflation countries in particular, the single currency also lowered the cost of debt service and so freed up fiscal resources for debt consolidation, new expenditure, or tax relief. This reduction in interest payments was very important for highly indebted countries such as Italy, which saw the ratio of debt service to gross domestic product (GDP) fall from 13.1 per cent in 1993 to 4.9 per cent in 2005. Although voices at the European Commission and in the European Central Bank have called for the whole of the windfall to be used for debt consolidation, most member states engaged in some combination of debt consolidation with higher spending and lower taxes.

The elimination of the balance of payments constraint is more striking. Absent the risk of currency crisis, the member states of the euro-zone are able to sustain important current account imbalances. This can be seen in Figure 2.6, which shows the unweighted standard deviation across member state current accounts as a percentage of GDP. The same figure also provides an unweighted average for current balances across the member states and an aggregate measure (or GDP-weighted average) for the euro-zone as a whole. While the average remains close to balance, the dispersion of member state performance has increased.

This increased variation in current account performance is due in part to the variation in fiscal policy across the member states – not all of which is in response to the requirements for aggregate demand stabilization (Jones 2003). On the contrary, as performance in GDP growth has converged across the member states, deficit to GDP ratios have not. This pattern is in contrast to the run-up to the single currency when deficit performance was more strongly convergent (Hallerberg 2004). Developments since the introduction of the euro can be seen in Figure 2.7, which shows the standard deviation in real GDP growth rates and deficit to GDP levels across member states. The convergence in real GDP growth can be seen also in terms of unemployment levels. This is shown in Figure 2.8, which also includes the weighted and unweighted average rates of unemployment across the euro-zone.

The point to note in looking across these figures is that those countries that have embraced the discipline of the Stability and Growth Pact are not those countries that have had an easy time in terms of either

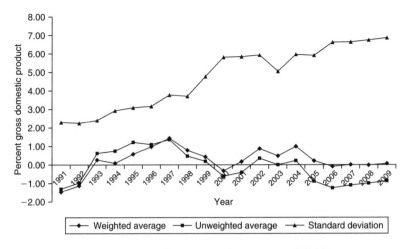

Figure 2.6 Current account performance in the euro-zone (EU-12)
Source: AMECO database, European Commission.

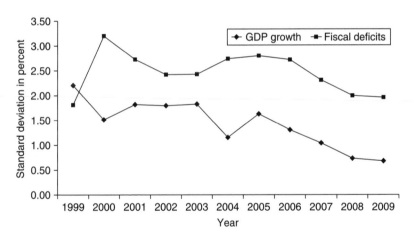

Figure 2.7 Cross-country variability in growth and deficits, euro-zone (EU-12)
Source: AMECO database, European Commission.

growth or employment. On the contrary, the divisions that emerged in the Council of Economics and Finance Ministers (ECOFIN Council) when the Pact was set aside in November 2003 pit small countries against large more obviously than strong performers against weak ones. Indeed, the staunchest proponent of enforcing the rules, the Netherlands, soon found itself in violation of the SGP (Jones 2004: 493–5).

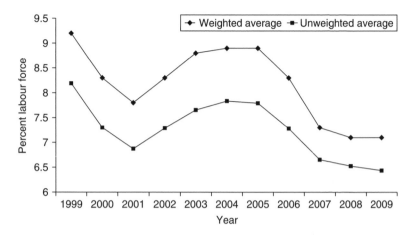

Figure 2.8   Unemployment in the euro-zone (EU-12)
Source: AMECO database, European Commission.

There are strong reasons for small countries to want to have clear guidelines for fiscal policy while larger countries would want to have greater discretion. Moreover, these reasons are not dissimilar to original arguments about the characteristics of an optimum currency area (McKinnon 1963). Small countries tend to be more open to trade than larger countries as a percentage of income. As a result the impact of fiscal stimulus on a small country economy tends to bleed out across import consumption onto foreign markets, offering few significant advantages to their larger neighbours for the high fiscal cost of achieving any demand stimulus at home. By contrast, large countries tend to be more closed, meaning that domestic fiscal stimulus is more effective at generating domestic fiscal activity. Large countries are also more important to the economies of small countries than small countries are to the economies of large ones. Hence domestic stimulus in large countries offers significant advantages for their smaller neighbours; a failure to stimulate the large-country economy during a time of recession offers a significant downside as well. This asymmetry in economic interdependence is very well known (Cooper 1968). Nevertheless, the implication that different countries should have different fiscal rules has never been accepted in the European Union. Instead, Europe's heads of state and government have insisted that everyone be bound by the same framework – and then ignored that framework when it obviously did not make sense.

The reform of the SGP adopted in March 2005 continued along these lines and eschewed any categorical differentiation between member states in the handling of the rules. To my knowledge, no one even raised the possibility that small countries and large countries should be given separate treatment. Instead, government representatives used large-country/small-country distinctions as an implicit critique of the status quo. Hence, while the Council of Ministers endorsed a wider range of conditions in defining exceptional circumstances, these have more to do with historical factors like German unification than the logic of economic interdependence per se (Jones 2006). The result has been to decrease the importance of the rules per se and to strengthen the notion of national ownership or fiscal responsibility.

The new SGP is more flexible and – if past behaviour is any guide to the future – the member states are willing to take advantage of that flexibility. The member states are also willing to take advantage of the low interest payments and light balance of payments constraint that the single currency has brought about. The fact remains, however, that national fiscal authorities are not equally able to stabilize their economies using fiscal policy alone. Monetary policy is not available and exchange rates are irrevocably fixed. Although these latter constraints are not as burdensome as many believe, that does not make them politically palatable. Hence there is strong incentive to imagine institutions that can share the burdens of fiscal stabilization automatically from one member state to the next.

4   International fiscal stabilization

The belief that common fiscal institutions can provide stabilization across geographic regions (and therefore across member states) dates back to early debates about economic interdependence and optimum currency areas. Peter Kenen (1969) introduced the possibility in a 1967 conference paper and it was quickly picked up in work by Cooper (1968: 19) and Fleming (1971: 478). By the end of the 1970s, the possibility of international fiscal stabilization even became part of the European Economic Community's plans to revitalize efforts at monetary integration in the 'Report of the study group on the role of public finance in European integration', also known as the McDougal report.

The argument for international fiscal stabilization is attractive because it follows the same pattern as the case for automatic fiscal stabilization within countries. When income falls, tax payments decline as well, thus absorbing some of the gross impact of the original shock. When unemployment rises, transfers also increase, thus cushioning the loss of income resulting from unemployment. The only difference between the international story and the national one is the pattern of income redistribution. In the national story, income is redistributed across time (through deficit spending) or across society (from haves to have nots). In the international story, income is redistributed across geographic space as well, with more prosperous regions implicitly transferring resources to less prosperous regions in response to the exogenous shock. Moreover, the scale of this stabilization is potentially significant – with recent estimates of the cushion provided by interregional stabilization within existing monetary union ranging from 10 to 30 per cent of the shock (Sala-i-Martin and Sachs 1992; Bayoumi and Masson 1995; Mélitz and Zumer 1998; Mélitz 2004).

The only real complication in the argument is that the interregional dimension of the transfers is largely unintended. Apart from a few specialized arrangements, like the German system for *Finanzausgleich* between regional or *Land* governments, most federal fiscal systems provide interregional stabilization because they choose to monopolize control over income taxation and to standardize patterns of income replacement. Moreover, once the size of interregional transfers becomes politically significant, the tendency is to reduce the level of interregional redistribution rather than to celebrate it. Hence, for example, the German federal government had to absorb much of the cost of *Finanzausgleich* during the process of German unification because the western *Länder* were reluctant to make further additional transfers to the East. In the United States, transfers in aid to state and local government are usually provided on a matching basis – which has the perverse effect of benefiting rich parts of the country rather than poor.

The advocates of international fiscal stabilization are well aware of this contrary political logic. As De Grauwe (2006: 722–3) explains:

> A warning note should be sounded here. When we argue that some form of budgetary centralization is necessary to allow for an insurance mechanism against asymmetric shocks, we should avoid the pitfalls of such mechanisms that have been observed within countries. These pitfalls have to do with moral hazard. We observe that this is often a serious problem when the transfers reduce the incentives of the receiving regions to adjust to shocks. As a result, temporary transfers can become chronic, thereby losing their insurance character. This feature will often lead to conflicts within the country (e.g. in Belgium) that are difficult to manage.

What they do not consider is that the standards for political significance are likely to change from one level of aggregation to the next. What passes for a reasonable level of redistribution in a close-knit society would not be tolerated in a larger group and would be actively opposed across different groups. The dilution of German *Finanzausgleich* illustrates this effect directly. It was not just the size of the transfers involved, but also the sense that the new *Länder* did not belong in the system.

There is an added problem. For any stabilization system to operate there has to be a progressive and continuous redistribution of resources through taxes and transfers. This can be designed along mutually accept-able principles where those who have support those who have not. However, the stabilization takes place in response to a shock. The mecha-nism does not operate through income levels but rather through income changes. Hence if a wealthy country were to suffer an exogenous shock, part of the income lost by the wealthiest members of that society would be absorbed by declining tax outlays and part of the income lost by less wealthy members who are pushed into unemployment would be replaced by transfer payments. In interregional terms, this cushion would be provided by the poorer countries that did not suffer from the shock. In the most recent recession, Spain and Greece would have transferred resources to France and Germany.

The problem with this situation is twofold. First, wealthy countries do not want to introduce progressive distributive mechanisms at the European level beyond those that already exist. Second, even if it were possible to introduce such mechanisms, the poorer member states would resent the implications should they actually work to stabilize the income of the wealthier member states in response to exogenous shocks. Both parties would prefer to accept the risk that if something bad happens, they are on their own. And, as it happens, that is what they have got.

5 Where do we go from here?

The status quo is not optimal, even if it is far from being as bad as many would like to believe. At the end of the analysis we are still left with the problem introduced at the start: the problem where countries like Italy join the single currency only to have their competitiveness inflate away as a result. If such countries can no longer rely on changes in the exchange rate to bail them out, so the reasoning runs, then they must either be subsidized or withdraw from the monetary union as a whole. The problem is one of perspective. Sure it is true that Italian competi-tiveness has worsened relative to Germany's since the start of monetary union – but perhaps that is less dramatic when viewed over the longer term. Indeed, we could tell a very different story if we started from a

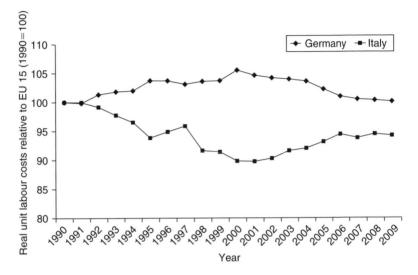

Figure 2.9   German and Italian competitiveness after 1990
Source: AMECO database, European Commission.

more unambiguous shock – like, for example, German unification. This can be seen in Figure 2.9, which repeats the data from Figure 2.1 using 1990 as the base year instead of 1999. In this figure, Italy only surrenders some of the gains that it made in the run-up to monetary union to a Germany that had grown grossly uncompetitive after unification. And here it is important to recall that as Italy has surrendered some of the advantage it held in the relative cost of labour, it has gained considerably on Germany in terms of the relative cost of capital. The situation is not optimal, but it is much better than many have feared. Moreover, the alternatives are worse. A return to fixed but adjustable exchange rates would not improve the prospects for stabilization via currency movements and it would impose a considerable cost in terms of interest rates and balance of payments concerns on fiscal policy-makers.

Monetary policy-makers would get back some room for manoeuvre in matching domestic interest rates to meet the needs of the non-traded service sector and the housing market, but only at the expense of higher borrowing costs across the economy as a whole. Policy response to exceptional circumstances would be marginally better, while normal conditions in the macroeconomy would be considerably worse.

The alternative of increasing the centralization of fiscal policy at the European level is equally unappealing. In order to prevent a political conflict that might arise if countries perceived themselves to be disadvantaged by the existence of the single currency and the conduct of the common monetary policy, we would be creating institutions that assign very transparent winners and losers across the member states. The cost of the European Union is already a push-button issue in the net-contributor countries when the total level of expenditure is around 1 per cent of income. By increasing that figure we may be able to make the process of stabilization marginally better, but normal political conditions would be considerably tenser.

The challenge in Europe is to get the right balance between unity and diversity, solidarity and independence. This is obvious (a cliché even) but it is also instructive. Fixed exchange rates help, not because of the political symbolism of a common currency but because exchange rates were not floating freely in any event and they were imparting too many different shocks on different parts of the European economy. The common monetary policy is only a partial success – particularly with respect to housing bubbles. But that suggests that member states should use transaction taxes and capital gains rules to cool domestic housing markets in response to the monetary integration shock. Finally, it is clear (or at least should be clear) that treating economic policy as a matter of common interest does not entail every member state doing everything in the same way. France and Germany are more important as markets for other European countries; Greece and Portugal are more important as potential sources of default risk. Fiscal policy co-ordination should take these factors into account and not the requirements for stabilization per se. European fiscal policy involves many different countries with different needs and implications. That is the reality. By contrast, the need to organize some sort of European fiscal stabilization in response to asymmetric shocks is a myth.

References

Bayoumi, T. and Eichengreen, B. (1997), 'Ever closer to heaven? An optimum-currency-area index for European countries', *European Economic Review*, 41: 761–70.

Bayoumi, T. and Eichengreen, B. (1998), 'Exchange rate volatility and intervention: implications of the theory of optimum currency areas', *Journal of International Economics*, 45: 191–209.

Bayoumi, T. and Masson, P. R. (1995), 'Fiscal flows in the United States and Canada: lessons for monetary union in Europe', *European Economic Review*, 39: 253–74.

Cooper, R. N. (1968), *The Economics of Interdependence: Economic Policy in the Atlantic Community*, New York: McGraw-Hill for the Council on Foreign Relations.

De Grauwe, P. (2006), 'Monetary integration since the Maastricht Treaty', *Journal of Common Market Studies*, 44(4) (November): 711–30.

Enderlein, H. (2006), 'Adjustment to EMU: the impact of supranational monetary policy on domestic fiscal and wage-setting institutions', *European Union Politics*, 7(1) (March): 113–40.

Fleming, J. M. (1971), 'On exchange rate unification', *Economic Journal*, 81(323) (September): 467–88.

Galí, J. and Perotti, R. (2003), 'Fiscal politics and monetary integration in Europe', in R. Baldwin, G. Bertola and P. Seabright (eds), *EMU: Assessing the Impact of the Euro*, Oxford: Blackwell, pp. 241–72.

Goodhart, C. A. E. (2006), 'The ECB and the conduct of monetary policy', *Journal of Common Market Studies*, 44(4) (November): 757–78.

Gowa, J. and Mansfield, E. D. (2004), 'Alliances, imperfect markets, and major-power trade', *International Organization*, 58: 775–805.

Hallerberg, M. (2004), *Domestic Budgets in a United Europe: Fiscal Governance from the End of the Bretton Woods System to EMU*, Ithaca and London: Cornell University Press.

Jones, E. (2003), 'Liberalized capital markets, state autonomy, and European Monetary Union', *European Journal of Political Research*, 42(2) (March): 111–36.

Jones, E. (2004), 'The politics of Europe 2003: differences and disagreements', *Industrial Relations Journal*, 35(6) (November): 483–99.

Jones, E. (2006), 'European macroeconomic governance', in Jeremy Richardson (ed.), *European Union Power and Policymaking*, 3rd edition, London: Routledge, pp. 329–49.

Kavanagh, E. et al. (1998), 'The political economy of EMU in Ireland', in E. Jones, J. Frieden and F. Torres (eds), *Joining Europe's Monetary Club: the Challenges for Smaller Member States*, New York: St. Martin's Press, pp. 123–48.

Kenen, P. B. (1969), 'The theory of optimum currency areas: an eclectic view', in R. A. Mundell and A. K. Swoboda (eds), *Monetary Problems of the International Economy*, Chicago: University of Chicago Press, pp. 41–60.

McKinnon, R. I. (1963), 'Optimum currency areas', *American Economic Review*, 53(4) (September): 717–25.

Mélitz, J. (2004), 'Risk sharing and EMU', *Journal of Common Market Studies*, 42(4) (November): 815–40.

Mélitz, J. and Zumer, F. (1998), 'Redistribution régionale et stabilisation par le gouvernement central', *Economie Internationale*, 75(3): 3–31.

Mundell, R. A. (1973), 'Uncommon arguments for common currencies', in H. G. Johnson and A. K. Swoboda (eds), *The Economics of Common Currencies*, London: George Allen & Unwin Ltd., pp. 114–32.

Sadeh, T. (2005), 'Who can adjust to the euro?', *The World Economy*, 28(11) (November): 1651–78.

Sadeh, T. (2006a), 'Adjusting to EMU: electoral, partisan, and fiscal cycles', *European Union Politics*, 7(3) (September): 347–72.

Sadeh, T. (2006b), *Sustaining European Monetary Union: Confronting the Cost of Diversity*, Boulder: Lynne Rienner.

Sala-i-Martin, X. and Sachs, J. (1992), 'Fiscal federalism and optimum currency areas: evidence for Europe from the United States', in M. B. Canzonieri, V. Grilli and P. R. Masson (eds), *Establishing a Central Bank: Issues in Europe and Lessons from the United States*, Cambridge: Cambridge University Press, pp. 195–219.

Steil, B. (2007), 'The end of national currency', *Foreign Affairs*, 86(3) (May/June): 83–96.

Tamborini, R. (2006), 'The "Brussels consensus" on macroeconomic stabilization policies in EMU: a critical assessment', in F. Torres, A. Verdun and H. Zimmermann (eds), *EMU Rules: the Political and Economic Consequences of European Monetary Integration*, Baden-Baden: Nomos Verlagsgesellschaft, pp. 137–59.

Tavlas, G. S. (1993), 'The "new" theory of optimum currency areas', *The World Economy*, 16(6) (November): 663–85.

Tilford, S. (2006), *Will the Eurozone Crack?* London: Centre for European Reform.

Tsoukalis, L. (2005), *What Kind of Europe?* Updated and expanded edition, Oxford: Oxford University Press.

3
The Role of Preferences and the Sustainability of EMU[1]

Francisco Torres

1 Introduction

Failed political attempts and successful political compromises on European monetary integration can be explained in terms of convergence of preferences over time. This is obviously tempered by the circumstances of each political and economic phase of European integration and the corresponding bargaining power of countries with different preferences.

During the 1990s, and in spite of the European recession cum exchange rate crisis, preferences on inflation and on the role of monetary policy and institutions did not seem to have diverged much. However, preferences regarding other elements of the governance structure of European Monetary Union (EMU), namely the Stability and Growth Pact (SGP) added later, may have not converged to the same degree.

There is thus a possibility that disagreements over monetary policy in the context of its broader macroeconomic framework may at some point result in a change in commitments towards EMU. Such a divergence might happen in the case of an asymmetric shock or due to the incapacity of some countries to adjust to EMU's macroeconomic framework. Preferences may converge or diverge depending on the very functioning of EMU. Preferences are therefore a key element in analysing the sustainability of EMU.

The next section looks back at the two main divergent views on how to achieve monetary integration in Europe. Section 3 discusses some of the main factors that contributed to the convergence of preferences on inflation and on the role of monetary policy in the European Monetary System (EMS). Section 4 analyses the first test to the commitment to exchange rate and price stability. Section 5 presents a framework of analysis for EMU's sustainability. Section 6 examines how preferences might (endogenously) respond to EMU governance. Section 7 concludes.

2 Two divergent views on the means to achieve monetary integration in Europe

From the beginning of the debate on EMU there were two main divergent views (or camps) on how to co-ordinate monetary policies and on the need to achieve monetary integration in Europe. The debate pitted the so-called monetarists, who thought that monetary integration would promote economic (and indeed political) convergence, against the so-called economists, who stressed the need for a higher level of co-ordination of economic policies and integration prior to the establishment of a monetary union, that is, for some prior convergence of economic (and necessarily political) integration.[2] The label 'monetarists' (not to be confused with the doctrine on the quantity theory of money) encompassed the view that a tight and unconditional agenda was needed for the creation of common monetary institutions, as an open-ended way not only of responding to the monetary problems of the moment but also of driving political integration, given that heightened economic integration and new institutions reflecting heterogeneous preferences would lead to a higher degree of political integration (compatible with a functionalist view). The 'economists' justified their label by advocating a prior convergence of economic developments and/or of preferences regarding a culture of (price) stability (compatible in a less obvious way with a federalist view).

Those divergent views amounted to two different approaches at two distinctive levels. The first point of contention concerned the nature of the transition to EMU, i.e. whether it should be more immediate or more gradual. A second point of dispute centred around divergent preferences on the role and institutional design of monetary policy, namely on the degree of centralization and independence of monetary policy required to guarantee price stability. Such a role and design were clearly not independent of the degree of economic and political integration which was necessary in order to share monetary sovereignty, which in turn conditioned the way in which the transition to EMU could be made.

As far as the first level (views on the transition) was concerned, the so-called monetarists (notably France, Belgium and Luxembourg and eventually also Italy, whose position was less clear-cut) adopted a functionalist view of European integration insofar as they perceived monetary co-operation, such as the narrowing of fluctuation bands or mutual credit lines, as a means of bringing about economic and political integration without surrendering too much of their political sovereignty. As for the second level (views on monetary policy), the building up of economic and monetary union would very much be an open-ended strategy to solve problems as they appeared and one which was to contribute to a deeper step-by-step political integration. This approach to monetary integration corresponds very much to a functionalist view of European integration.

On the other hand, the so-called economists (by and large the Germans and the Dutch) argued that, with a view to transition, economic convergence and close co-ordination of other policies such as fiscal and wage policies would have to come first. As for the second level (views on monetary policy), they would only agree to move on to EMU after making sure that there had been a prior convergence in terms of economic developments and/or the previous establishment of a federal institution with well-defined objectives. This position can be described as a federalist view of European integration insofar as its proponents would advocate the creation of new common supranational institutions with clearly defined goals for which there was a need for prior agreement.

At first glance, the 'economist's' requirement of a prior convergence in terms of economic developments might seem contradictory with respect to an institutional approach setting up the appropriate rules for the automatic attainment of a non-inflationary environment that is also more conducive to long-term growth. Of course, the prior convergence of economic developments as a political requirement amounts very much to a step-by-step (gradualist) approach and does not necessarily ensure a genuine convergence of preferences nor the sustainability of new common rules.[3] Only institutional arrangements, such as the rules governing the European Central Bank (ECB), would guarantee that all EMU members abided by a common preference for low inflation for the entire eurozone. However, such a prior (entry) requirement, understood as a test for a genuine convergence of preferences, is compatible with a federalist view and the defence of new institutions with clearly defined political objectives (basically, a monetary constitution). Considered from the perspective of different but converging preferences, it may also be easier to comprehend the coherence of the different positions as far as EMU is concerned throughout recent decades and the rationale behind the compromise reached at Maastricht.[4]

The Werner plan[5] and the experience with the Snake[6] clearly show that the preferences between the two camps were too different for a compromise to be possible. However, the creation of the European Monetary

System (EMS) indicates some increased flexibility (in the context of relaunching Franco-German co-operation[7]) on the part of both camps, which boils down to the creation of a temporary and open-ended institution. This in turn implied delaying discussions about preferences over the goals of monetary policy.

The EMS was then possible (although with opposition from the Bundesbank[8]) as it was a way to solve immediate problems (see below) while leaving the door open for realignments whenever monetary policy goals (preferences) were not compatible. Eventually, during the second phase of the transforming EMS, when it became essentially a Deutschmark zone, preferences between the two camps converged significantly. That made it possible to agree on a blueprint for economic and monetary union, with clearly defined goals to be implemented by a common federal institution.

Again, in the transition to EMU another compromise was struck. On the one hand, the 'monetarists' proposed a tight and quasi-irreversible agenda (with a very precise calendar), partly in order to anchor post-reunification Germany to the European Union. On the other hand, the 'economists' established the entry criteria and the SGP. They envisaged these as a guarantee for a prior and genuine convergence of preferences or at least as a means of addressing the potential opposition of German public opinion to the loss of the Deutschmark. This compromise was clearly political but it does reflect a true convergence of preferences over the years.

The different unsuccessful political attempts (Werner plan, Snake) and successful political compromises (EMS, EMU) can be explained in terms of convergence of preferences over time, tempered of course by the circumstances of each political and economic phase of European integration and the corresponding bargaining power of each camp.

3   Converging preferences on inflation and the role of monetary policy

In the 1970 Werner report the European Economic Community's (EEC) main objective appeared to consist in achieving the political independence of Europe in monetary affairs. At that time, conflicts over the course of monetary policy were already undermining the good functioning of the Bretton Woods system, with the US becoming an increasingly reluctant leader. The project of monetary unification in Europe envisaged by the Werner report involved the creation of an area in which goods, services, people and capital would circulate freely and without competitive distortions and thereby reinforce the European Community's (EC) contribution to European economic and monetary equilibrium (Werner Committee 1970: 9).

At that stage, as far as Germany was concerned, a European monetary union would have to have an independent European central bank basically modelled on the Bundesbank.[9] This position, however, was not compatible with the requirements of other countries, including in particular France, which would like to preserve more active monetary policies. As a consequence, the Werner plan for an economic and monetary union did not go ahead.[10]

The EMS began to operate in 1979, reflecting a functionalist approach to European integration and corresponding to the perspective of the so-called monetarists (France, Belgium and Luxembourg). During the first years of its life, between 1979 and 1983–4, the EMS was still characterized if not by symmetry then at least by frequent realignments. The latter would allow for the accommodation of inflation differentials through devaluations of the weaker currencies (their central parities) in order to compensate for the corresponding loss of competitiveness. From the mid-1980s, however, and up until the exchange rate crisis of 1992–3, the EMS essentially became an asymmetric mechanism, a Deutschmark area, with fewer (and smaller) realignments, which would allow only for the partial accommodation of inflation differentials.[11] Starting from a mechanism of exchange rate stability (with many adjustments) the EMS became a disciplinary mechanism. This change in the nature of the EMS, from a symmetrical arrangement to an asymmetric arrangement anchored in the Deutschmark, was the result of a convergence of the preferences of policy-makers and politicians from the different participating countries.

Let us consider some of the factors that contributed to the convergence of preferences in the EMS. The first of these factors concerned two important policy and political changes, one in France and the other one in Italy.[12] France came to accept what it had not accepted in the compromise that established the EMS, namely a surrender of its monetary sovereignty and following the anti-inflationary policy of the Bundesbank and thereby allowing at the same time the engine of Franco-German integration to be relaunched. Italy took a bit longer but in 1985, when the lira was forced to devalue again against the Deutschmark, the wage indexation mechanism, known as the *scala mobile*, was abolished with a view to breaking the wage-inflation spiral.

To help us better understand the changes which occurred, these policy and political changes in France and Italy but also in several other countries need to be put in the context of domestic political struggles between stability-oriented national central banks and treasuries on the one hand and non-stability oriented spending ministries and politicians constrained by the political business cycle on the other. Stability-oriented policy-makers rightly anticipated that these changes would also transform the EMS into an external constraint, and thereby also into a guarantee for monetary, and hopefully budgetary, discipline.

Another important factor involves the changes which occurred in international politics, namely the so-called conservative revolution and the consequent establishment of 'supply-side economics' and monetarist doctrines. Those doctrines banned the use of stabilization policies for structural purposes and favoured price stability over other goals of economic policy.

Last but not least, there was also a revolution in economic thinking – the rational expectations revolution – consisting in the assumption that economic agents were rational (which led to the award of the Nobel Prize to Robert Lucas in 1995 precisely for having developed and applied rational expectations and by having thereby transformed the understanding of economic policy). It drew attention to the costs in terms of inflation and unemployment of the lack of credibility of policy-makers in relation to economic agents (which led to the award of the Nobel Prize to Finn Kydland and Edward Prescott in 2004, for their analysis of the time inconsistency of economic policy[13]).

Following the seminal paper by Barro and Gordon (1983), Giavazzi and Pagano (1988) stressed the usefulness of EMS discipline as a means of effectively reducing inflation with a lower cost in terms of output and unemployment. Fixed exchange rates, unlike other policy targets, can easily be tracked by the private sector and easily implemented by the authorities. With a credible exchange rate peg to a strong currency (such as the Deutschmark), the monetary authorities of higher-inflation countries could draw on the anti-inflationary reputation of the strong currency country (Germany) so as to strengthen the credibility of national institutions and modify the expectations of private agents. In this way the authorities of the higher-inflation countries raised the political costs of inflation because any divergent behaviour would imply a self-inflicted loss of competitiveness. Moreover, the anti-inflation commitment of the monetary authorities could constantly be monitored by the private sector. Giavazzi and Pagano's contribution was one of the most influential academic contributions leading to the creation of a consensus (and epistemic communities) in favour of EMU.

By the late 1980s and early 1990s a general consensus had been established among economists but also, in part thanks to various networks among policy-makers (i.e. members of the monetary committees and national central banks and treasuries which may have constituted an epistemic community[14] in favour of sound rules to guarantee price stability), the private sector and eventually also politicians, on the need to radically change the attitude towards inflation. There was also a relative consensus among those actors on the powerful disciplinary and disinflationary role of the EMS.

Such a growing consensus may have contributed to the stability of the EMS between 1987 and 1992. There were no realignments, except for a technical adjustment of the lira to a narrow band of fluctuation in 1990, and policy-makers became used to the idea of living in a system of irrevocably fixed exchange rates.

At Maastricht, all EU countries seemed to have come around to the view that a credible and sound counter-inflationary monetary constitution should be adopted (although not necessarily a European monetary constitution, according to the UK, Denmark and Sweden). As has been pointed out in the modern political economy literature, joining a monetary union based on institutions that deliver price stability is probably the best way to implement such a strategy.

4   The first test to the commitment to exchange rate and price stability

German reunification in 1990 was a typical asymmetric shock that put to the test EMS members' commitment to exchange rate and price stability. Policy-makers and politicians remained firmly committed to fixed exchange rates in order not to lose credibility. A revaluation of the Deutschmark against all other currencies could have been the textbook answer to such an asymmetric shock. Yet the other EMS members resisted that option, fearing a loss of the credibility gained over the previous years inside the EMS.

With the elimination of capital controls – an efficiency objective of the Single Market Programme – the markets could easily test the commitment of each EMS member regarding their degree of adherence to the German tight monetary stance. The British pound and Italian lira, which were considered by the markets to be strongly overvalued in real terms, were forced out of the system by two speculative attacks. All the other currencies remained in the system but the EMS fluctuation bands had to be enlarged less than a year later.[15]

Yet, that enlargement of the fluctuation bands in most EU countries did not imply an abandonment of the anti-inflationary stance, as they maintained, and in some cases even accelerated, the pace of convergence with the satisfaction of the approved nominal criteria established in the Maastricht Treaty. As a matter of fact, fixed exchange rates and the commitment to the internal market objective of liberalizing all capital movements implied the end of any monetary policy autonomy for the 'followers' of Germany. The only chance to hold on to any monetary sovereignty was to share it in a common institution such as a European central bank. However, not all countries managed to fulfil the convergence criteria necessary to enter EMU in 1999.

From a strictly economic point of view, waiting for the convergence of economic conditions to form a monetary union did not make sense. In fact, according to some authors, including for instance De Grauwe,[16] the gradual approach inscribed in the Maastricht Treaty was nothing but a mechanism for delaying a political conflict between the German (i.e. Bundesbank) preference for not sharing monetary sovereignty in EMU and the French preference for a larger influence in European monetary affairs. In fact, from an economic standpoint it would make sense to allow high inflation and/or high debt countries into EMU, provided that they had decided to participate in any case, so that it would be easier (in other words less costly) for them to reduce inflation and their public debt ratios. This is because the institutional differences, which reflect different preferences and which imply different inflation and interest rates, would then disappear. Therefore, it would have been sufficient to guarantee an adequate institutional design of the ECB for it to fulfil its task of assuring price stability and resist any pressures to accommodate problems in the area of public finance. In fact, the works of Frankel and Rose and of others[17] suggest that the very participation in a monetary union may well contribute to fulfilling the optimal currency area (OCA) criteria. This is because monetary integration seems to lead to greater trade (openness) integration *cum* greater output correlation between different regions (countries)[18] and also to greater financial market integration in the currency area. This higher integration of capital markets provides an additional (private insurance) mechanism of adjustment to asymmetric shocks (a point already raised by Mundell in 1973).[19]

Nevertheless, convergence requirements were imposed in order to show the commitment to a culture of price stability. Criteria on the convergence of long-term nominal interest rates and ERM membership reflected the view that countries had to convince the markets of their determination to maintain an anti-inflationary stance.[20] Fiscal criteria were motivated by the idea that some prerequisites in the area of public finance would provide an incentive for fiscally weak countries to avoid politically motivated deficits that could endanger, through the insolvency of the respective public sectors, the monetary stability of the entire union.

The idea that fiscal policy should play a greater role in cushioning the impact of shocks is best reconciled with the convergence requirements set out in the Treaty on European Union, according to which national fiscal policies are constrained by binding rules, if one takes into account that the level of public deficits in the early 1990s was very high throughout most of the countries of the European Union.[21] The compromise involved a rapid leap forward to a one-speed monetary union entailing a number of entry requirements which would test whether (or show to those opposing EMU that) there was a 'sufficient' prior convergence of preferences.

During the 1990s, preferences on inflation and on the role of monetary policy and institutions did not seem to have diverged much. That notwithstanding, preferences regarding the SGP and other elements of the governance structure of EMU added later may not have converged to the same extent, although they were accepted within the 'package'.

This raises the possibility that disagreements over monetary policy in the context of its broader macroeconomic framework may at some point result in a change in commitments towards EMU.[22] Such a divergence might happen in the case of an asymmetric shock or due to the incapacity of some countries to adjust to EMU's macroeconomic framework.[23]

5   A framework of analysis for the sustainability of EMU

In order to analyse the sustainability of EMU, I suggest the framework of 'sustainable currency areas' (SCA) criteria. While the traditional OCA criteria tend to focus on the economic dimension of a monetary union, the SCA criteria encompass also a political dimension.

In the economic dimension, the three criteria relate to the cost of a monetary union, namely the loss of the exchange rate as an adjustment mechanism. For the traditional OCA theory, a monetary union is above all a problem of macroeconomic stabilization, of retaining or forgoing control over national currencies and domestic monetary policy. The first criterion concerns the degree of diversification of production (Kenen 1969) and to some extent consumption and spending patterns.[24] The second criterion is the existence of alternative adjustment mechanisms to the exchange rate such as labour mobility (Mundell 1961), wage flexibility and integration of capital markets, the latter one taken as a private insurance mechanism against shocks (Mundell 1973). Finally, the third criterion consists in the degree of openness of the economy (McKinnon 1963), which conditions the effectiveness of the stabilization role of exchange rates[25] (the relinquished instrument of macroeconomic adjustment).

In the political dimension, defined along the lines of Baldwin and Wyplosz (2006) where economic and political OCA criteria are explicitly set out, I include the traditional (adjustment) fiscal transfers and/or budget centralization mechanism, in terms of a public insurance mechanism. The other two political criteria concern the degree of homogeneity of preferences and the degree of openness to further political integration in the currency area.

The two dimensions (economic and political) are complementary in the analysis of the sustainability of a monetary union. This is because political criteria can compensate for insufficient compliance with the economic criteria. For instance, a scheme of automatic fiscal transfers can alleviate the burden of adjustment to asymmetric shocks, although, as argued by Jones (Chapter 2, this volume), in the present conditions (significantly different levels of income across different member states) it may well trigger dissatisfaction with EMU in the same way as other spill-overs of EMU to the social and labour market areas. Also, converging preferences and openness to further political integration (which are intended to capture what Paul De Grauwe in this volume calls the deep variable whose lack may lead to secession from and/or disruption of EMU, and Baldwin and Wyplosz (2006) denominate as the solidarity criterion) may assure the sustainability of EMU even when the adjustment capacity and the degrees of homogeneity of production structures and consumption patterns and openness to trade seem insufficient.[26]

Table 3.1 summarizes the different SCA criteria (degree of homogeneity, adjustment capacity and degree of openness) along their two dimensions (economic and political).

To be sustainable monetary unions require a certain degree of homogeneity between their member states both in terms of their production structures (so that shocks do not hit them in too different ways) and preferences (so that the common monetary policy responds to the problems that any given country perceives as more urgent to be addressed in the case of a particular shock). They also need some adjustment capacity in their labour markets and through private (financial market integration) or public insurance mechanisms (fiscal transfers). Finally, they require a certain degree of openness both in terms of trade among their members

Table 3.1   Sustainable currency areas (SCA) criteria

	Dimensions	
Criteria	Economic dimension:	Political dimension:
Degree of homogeneity:	in required response to shocks	of national preferences
Adjustment capacity:	of labour markets and by means of financial market integration	by means of fiscal transfers/budget centralization
Degree of openness:	to trade among CA regions	to further political integration in the currency area

(so that the loss of the exchange rate instrument, used to affect cost competitiveness, is not too costly) and in terms of further political integration (given that only if a country expects to benefit from further integration will it endure some of the costs associated with the monetary union, thus resisting the temptation to secede).[27]

Along the lines of De Grauwe (2006 and Chapter 1, this volume),[28] one may summarise this framework of analysis by means of graphical representations. In Figures 3.1 and 3.2, the SCA line defines the combinations of homogeneity and adjustment capacity (Figure 3.1) and the combinations of homogeneity and openness (Figure 3.2) for which EMU is sustainable. That is, the lack of homogeneity in terms of the required response to optimally address different shocks and/or regarding member states' preferences can be compensated for by labour mobility and/or wage flexibility and/or financial market integration and/or some form of budget centralization or a scheme of fiscal transfers between the regions. It can also be compensated for (second trade-off) by openness to trade among the countries of the monetary union and/or to political integration of the currency area. Figure 3.1 represents the trade-off between the degree of homogeneity in the required response to shocks and of national preferences and the adjustment capacity. Figure 3.2 represents the trade-off between the degree of homogeneity in the required response to shocks and of preferences and the degree of openness to trade and to further political integration.

An increase in trade between the member states and/or a more open stance towards political integration of the currency area has the effect of shifting the euro-zone from its initial position more into the sustainability area as far as the trade-off between the degree of homogeneity and adjustment capacity is concerned. Recent wage developments in the

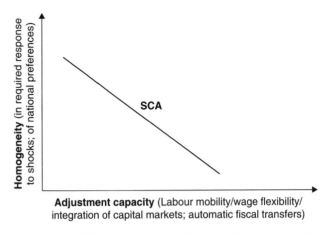

Figure 3.1   The trade-off between homogeneity and adjustment capacity

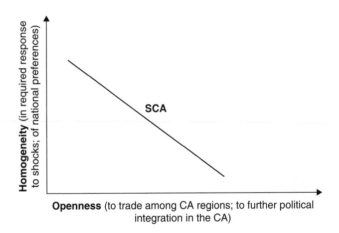

Figure 3.2   The trade-off between homogeneity and openness

euro-zone might reflect a convergence of preferences towards increased labour market flexibility, thereby contributing also to a more sustainable position of the euro-zone in regard to the trade-off between the degree of homogeneity and the degree of openness. Any exogenously determined leap forward in European political integration, by co-ordinating actions in other policy areas, would also shift the euro-zone more into the sustainability area in terms of both trade-offs.

The advantage of this multi-dimensional framework is that one can see that a partial fulfilment of the different political criteria compensates for the non-satisfaction of OCA criteria, making EMU sustainable even without exogenous political unification. Apart from the existence of a scheme of automatic fiscal transfers, which depends very much on the degree of political integration, openness to further political integration and the homogeneity of preferences inside the euro-zone contribute to sustaining EMU. Homogeneity of preferences and openness to further political integration mean that member states can better accept both the objectives of the common monetary policy (preferences) and the costs of non-adequate stabilization in the presence of asymmetric shocks. Also, both tend to diminish political home-grown shocks as countries might converge on similar views towards common principles in other areas of the economy (take for instance the case of flexicurity – increased labour market flexibility compensated for by increased social protection).[29]

6   Endogenous preferences

One of the most interesting features of the EMU is that preferences seem to have converged sufficiently for its construction and general acceptance. Furthermore, the dynamic nature of preferences suggests that one should consider how they might evolve inside EMU as they condition its sustainability. Let us take the trade-off between the benefits from monetary integration and the heterogeneity costs of a common monetary policy. Benefits arise from the centralization of monetary policy. Costs are associated with the loss of an independent monetary policy: a common monetary authority cannot react to the specificities of each country and take into account different preferences about the various trade-offs that arise when setting its monetary policy for the whole area.

Figure 3.3 provides a simplified and static graphical version of the trade-off. Marginal benefits are always positive although declining as the benefit of adding a new member to EMU gets smaller. Marginal costs are positive but also rising as the heterogeneity costs for the euro-zone of letting in an additional member increase.[30] The optimal size of the monetary union is given by the point where the marginal costs and benefits of a common monetary policy equalize.[31] The trade-off is also conditioned by EMU's regulatory system (the common monetary policy in the context of its macroeconomic framework). This is depicted in Figure 3.4: the optimal size of the monetary union might increase to OS1 or decrease to OS2.

Preferences are therefore a key element for analysing the sustainability of EMU. They will tend to diverge if EMU's regulatory system (monetary policy within its also evolving macroeconomic framework) is not adequate but might well converge and sustain EMU when it is perceived as

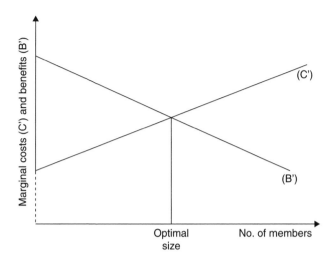

Figure 3.3 Benefits from monetary integration versus heterogeneity costs of a common monetary policy (political plus economic dimension)

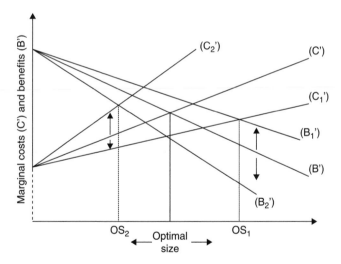

Figure 3.4 Impact of EMU's regulatory system on costs and benefits

adequate. On the other hand, monetary policy and/or EMU's governance might also take into account, to different extents, the evolution of preferences. One case in point is reform of the SGP in 2005.

Eurobarometer evidence (Figures 3.5, 3.6 and 3.7) indicates that support for EMU has remained stable in the euro-zone (72 per cent in favour

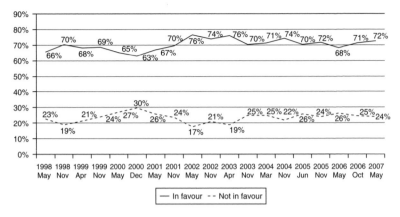

Figure 3.5   Single European currency: for or against (euro-zone)

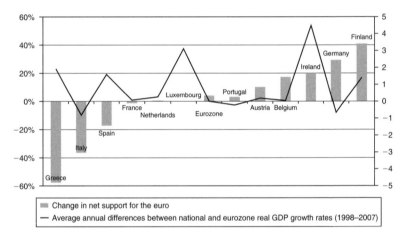

Figure 3.6   Changes in net support for the euro and average annual differences between national and euro-zone real GDP growth rates (1998–2007)

and 24 per cent not in favour in 2007) although it varies among different countries. For the period 1998–2007, in Italy, which has been growing below the average of the euro-zone, net support for the single currency dropped significantly although it is still fairly high (67 per cent in favour against 25 not in favour). In Ireland and Finland, two fast-growing countries, net support went up significantly. What is somewhat more puzzling is that net support for the single currency went up (significantly) in Germany and (marginally) in Portugal, the other two

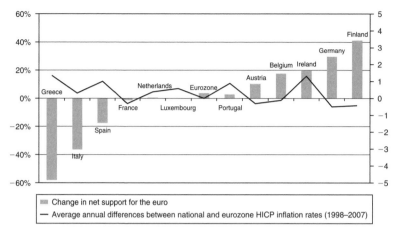

Figure 3.7 Change in net support for the euro and average annual differences between national and euro-zone HICP inflation rates (1998–2007)

slow-growth countries during the period considered, and decreased substantially in Spain (which, however, still enjoys a large net support for the single currency) and Greece (the only euro-zone country without a majority in favour of the single currency), both of which were among the fastest growing countries in the euro-zone.[32]

7 Conclusion

Preferences on inflation and on the role of monetary policy and institutions converged sufficiently during the second phase of the transforming EMS (when it became essentially a Deutschmark zone) to allow for the creation of EMU and clearly defined goals to be implemented by the ECB. During the convergence phase to EMU in the 1990s there might not have been much divergence of those preferences. Still, preferences regarding the SGP and other elements of the governance structure of EMU that were added later may have not converged to the same extent. This raises the possibility that disagreements over EMU's macroeconomic framework may at some point result in a change in commitments in the case of an asymmetric shock or due to the incapacity of some countries to adjust.

The sustainability of monetary unions presupposes a certain degree of member state homogeneity, in terms of their production structures (a traditional OCA criterion) but also in terms of preferences, so that the common monetary policy is seen by a given country to respond to the problems perceived as more urgent in the context of a particular shock. It also requires a certain degree of openness, in terms of trade (another classical OCA criterion) but also in terms of further political integration. Only if a country expects to benefit from further integration will it be prepared to endure some of the costs associated with the monetary union, and resist the temptation to secede.

Preferences and their evolution therefore stand out as a key element for analysing the sustainability of EMU. They will tend to diverge if EMU's regulatory system is not adequate but might well converge and sustain EMU when it is perceived as delivering. On the other hand, monetary policy and/or EMU's governance might also take into account, to different extents, the evolution of preferences. The reform of the SGP in 2005 is a case in point but possible refinements such as the institutionalization of the euro-group and of euro-zone diplomacy or developments in the area of financial supervision might also reflect the need to respond to shared preferences among euro-zone countries.

Notes

1. I wish to thank seminar participants at the London School of Economics, IEE, Universidade Católica, Lisbon, and the University of Rome 'Tor Vergata' for comments and criticism on this chapter, which partly draws on a previous paper on 'The long road to EMU' presented at the European University Institute, Florence. I also thank Luísa Benta for providing me with Eurobarometer evidence. This contribution is based on my on-going research at IEE, Universidade Católica, on 'The political economy of European monetary governance: the role of preferences, policies and strategies' and is also part of an FCT project on Economic Growth, Convergence and Institutions (research grant POCI/EGE/55423/2004, partially funded by FEDER).
2. Describing the controversy over the Maastricht convergence criteria, Wyplosz (2006) classifies these two old labels as bizarre, questioning the reasons behind them. In this section I go a bit beyond the established definitions of those two labels (see for instance Ungerer 1997).
3. De Grauwe (1996).
4. Wyplosz (2006); Torres (2007).
5. The Werner group set out a three-stage process to achieve EMU within ten years, including the possibility of a single currency. The member states agreed in principle in 1971 and began the first stage – narrowing currency fluctuations. However, a fresh wave of currency instability on international markets quashed any hopes of tying the Community's currencies closer together (see European Commission, http://ec.europa.eu/economy_finance/the_euro/em_union9377_en. htm, accessed 30 August 2008).
6. The Snake entered into force on 24 April 1972 and allowed central banks to buy and sell European currencies provided that the exchange rate fluctuation margin of 2.25 per cent, corresponding to the authorized margins between

the dollar and the currencies of the Six, was not overstepped. See European Navigator website http://www.ena.lu/ (accessed 30 August 2008)

7. For different explanations of the importance of Franco-German co-operation throughout the process of monetary integration and the implications of such integration and ensuing economic convergence of the two countries for that relationship, see Collignon (2004) and Jones (2002).

8. As the Bundesbank feared that the arrangement might condition its very monetary policy it could not reveal the flexibility of the German government that also considered other political goals besides price stability.

9. See Zimmermann (2004) for a citation of the precise wording used by the German negotiator in the Werner Committee, J. Schöllhorn, in his Memorandum on EMU, 23/4/7, 0PA-AA, IIIA1, vol. 590.

10. See Gros and Thygesen (1998) for a thorough analysis of the failure of the Werner plan.

11. According to Mundell (1994), the Exchange Rate Mechanism (ERM) of the EMS in theory was symmetrical with respect to its member countries, but in practice the Deutschmark became the 'inflation anchor' of the system. See Torres (2007) for a more detailed analysis and a graphical representation.

12. According to Quaglia and Maes (2004), the lack of convergence of France and Italy with Germany in the process of European monetary integration was mainly explained by their difficulties in accepting a common and independent European central bank and by problems in achieving macroeconomic stability, respectively.

13. Kydland and Prescott (1977).

14. See Haas (1992: 3) for a definition of epistemic communities. Collignon and Schwarzer (2003), who also provide an excellent discussion on how epistemic communities create consensus as well as a thorough discussion of the concept, apply the concept of epistemic communities to the private sector, namely to two important non-governmental organizations representing the views of the business and banking communities that took a very active role in favour of European Monetary Union: the Giscard-Schmidt Committee for the Monetary Union of Europe (CMUE) and the Association for the Monetary Union of Europe (AMUE). See also Verdun (1999) for an application of the concept to the Delors Committee.

15. For an account of this episode, according to which the British Chancellor of the Exchequer, Kenneth Clarke, had a decisive role, see Collignon and Schwarzer (2003: 122).

16. De Grauwe (1993).

17. See Frankel and Rose (1998), Rose (2000) and successive empirical studies for estimates of the effect on trade of the elimination of exchange rate volatility in monetary unions.

18. See Frankel and Rose (1998). The growing importance of the service sector in the economy might have contributed to mitigate Krugman's (1993) argument that an initial OCA might lead to increased regional specialization and thus become more prone to asymmetric shocks.

19. A critique of Frankel and Rose may be found in Chapter 4, this volume.

20. Baldwin and Wyplosz (2006).

21. See Corsetti and Roubini (1993) for an analysis of the trade-off between the benefits of fiscal rules and the possibility of using fiscal policy as a stabilization

instrument. See also Jones (2007) for a discussion of the role of fiscal stabilization in EMU. Interest rate payments on public debt amounted to 40 per cent of total household savings in Europe, hitting private investment and jeopardizing the financing of social protection.

22. In the case of EMU's sustainability, one should take into account that there are important economic and political exit costs. See Eichengreen (2007) for an excellent account of the various implications of EMU exit.
23. See Torres (2008) for a discussion of the fact that EMU's functioning triggers spill-over effects across various policy areas which might in turn lower heterogeneity costs by leading to some co-ordination and/or reform in those very areas.
24. According to Corsetti (2008), even in the case of uncorrelated regional shocks and production specialization, the convergence in spending patterns makes the policy stance that is optimal at the regional level more symmetric across the different regions.
25. New micro-founded OCA models tend to share Mundell's (1973) scepticism about the stabilizing role of exchange rate movements (see Corsetti 2008). See also De Grauwe (2006 and this volume) for a discussion of the respective implications for the OCA theory.
26. The different degrees of compliance with OCA criteria have led us to talk about increases or decreases in optimality. Yet, from a linguistic point of view, 'optimum' is already a superlative.
27. Linkages between EMU and EU integration tend to reinforce the sustainability of EMU; see Torres (2008).
28. De Grauwe (this volume) represents the trade-offs between symmetry and flexibility and between symmetry and integration, within the classical economic OCA criteria.
29. The fact that EMU gives rise to spill-overs into other policy areas has resulted in different degrees of coordination at the European level; see Torres (2008).
30. Of course, in the hypothetical case of Germany joining a monetary union already consisting of the Benelux countries, the extra benefit would be superior to the extra benefit brought by the entry of the previous member (say, Luxembourg). Different sizes (assumed away in this very simplified graphic representation) matter. Also, it would not be a matter of indifference (in terms of heterogeneity costs, both political and economic) whether it was France or the UK that joined the monetary union between the Benelux countries and Germany.
31. The trade-off endogenously determines size, composition and scope of the union (Alesina et al. 2005).
32. Developments in Greece and in Italy with regard to the net support for the euro might also relate to the perceived impact of the euro changeover on price rises (Deroose et al. 2007).

References

Alesina, A., Angeloni, I. and Etro, F. (2005), 'International unions', *American Economic Review*, 95(3): 602–15.

Baldwin, R. and Wyplosz, C. (2006), *The Economics of European Integration*, 2nd edition, Maidenhead: McGraw-Hill.

Barro, R. and Gordon, D. (1983), 'Rules, discretion and reputation in a model of monetary policy', *Journal of Monetary Economics*, 12: 101–21.

Collignon, S. (2004), 'Learning to live in euroland: the role of France and Germany', paper presented at the conference 'France and Germany in the International Division of Labour', Paris, 9–10 December.

Collignon, S. and Schwarzer, D. (2003), *Private Sector Involvement in the Euro: the Power of Ideas*, London: Routledge.

Corsetti, G. (2008), 'A modern reconsideration of the theory of optimal currency areas', CEPR Discussion Paper, February.

Corsetti, G. and Roubini, N. (1993), 'The design of optimal fiscal rules for Europe after 1992', in F. Torres and F. Giavazzi, *Adjustment and Growth in the European Monetary Union*, Cambridge: Cambridge University Press, pp. 46–82.

De Grauwe, P. (1993), 'The political economy of monetary union in Europe', Documento de Trabalho do Centro de Estudos Europeus, Universidade Católica Portuguesa, September.

De Grauwe, P. (1996), 'The economics of convergence towards monetary union in Europe', in F. Torres (ed.), *Monetary Reform in Europe*, Lisbon: Universidade Católica Editora, pp. 121–47.

De Grauwe, P. (2006), 'What have we learnt about monetary integration since the Maastricht treaty?', *Journal of Common Market Studies*, 44(4): 711–30.

Deroose, S., Hodson, D. and Kuhlmann, J. (2007) 'The legitimation of EMU: lessons from the early years of the euro', *Review of International Political Economy*, 14(5): 800–19.

Eichengreen, B. (2007), 'The break-up of the euro area', NBER Working Paper 13393.

Frankel, J. and Rose A. (1998), 'The endogeneity of the optimum currency area criteria', *Economic Journal*, 108: 1009–25.

Giavazzi, F. and Pagano M. (1988), 'The advantage of tying one's hands: EMS discipline and central bank credibility', *European Economic Review*, 32: 1055–75.

Gros, D. and Thygesen, N. (1998), *European Monetary Integration: From the EMS to EMU*, Essex and New York: Addison Wesley Longman.

Haas, P. (1992), 'Introduction: epistemic communities and international policy coordination', *International Organization*, 46: 1–35.

Jones, E. (2002), *The Politics of Economic and Monetary Union: Integration and Idiosyncrasy*, Lanham, MD: Rowman and Littlefield.

Jones, E. (2007), 'Populism in Europe', *SAIS Review* 27(1) (Winter–Spring): 37–47.

Kenen, P. (1969), 'The optimum currency area: an eclectic view', in R. Mundell and A. Swoboda (eds), *Monetary Problems of the International Economy*, Chicago: University of Chicago Press.

Krugman, P. (1993), 'Lessons of Massachusetts for EMU', in F. Torres and F. Giavazzi (eds), *Adjustment and Growth in the European Monetary Union*, Cambridge: Cambridge University Press.

Kydland, F. and Prescott, E. (1977), 'Rules rather than discretion: the inconsistency of optimal plans', *Journal of Political Economy*, 85: 473–91.

McKinnon, R. (1963), 'Optimum currency areas', *American Economic Review*, 53: 717–25.

Mundell, R. (1961), 'A theory of optimal currency areas', *American Economic Review*, 51: 657–65.

Mundell, R. (1973), 'Uncommon arguments for common currencies', in H. Johnson and A. Swoboda (eds), *The Economics of Common Currencies*, London: Allen & Unwin.

Mundell, R. (1994), 'The European Monetary System 50 years after Bretton Woods: a comparison between two systems', paper presented at Project Europe 1985–95, the 10th edition of *Incontri di Rocca Salimbeni* meetings, in Siena, 25 November.

Quaglia, L. and Maes, I. (2004), 'France and Italy's policies on European monetary integration: a comparison of "strong" and "weak" states', *Comparative European Politics*, 2(1): 51–72.

Rose, A. (2000), 'One money, one market: the effect of common currencies on trade', *Economic Policy*, 15(30): 7–46.

Torres, F. (2007), 'The long road to EMU: the economic and political reasoning behind Maastricht', NIPE Working Paper 23.

Torres, F. (2008), 'EMU's wider output legitimacy', work in progress, IEE, Universidade Católica Portuguesa.

Ungerer, Horst (1997), *A Concise History of European Monetary Integration: From EPU to EMU*, Westport and London: Quorum Books.

Verdun, A. (1999), 'The role of the Delors Committee in the creation of EMU: an epistemic community?', *Journal of European Public Policy*, 6(2) (June): 308–28.

Werner Committee (1970), *Report to the Council and the Commission on the Realisation by Stages of Economic and Monetary Union in the Community*, definitive text (Werner Report), Bulletin of the European Communities (supplement), 11.

Wyplosz, C. (2006), 'European Monetary Union: the dark side of a major success', *Economic Policy* (April): 207–62.

Zimmermann, H. (2004), 'Regaining autonomy: the German government, the Bundesbank, and the breakdown of "Bretton Woods", 1965–1978', paper prepared for delivery at the 2004 Annual Meeting of the American Political Science Association, 2–5 September.

4
Globalization vs. Europeanization: Assessing the Impact of EMU on Business Cycle Affiliation

Michael Artis[1]

1 Introduction

At the onset of EMU, underlying the political debate between 'monetarists' and 'economists' (Tsoukalis 1997) was the idea that the creation of a single monetary area would produce the convergence of business cycles of its member states leading to a single, synchronized, 'European business cycle'. This would mean a de facto elimination of the risk of asymmetric shocks, and would make the 'one size fits all' monetary policy of the ECB most effective. There are several papers which claim to discern the existence of such a cycle (e.g. Artis et al. 2004; Kaufmann 2003). The European business cycle forms the subject of analysis for the CEPR's Euro Area Business Cycle Dating Committee and its coherence is a positive indicator for monetary union. But is 'globalization' overwhelming 'Europeanization'? This chapter addresses this question focusing on business cycle affiliations, meaning the alleged tendency for some countries' business cycles to cluster together with others. To this aim, the chapter derives deviation cycles for OECD countries and examines their synchronization through the application of fuzzy clustering techniques.

Dividing the whole period (1970–2003) into three sub-samples allows an assessment of changes in business cycle affiliation over time. The UK, for example, appears to move from a US association to a European one. The chapter also reports the results of applying a non-parametric procedure to test for business cycle association. This test suggests that the European grouping is not a very distinctive one. 'Globalization' may be overwhelming 'Europeanization'.

2   Is there a European business cycle?

The first question to answer in assessing the impact of EMU on business cycle affiliation is whether there has ever been evidence of a European business cycle.

Some years ago, with my colleague Wenda Zhang, I wrote a paper (Artis and Zhang 1997) in which we employed the OECD's trade cycle database and a presentational device first deployed by Baxter and Stockman (1986) to indicate the possible arrival of a European cycle, associated with the Exchange Rate Mechanism (ERM) of the European Monetary System (EMS). In that paper we took industrial production deviation cycles estimated by the OECD on the basis of a modified NBER algorithm and showed the cross plots of the cross-correlations of those cyclical deviates vis-à-vis the US and vis-à-vis Germany for a sequence of two periods. The first of these was typified as a 'pre-ERM period' (1961:1 to 1979:3), the second as the ERM period (1979:4 to 1993:12). The interest in the picture was that where the observations for the first period suggested a broad 'world cycle', in the second a number of countries could be seen as having moved strongly towards a stronger affiliation with Germany, with Germany and the US themselves much less closely related to each other. The UK was a prominent exception, with the European countries that had moved towards a stronger identification with Germany being those that were associated with the ERM either as full or as 'apprentice' (shadowing) members. It might have been thought that this movement would be strengthened in subsequent years for at least two reasons: first, the establishment of the EMU would reduce the impact of idiosyncratic policy shocks on national business cycles; second, the trade creation brought about by the establishment of monetary union would lead to a closer association of business cycles. This latter effect indeed seemed to be substantiated by Frankel and Rose in later work (e.g. Frankel and Rose 1998) and lay behind their claim that the optimal currency area criteria were substantially endogenous. Indeed some later papers, as already mentioned – e.g. those by Kaufmann (2003) and by Artis et al. (2004) – provided evidence for a strengthening of the European cycle. Perhaps significantly, both these papers worked with industrial production data rather than GDP;[2] more to the point, though, they tackled the problem by asking whether European countries were becoming closer together – this is, so to speak, looking out from inside. Yet, clearly, the finding that the European countries have been getting closer together does not offer sufficient identification of a distinctively European cycle if there is a general tendency for all countries to be drawing closer together. This is what seems to be revealed when the original Artis and Zhang (1997) paper is replicated on later data, as documented in Artis (2006). More recent papers still – e.g. those of Canova et al. (2007) or Kose et al. (2008) – do not appear to find striking evidence of a European grouping.[3] In the rest of this chapter we will adduce some evidence based on a fuzzy clustering of cross-correlations which corroborates these broad findings.

3 Measuring business cycle affiliations

In order to comment on business cycle affiliation it is necessary in the first instance to have a good idea of how to measure the cycle. Economists have made considerable progress in this respect in recent decades (Harding and Pagan 2001, 2002; Artis et al. 2002). Business 'cycles', as such, are not entirely well-termed, since the word 'cycle' suggests a degree of regularity which is not found in practice. Nevertheless the idea is that it is possible to observe broad-based movements in the economy which have an oscillatory character, even if those oscillations do not occur with a strictly uniform periodicity and vary in the total length of time taken to work themselves out. Recent work seems to have allowed the efficient identification of cycles, from which one may proceed at least to *measure* affiliations between countries with some confidence (Harvey and Jaeger 1993; Baxter and King 1999; Harvey and Trimbur 2003).

Commonly, measures of affiliation between business cycles are in fact measures of synchronization and a standard means of assessing this is to measure the cross-correlation between the detrended series. A standard product is therefore a cross-correlogram showing the cross-correlations of the countries analysed in the sample under consideration. The cross-correlogram shows all the pair-wise cross-correlation coefficients that can be estimated and lends itself to an application of clustering techniques. However, there are still other characteristics of business cycles that could be taken into account, although as soon as more than one characteristic is involved a weighting problem arises.

Table 4.1 indicates the data set we are using, the countries involved and the time periods for which the (quarterly) GDP series are available. Using these data we proceed to derive deviation cycles using the H-P band-pass method described in Artis et al. (2002). That is, the data are filtered twice through low-pass Hodrick-Prescott band-pass filters to isolate those frequencies with periodicities that correspond to the business cycle (i.e. 1.25 to 8 years in this case). Then the pair-wise cross-correlations can be calculated as the basic measure of synchronization and the techniques of fuzzy clustering applied. Finally, in order to pave the way for the

Table 4.1   The country samples

Country	Code	Sample size
Austria	AUT	1970–2003
Finland	FIN	1970–2003
France	FRA	1970–2003
Germany	DEU	1970–2003
Italy	ITA	1970–2003
Spain	ESP	1970–2003
Sweden	SWE	1970–2003
United Kingdom	GBR	1970–2003
EU-15	EU-15	1970–2003
United States	USA	1970–2003
Canada	CAN	1970–2003
Japan	JPN	1970–2003
Switzerland	CHE	1970–2003
Australia	AUS	1970–2003
Korea	KOR	1970–2003
Netherlands	NLD	1977–2003
Portugal	PRT	1977–2003
Norway	NOR	1978–2003
Belgium	BEL	1980–2003
Mexico	MEX	1980–2003
New Zealand	NZL	1982–2003
Denmark	DNK	1988–2003
Ireland	IRL	1997–2003

non-parametric exercise reported in section 5 of this chapter, the cycles have to be dated so that at any and all points of time it is possible to say what cyclical phase (upturn/downturn) a particular economy is in. The dating is accomplished using the algorithm described in Artis et al (2002).

4   Clustering

4.1   Hard clustering

A 'hard' clustering algorithm starts with a distance matrix showing some measure of dissimilarity between the countries located along the axes; this will be a square matrix with a diagonal of zeroes and symmetric above and below the diagonal.

The algorithm then first forms a cluster from the two observations which are closest together; replacing these by another value, the algorithm then proceeds to find the next smallest difference between any two observations (counting the just completed first cluster as one of these) and so on. The initial values entering the distance matrix are in the form of dissimilarities between (in our case) countries in respect of some characteristic (possibly several characteristics) – so the algorithm will cluster together countries which are similar in respect of that characteristic (or set of characteristics).

In our own case x_{ki} is a measure of the cyclical synchronicity of the country in question *with all the other countries*. Clustering algorithms are long on alternative measures of distance (the measurement of the difference between observations) and on alternative ways to compute the 'replacement' value of a cluster after one has been identified; by contrast they are rather short on measures of significance or adequacy. The distance measure we are using is the Euclidean distance,

$$\sqrt{\sum_{k=1}^{22} (x_{ki} - x_{kj})^2}$$

and the cluster replacement measure that of average linkage. Experimentation with alternative distance measures did not in general reveal any significant difference.

Contemporaneous cross-correlation is not the only dimension in which we might want to measure similarity of business cycle experience. Some investigators (e.g. Massman and Mitchell 2002; Barrell and Weale 2003) have suggested as an alternative the distance *between* cycles, as might be measured for example by the RMS of the squared differences over a period of time. The suggestion responds to the idea that whilst (for example) synchronization may not change over time, the amplitude of cycles may do so and thus the difference between cycles, for a given degree of synchronization, may increase, or diminish. However, we do not pursue this idea further here.

4.2 Why fuzzy is better than hard

We may now turn to the fuzzy clustering analysis. In fuzzy clustering less information is wasted than in hard clustering: countries may be typified as having 'membership coefficients', belonging (say) as to x% to one group or cluster and as to (1 – x)% to the other (in the case that only two clusters are distinguished). Clearly this is preferable to forcing the country to belong to a particular cluster as hard clustering does.

More generally the analysis gives the possibility of discerning whether there is a 'distinct' set of groupings or not. To approach this question

Table 4.2 Fuzzy clustering, correlation of business cycles, full sample: 1970–2003

	Coefficients		Silhouette width	Belongs to cluster
Austria	0.64	0.36	0.79	1
Finland	0.52	0.48	0.49	1
France	0.70	0.30	0.81	1
Germany	0.67	0.33	0.78	1
Italy	0.72	0.28	0.79	1
Spain	0.69	0.31	0.76	1
Sweden	0.38	0.62	0.25	2
United Kingdom	0.55	0.45	0.50	1
EU-15	0.74	0.26	0.81	1
United States	0.51	0.49	0.41	1
Canada	0.51	0.49	0.46	1
Japan	0.51	0.49	0.45	1
Switzerland	0.71	0.29	0.77	1
Australia	0.38	0.62	0.06	2
Korea	0.45	0.55	−0.11	2
Netherlands	0.72	0.28	0.75	1
Portugal	0.55	0.45	0.51	1
Norway	0.35	0.65	0.61	2
Belgium	0.76	0.24	0.76	1
Mexico	0.39	0.61	0.19	2
New Zealand	0.32	0.68	0.54	2
Denmark	0.34	0.66	0.62	2
Ireland	0.70	0.30	0.72	1
Silhouette width	0.66	0.31		

Number of clusters 2
Average silhouette width 0.55
Dunn's coefficient 0.55
Normalized Dunn's coefficient 0.10

we use one of the 'goodness of fit' measures associated with fuzzy clustering, which is the measure of average silhouette width. Maximizing the average value of the cluster silhouette width seems a plausible way to determine the 'optimal' number of clusters (Kaufman and Rousseow 1990 provide a definition of this and of other measures associated with fuzzy clustering).

The average silhouette measure is bounded by ± 1, with positive values indicating that the clusters are relatively well defined. In Table 4.2, which covers the whole period, this criterion produces two clusters, of which one (cluster 1) is a good deal larger than the other. It involves most of the advanced industrial countries including both (most of) Europe and North America.

Table 4.3   Fuzzy clustering, correlation of business cycles, sample: 1970–1980

	Coefficients		Silhouette width	Belongs to cluster
Austria	0.55	0.45	0.55	1
Finland	0.44	0.56	0.17	2
France	0.50	0.50	0.40	1
Germany	0.58	0.42	0.56	1
Italy	0.53	0.47	0.51	1
Spain	0.53	0.47	0.49	1
Sweden	0.45	0.55	0.09	2
United Kingdom	0.49	0.51	0.00	2
EU-15	0.53	0.47	0.51	1
United States	0.47	0.53	0.24	2
Canada	0.45	0.55	0.23	2
Japan	0.58	0.42	0.50	1
Switzerland	0.55	0.45	0.50	1
Australia	0.41	0.59	0.50	2
Korea	0.54	0.46	0.29	1
Netherlands	0.60	0.40	0.56	1
Portugal	0.53	0.47	0.37	1
Norway	0.49	0.51	0.21	2
Belgium	0.57	0.43	0.53	1
Mexico	0.51	0.49	−0.03	1
New Zealand	0.45	0.55	0.35	2
Denmark	0.41	0.59	0.43	2
Ireland	0.59	0.41	0.57	1
Silhouette width	0.45	0.27		

Number of clusters 2
Average silhouette width 0.37
Dunn's coefficient 0.51
Normalized Dunn's coefficient 0.01

Two clusters are also detected in the first sub-period (Table 4.3), more or less even in numbers of members. The UK is clustered with Canada and the USA; most other European countries are clustered separately. The second sub-period (Table 4.4) finds a larger number (5) of clusters to be optimal, suggesting a higher degree of idiosyncrasy in the period. Not even France and Germany are found to be in the same cluster in this period, although they are in the same clusters in the preceding and succeeding periods.[4] Table 4.5, finally, finds 3 clusters to be optimal for the most recent decade, one of these being a fairly prominent 'European' grouping, including the UK. Thus while the evidence is not totally hostile to finding a coherent 'European' grouping it is far from being fully supportive.

Table 4.4   Fuzzy clustering, correlation of business cycles, sample: 1980–1992

	Coefficients					Silhouette width	Belongs to cluster
Austria	0.09	0.13	0.16	0.33	0.29	0.25	4
Finland	0.23	0.06	0.15	0.46	0.10	0.47	4
France	0.11	0.06	0.10	0.61	0.12	0.66	4
Germany	0.12	0.14	0.42	0.17	0. 15	0.80	3
Italy	0.13	0.05	0.24	0.49	0.10	0.34	4
Spain	0.07	0.05	0.08	0.64	0.16	0.62	4
Sweden	0.10	0.05	0.18	0.55	0.13	0.48	4
United Kingdom	0.17	0.07	0.13	0.41	0.21	0.51	4
EU-15	0.09	0.04	0.18	0.59	0.10	0.43	4
United States	0.40	0.07	0.35	0.10	0.08	0.60	1
Canada	0.58	0.05	0.24	0.08	0.05	0.76	1
Japan	0.14	0.08	0.25	0.42	0.12	0.26	4
Switzerland	0.12	0.03	0.73	0.08	0.04	0.68	3
Australia	0.69	0.04	0.16	0.06	0.04	0.76	1
Korea	0.03	0.07	0.04	0.06	0.80	0.63	5
Netherlands	0.10	0.05	0.73	0.08	0.05	0.84	3
Portugal	0.13	0.24	0.11	0.19	0.33	0.67	5
Norway	0.13	0.47	0.15	0.09	0.16	0.73	2
Belgium	0.04	0.79	0.05	0.04	0.08	0.71	2
Mexico	0.62	0.06	0.13	0.12	0.07	0.68	1
Silhouette width	0.70	0.72	0.78	0.45	0.65		

Number of clusters 5
Average silhouette width 0.55
Dunn's coefficient 0.39
Normalized Dunn's coefficient 0.24

5   Globalization vs. Europeanization?

In this section of the chapter we complement the results of the fuzzy clustering analysis with a non-parametric technique to ask questions about the coherence of particular groupings. The procedure involves the 'McNemar test' and has been given prominence recently by Bovi (2003, 2005). As we have already noted, many of the papers in the stream of literature associated with the identification of the European business cycle look outwards, over a period of time, from inside a European group, seeking to identify a closer union (or otherwise).

The important point made by Bovi is that this should be complemented by an analysis of whether any such development has proceeded faster or slower than similar processes elsewhere. Bovi himself uses long-run data on classical cycles to look at this question, focusing in particular

Table 4.5 Fuzzy clustering, correlation of business cycles, sample: 1992–2003

	Coefficients			Silhouette width	Belongs to cluster
Austria	0.33	0.11	0.56	0.79	3
Finland	0.57	0.18	0.26	0.43	1
France	0.23	0.11	0.66	0.82	3
Germany	0.22	0.13	0.65	0.82	3
Italy	0.22	0.20	0.58	0.74	3
Spain	0.34	0.11	0.54	0.71	3
Sweden	0.32	0.42	0.26	0.12	2
United Kingdom	0.26	0.11	0.63	0.74	3
EU-15	0.32	0.10	0.58	0.68	3
United States	0.63	0.17	0.20	0.61	1
Canada	0.25	0.09	0.67	0.78	3
Japan	0.26	0.56	0.18	0.54	2
Switzerland	0.24	0.08	0.68	0.76	3
Australia	0.42	0.37	0.21	0.52	1
Korea	0.15	0.71	0.14	0.58	2
Netherlands	0.37	0.08	0.54	0.65	3
Portugal	0.38	0.19	0.43	0.50	3
Norway	0.24	0.61	0.16	0.47	2
Belgium	0.35	0.10	0.54	0.67	3
Mexico	0.65	0.16	0.19	0.61	1
New Zealand	0.13	0.76	0.10	0.67	2
Denmark	0.23	0.10	0.67	0.73	3
Ireland	0.19	0.07	0.74	0.81	3
Silhouette width	0.55	0.48	0.73		

Number of clusters 3
Average silhouette width 0.51
Dunn's coefficient 0.44
Normalized Dunn's coefficient 0.20

on the position of the UK. Our data sample in this section of the chapter is much shorter and we shall not ask exactly the same questions of the data. How does Bovi's procedure work? Bovi himself recognizes a contribution by McNemar, made as long ago as 1947 (McNemar 1947). The key here is a contingency table approach, as in Table 4.6. At this point we use the information that the application of the cycle-dating algorithm provides. We can divide our observations into four cells (as in the table). When all the countries in Group 1 are in the same business cycle phase (that is, 'in synch'), there will be some periods in which the countries making up Group 2 are also 'in synch' – the intersection of these two sets gives the cell labelled N_{11}, the number of observations in which both groups are 'in synch'. Similarly, while the members of

Table 4.6   A contingency table approach

| | | Group 2 | |
		In-synch	Out-of-synch
Group I	In-synch	N_{11}	N_{12}
	Out-of-synch	N_{21}	N_{22}

Group 1 are 'out of synch' with each other, there will be some periods when the members of Group 2 are also out of synch: the intersection of these two sets corresponds to the cell labelled N_{22} in Table 4.6

The cells labelled N_{12} and N_{21} correspond to the remaining intersections. The information in the contingency table can be used to test whether Group 1 is more (or less) coherent than Group 2, in the sense that it is (or not) more often 'in synch' than Group 2.

McNemar offers the scaled difference $(N_{12} - N_{21})^2/(N_{12} + N_{21})$ as a suitable test statistic for which a χ^2 distribution is suggested (provided that numbers are large enough). Bovi points out that a continuity correction (due to Sheskin 2004) may also be applied. In principle, the test can also be applied, *mutatis mutandis*, to the information in the leading diagonal cells, which we have done here as a check on the main results. Whilst the attraction of the approach is that it can be applied to groups of countries, it can also be applied to individual countries or to groups that are represented by a single aggregate number – it is just that in these cases the country in question (or the aggregate) can only ever be typified as being 'in synch' with itself. If a single country or aggregate takes the place of group 1 (2) in the formula, then the cells N_{22} (N_{12}) and N_{21} (N_{22}) are null. For this reason we have not included individual countries or aggregates in the test. There is also a problem in comparing groups of unequal size in that it is 'harder', other things equal, for a large group to be in synch with itself than for a smaller group. Here we have made the ad hoc adjustment that in comparisons of groups of unequal size, only 80 per cent of the members of the larger group need to be in synch for the group as a whole to be regarded as such; clearly this is an arbitrary adjustment. For these reasons the clearest comparisons are those between the 'core EMU' and the 'Anglo' group – which happen to be the focus of Bovi's attentions in his original papers.

Table 4.7 Bovi-McNemar test statistics, full sample: 1970–2003

	Core EMU	Non-EMU	EU-15	G7	ROW	OECD	ANGLO	EMUUK	NAMU
EMU	0.33	0.20	–	1.29	–1.64	3.86	0.17	–	–1.09
Core EMU		0.00	0.09	0.57	–2.46	5.26	0.00	0.09	–1.96
Non-EMU			0.06	0.53	–2.91	5.76	0.00	0.06	–2.88
EU-15				0.31	–3.52	6.55	0.05	–	–2.91
G7					–9.00	13.24	1.33	0.31	–6.37
ROW						–	4.57	3.52	0.09
OECD							9.31	6.55	1.60
ANGLO								0.05	–
EMUUK									–2.91

Notes:
Critical values: $\chi^2(1)$ at 1% = 2.71 / at 5% = 3.84 / at 10% = 6.63
Clusters of countries:
EMU: all EMU countries Core EMU: FRA, DEU, ITA; non EMU: GBR, SWE, DNK; EU15; all EU
countries G7: USA, CAN, JPN; ROW: all non-EU countries; OECD: all OECD, not EU; ANGLO:
only USA, CAN, GBR; EMUUK: EMU with UK included; NAMU: USA and UK.

In the current application we recognize nine groups of countries. The
groups are: Core EMU (Germany, France and Italy); EMU (all current
members of EMU except Greece, and Luxembourg for which data are
not available); non-EMU (Denmark, UK, Sweden); EU-15 (all except
Greece and Luxembourg); the G-7; the rest of the world (ROW) – all
countries listed in Table 4.1 (i.e. OECD) minus the groups already mentioned; the OECD (all countries in Table 4.1 minus the EU countries;
'ANGLO' – the USA, UK and Canada; EMUUK – the EMU plus the UK;
and NAMU, the US and UK.

Table 4.7 gives a set of results. For their interpretation, bear in mind
that in terms of the formulae quoted above, the countries reported in the
column heads are Group 1 whilst those reported in the rows are Group 2.
This means that a positive and significant value of the figure reported
would indicate that the group defined in the column is more coherent
than that reported in the row, whilst a significant negative figure would
have the opposite implication.

Bearing in mind the critical values listed at the foot of the table, it
is clear that rather little is significant that does not involve one of the
individual countries or the EU-15 aggregate. The main exception is that
some of the figures in the OECD column border acceptable levels of
significance. But significance here means that there is a difference in the
coherence of the groups compared. On this basis there is little to support

the view that there is a distinctive coherent European grouping – only the EU-15–OECD pairing might suggest otherwise (the same can be said at a lower level of significance for Core EMU and non-EMU pairings with OECD here).

6   Conclusion

The object of the chapter was to see whether measures of business cycle synchronization or coherence support the view that there are 'business cycle clubs'. We had particularly in mind that it might be possible to detect the emergence of a 'European business cycle'. The results we have obtained seem to show that whilst some business cycle groupings can be detected for periods of time, only a few of these are reasonably persistent. The presence of a persistent – or growing – 'European' grouping seems particularly hard to detect, perhaps surprisingly given the common implicit acceptance of the contrary view. Among the possible explanations for this must be counted the following: changes in the relative frequency of global versus regional or national-idiosyncratic shocks; changes in the interrelationships between economies (to put it loosely, the growth of 'globalization'), and the habit of examining the European cycle by starting with Europe and looking at its development, so to speak from the inside out.

In acting in this way there is a clear risk of failing to distinguish globalization from Europeanization, when by globalization we mean to refer to a phenomenon embracing the group of advanced countries. (Kose et al. 2008 note that there is a decoupling of advanced from developing countries in recent years.) Something must be added also to account for differences in the results that may be obtained, either by working with industrial production or GDP data, or, in the case of some of the more recent papers reviewed, working with composites or factors based on an ensemble of macroeconomic variables.

Notes

1. The author wishes to acknowledge the helpful research assistance of Peter Claeys of the EUI and the hospitality of the European Commission (DG-ECFIN) during a stay as Research Fellow there during the month of May 2004, when work on this chapter was advanced.
2. Industrial production is more cyclical than GDP and relates more closely to tradable goods, biases which might conduce to a 'European cycle' finding.

On the other hand Camacho et al. (2006) use industrial production data and deliver a sceptical verdict on the existence of a 'European' cycle.
3. Note that this may not matter for the key policy question which is whether the cycles are close enough for a single monetary policy to be effective and acceptable.
4. The Netherlands and Switzerland are more constant companions for Germany.

References

Artis, M. J. (2006), 'What do we now know about currency unions?', *Quarterly Bulletin of the Bank of England*, 46(2): 243–55.

Artis, M. J. and Zhang, W. (1997), 'International business cycles and the ERM: is there a European business cycle?', *International Journal of Finance and Economics*, 2: 1–16.

Artis, M. J., Krolzig, H. M. and Toro, J. (2004), 'The European business cycle', *Oxford Economic Papers*, 56: 1–44.

Artis, M. J., Marcellino, M. and Proietti, T. (2002), 'Dating the Euro Area business cycle', CEPR Discussion Paper, no. 3696, London: CEPR.

Barrell, R. and Weale, M. (2003), 'Designing and choosing macroeconomic frameworks: the position of the UK after four years of the euro', *Oxford Review of Economic Policy*, 19: 132–48.

Baxter, M. and King, R. G. (1999), 'Measuring business cycles: approximate bandpass filters for economic time series', *Review of Economics and Statistics*, 81: 575–93.

Baxter, M. and Stockman, A. C. (1986), 'Business cycles and the exchange rate regime', *Journal of Monetary Economics*, 23: 377–400.

Bovi, M. (2003), 'A non-parametric analysis of international business cycles', ISAE Working Papers, no. 37.

Bovi, M. (2005), 'Globalization vs Europeanization: a business cycles race', *Oxford Bulletin of Economics and Statistics*, 67: 331–45.

Camacho, M., Perez-Quiros, G. and Saiz, L. (2006), 'Are European business cycles close enough to be one?', *Journal of Economic Dynamics and Control*, 30: 1687–1706.

Canova, F., Ciccarelli, M. and Ortega, E. (2007), 'Similarities and convergence in G-7 cycles', *Journal of Monetary Economics*, 54: 850–78.

Frankel, J. and Rose, A. (1998), 'The endogeneity of the optimal currency area criteria', *Economic Journal*, 108: 1009–25.

Harding, D. and Pagan, A. (2001), 'Extracting, analysing and using cyclical information', Melbourne Institute of Applied Economics and Social Research, mimeo.

Harding, D. and Pagan, A. (2002), 'Synchronization of cycles', Melbourne Institute of Applied Economic and Social Research, mimeo.

Harvey, A. C. and Jaeger, A. (1993), 'Detrending, stylized facts and the business cycle', *Journal of Applied Econometrics*, 8: 231–47.

Harvey, A. C. and Trimbur, T. (2003), 'General model-based filters for extracting trends and cycles in economic time series', *Review of Economics and Statistics*, 85: 244–55.

Kaufman, L. and Rousseow, P. J. (1990), *Finding Groups in Data*, New York: John Wiley and Sons.

Kaufmann, S. (2003), 'The business cycle of European countries: Bayesian clustering of country-individual IP growth series', Working Papers of the National Bank of Austria, no. 83.

Kose, M. A., Otrok, C. and Prasad, E. (2008), 'Global business cycles: convergence or decoupling?', mimeo.

Massmann, M. and Mitchell, J. (2002), 'Have UK and European business cycles become more correlated?', *National Institute Economic Review*, 192: 58–71.

McNemar, Q. (1947), 'Note on the sampling error of the difference between correlated proportions or percentages', *Psychometrika*, 12: 153–7.

Sheskin, D. J. (2004), *Handbook of Parametric and Nonparametric Statistical Procedures*, 3rd edition, Boca Raton: Chapman and Hall/CRC Press.

Tsoukalis, L. (1997), *The New European Economy Revisited*, Oxford: Oxford University Press.

5
EMU and the Euro-Mediterranean Dialogue: Trade Interdependence between Mediterranean and Euro-area Countries

Giorgio Fazio

1 Introduction

Economic interdependence and trade encourage international dialogue and represent a base for reducing international conflicts. Hence, international co-operation for the reduction of barriers to trade and capital flows can be important not only in inducing economic progress, but also in promoting peace (Polachek and Siegle 2006). In this respect, the introduction of the euro represents an epochal event for both the participants in the single European currency and for their external partners, and in particular those in neighbouring regions. However, whilst a large body of literature has focused on analysing the first, in particular, with respect to the impact of the euro on intra-regional trade, little effort has been devoted to investigating the role of the euro in shaping the relations of the EMU members with their non-EMU partners.

In particular, enhancing economic and trade relations among the EU countries and their Mediterranean neighbours can have substantial implications for the economic and political stabilization of the area, and especially for the Middle East peace process. After all, the Mediterranean Sea is the natural setting for the dialogue between the West and the Middle East. This chapter, therefore, focuses on the implications of the introduction of the European single currency for the process of Euro-Mediterranean integration and, in particular, for the Euro-Mediterranean Partnership (EMP), with a special attention to trade relations.

By design, the euro should enhance trade among its members. The common currency eliminates exchange rate uncertainty, reduces trading costs and uncertainty, and favours cross-national trade and investment. Over recent years, an intensive academic and policy debate, prompted by the birth of EMU and ignited by Rose's (2000) *Economic Policy* paper, has concentrated on the role of currency unions in promoting trade. Despite the considerable controversy on the proper estimated effect of currency unions, as reported by Baldwin (2006), the evidence that currency unions increase trade is overwhelming.

Importantly, currency unions are not usually associated with trade diverting effects. However, this hypothesis is of fundamental importance for the development of the Euro-Mediterranean dialogue, as the little existing evidence on non-EU Mediterranean trade indicates already too small levels of trade (see Al-Atreash and Yousef 1999). Yet academic and policy circles have devoted very little attention to this issue.

This chapter attempts to fill this gap with respect to the effects of the euro on the process of Euro-Mediterranean integration, as intended by the Barcelona Declaration, through greater trade. In particular, some crucial questions are asked: Has the introduction of the euro influenced the process of integration through trade conceived by the Barcelona Conference? If the common currency is, as expected, trade-creating among the members of the union, does this process come at the expense of trade with the Southern neighbours? Clearly, providing an answer to these questions entails some important political and policy implications for both European and Mediterranean countries.

Therefore, we perform an empirical investigation of the extent of trade integration between the countries that will form the Free Trade Area (FTA) in 2010. In particular, we look at the trade flows between Euro-Mediterranean countries using the toolbox provided by the gravity model in order to estimate the extent of trade within and between specific geo-political blocs identified along the North–North, the North–South and the South–South axes. Moreover, we monitor the progress of these trade blocs over time during the 1980s and up to 2004 with a greater focus on the more recent post-euro period. Bearing in mind these considerations, the next section briefly discusses the debate on currency unions and trade south of the Mediterranean. Section 3 briefly introduces the Euro-Mediterranean Partnership. Sections 4 and 5 outline the econometric methodology and present the data employed in the empirical analysis. Section 6 discusses the results and section 7 concludes.

2   Currency unions and trade integration south of the Mediterranean

Currency unions can promote economic integration in a number of ways: by reducing transaction costs and increasing the market size, they boost trade and allow the exploitation of economies of scale; by enhancing greater macroeconomic stability and reducing uncertainty, they improve the efficient allocation of resources and favour cross-border investment and financial integration; and by committing governments for the long term, they can improve political integration. Clearly, they also entail losses, depending on the need for an independent monetary policy.

As discussed above, the literature on trade interdependence in the Mediterranean is quite scarce. The little existing evidence seems to indicate too low levels of trade. In reference to the Middle East, Al-Atreash and Yousef's (1999) paper suggests that trade within the region is lower than what would be expected by economic theory and that, contrary to most of the evidence on trade blocs, group membership (such as the Gulf Cooperation Council and the Arab Maghreb Union) does not exercise any positive effect on trade between these countries.

Recently, however, some authors have tried to investigate whether the birth of the euro will inspire the future formation of monetary unions, especially south of the Mediterranean. In particular, Honohan and Lane (2000) discuss whether the European single currency is likely to promote the implementation of monetary unions in Africa. They stress the substantive differences between African and European countries and argue that the launch of single or regional African currencies is both unlikely and undesirable. However, they argue that the euro could represent a valid anchor currency to ensure greater African monetary stability.

Tsangarides et al. (2006) use the gravity model to analyse the relevance of currency unions in Africa and conclude that African countries do benefit from the trade-creating effect of currency unions as much as the rest of the world. Currency unions are also associated with further positive effects in terms of greater trade stability and price co-movements, but not of output co-movement (hence, in terms of the reduction of asymmetric shocks). Particularly important in promoting integration is the duration of currency unions, since the longer the life of a currency union, the greater the benefits for its members.[1] However, the low levels of trade among African countries probably implies that trade promotion in Africa depends more on other factors, such as the improvement of infrastructures, institutions and trade policies, than on the implementation of monetary unions.

Subramanian and Tamirisa (2003) investigate the extent of African trade integration with the world economy. Although they tend to confirm the conventional view that Africa is not well integrated with the rest of the world, they argue that this result is only valid for

Francophone Africa. Anglophone Africa, in contrast, is inverting the trend of disintegration, especially with industrialized countries.

Masson (2007) also discusses the feasibility and desirability of a single African Monetary Union (AMU) and concludes that the low level of current trade among African countries makes the potential benefits of a common currency too small. Even the doubling of trade would not outweigh the costs of existing asymmetries between African countries. However, he admits that regional currency unions in Africa could be a possibility.

Therefore, despite the fact that most of the studies in the literature tend to exclude the possibility of a single AMU, along the lines of the euro, they do not rule out the possibility that the experience of regional currency might develop in the future. Given the dominance of African trade with European countries, the euro might also serve as reference currency for possible future currency zones, along the lines of the experience of the CFA franc zone.

North African Mediterranean and Middle East countries have a substantial advantage compared to the rest of the African countries. The Euro-Mediterranean Partnership, founded in Barcelona, and the FTA in 2010 constitute the proper platform for promoting future economic co-operation and monetary integration in the area.

3   The Barcelona Conference and the Euro-Mediterranean Partnership

Building stronger ties among European and Mediterranean countries is the main agenda of the EMP. The EMP was established in the 1995 Barcelona Conference with the goal of beginning a process towards 'peace and shared prosperity' and 'sustainable and balanced economic and social development' in the Euro-Mediterranean area. Fifteen European Union member states and twelve non-EU members from the Mediterranean Sea area signed the Barcelona Declaration with the aim of achieving long-term objectives in the promotion of human rights, democracy, security, and socio-cultural co-operation in the area (see Table 5.1 for a full list of participants at the Barcelona Conference and the EMP).

The strength of the linkages between trade, peace and prosperity must have been clear to the conference participants, as they identified trade integration as the way to build and reinforce the partnership. The establishment of the Euro-Mediterranean Free Trade Area (EU-MeFTA) by the year 2010 represents the final and most significant step in this process.[2]

Table 5.1   The Euro-Mediterranean Partnership

EU members	Non-EU members
Austria, Belgium, Cyprus,* Denmark, Germany, Spain, Finland, France, Greece, Ireland, Italy, Luxembourg, Malta,* Netherlands, Portugal, United Kingdom and Sweden	Algeria, Egypt, Israel, Jordan, Lebanon, Morocco, Syria, Tunisia, Turkey, and the Palestinian Authority

* Entered the EU in 2004

Since the signing of the Declaration, a number of co-operation treaties have been signed by the EU with its future partners in the free trade area. While Turkey has been in a customs union with the EU since 1996, other association agreements have been negotiated with the Palestinian Authority (1997), Tunisia (1998), Israel (2000), Morocco (2000), Jordan (2002), Egypt (2004), Algeria (2005), Lebanon (2006) and Syria (under negotiation). In 2004, Malta and Cyprus officially joined the European Union.

Important steps to strengthen trade relationships have been under-taken or are being undertaken by non-EU Mediterranean countries. The most important of these is probably the Agadir Agreement, a free trade area established in 1994 between Jordan, Tunisia, Morocco and Egypt (Lebanon is currently negotiating its entry). A free trade area between Libya and Lebanon is also under negotiation.

Since the middle of the 1990s, a number of international events may have affected the progress towards a stronger Euro-Mediterranean part-nership. First of all, the financial crises of the second part of the 1990s undermined the general confidence of international investors towards emerging markets (Bayoumi et al. 2007). Secondly, the events follow-ing 11 September 2001 have produced a particular unsteadiness between Western and Arab countries with potential negative consequences for the peace process in the Middle East. Furthermore, the enlargement of the EU to some of the Central and East European (CEE) countries is seen by some commentators as an event that may well lead to greater integration with the Central and Eastern countries to the detriment of North–South and South–South integration. Indeed, in 2003 the European Commission for-mulated the European Neighbourhood Policy (ENP) with the objective of starting to draw into further integration neighbouring countries of the new and enlarged EU in 2004 and avoid frictions between the new EU and its neighbours.[3] Last, but not least, the introduction of the euro may have had asymmetric effects on the levels of trade among countries in the area.

Table 5.2 Trade blocs in EU-MeFTA

Northern Europe (NE)	Southern Europe (SE)	Middle East – North Africa (MENA)	Northern Europe – Middle East – North Africa (NEMENA)	Southern Europe – Middle East – North Africa (SEMENA)
Austria Belgium Denmark Germany Finland Ireland Luxembourg Netherlands, Portugal, UK Sweden	Spain, France Greece, Italy Malta, Cyprus	Algeria, Egypt Morocco Tunisia Israel Jordan Syria Turkey	Northern Europe & Middle East North Africa (trade intra-NE and intra-MENA excluded)	Southern Europe & Middle East North Africa (trade intra-SE and intra-MENA excluded)

In order to assess the extent of trade among the Euro-Mediterranean partners, we run a simple empirical investigation using the gravity model. Then, we investigate the trade patterns in the area along different geographical axes. In particular, we look at trade among Northern EU countries, Southern EU countries, Middle Eastern and North African countries and among the first two and the third. The country groupings are listed in Table 5.2. Finally, we monitor the evolution of the trade patterns between these blocs over time, with a particular eye on the introduction of the euro.

4 A simple empirical evaluation

4.1 The gravity model

In this section we provide a short review of the econometric techniques used to estimate the proposed gravity representation of trade flows.[4] The traditional formulation of the gravity model derives from Newton's universal law of gravitation, which states that the attraction between two bodies is proportional to their mass and inversely proportional to their distance. The most elementary formulation of the model reflects these assumptions:

$$T_{ij} = a \frac{W_i W_j}{d_{ij}},$$

where W_i and W_j denote the weights (the economic size) of countries i and j, d_{ij} is the distance between origin and destination, and a is a simple proportionality factor. In international trade, the most basic representation of the gravity model explains the amount of trade between two countries as increasing in the size of the two economies, measured by their national incomes, and decreasing in their geographical distance, which can be interpreted as a proxy for the cost of transporting goods from origin to destination (between the most populous cities). Since its first applications by Tinbergen (1962), the model has become the 'workhorse' of International Economics (Eichengreen and Irwin 1997), gaining popularity thanks to its applicability to a wide variety of empirical experiments.[5] In the past, the use of the gravity equation was criticized because of a substantial lack of theoretical foundations.[6] These criticisms have, however, been cast aside after a number of papers have shown how the gravity equation can be derived from different trade models.[7]

Empirically, the most common representation of the gravity equation takes the following log-linear form:

$$\log(X_{ijt}) = a_0 + a_t + a_{ij} + B_{ijt}G_{ijt} + \varepsilon_{ijt}, \quad \text{with } t = 1, \ldots, T, \qquad (5.1)$$

where X_{ijt} is the volume of exports from country i to country j. The intercept is composed of three parts: a_0 is common to all country pairs and all years, a_t is common to all pairs, but year-specific, and a_{ij} is the country-pair specific part. Disturbances ε_{ijt} are assumed normally distributed and pair-wise uncorrelated errors. G_{ijt} is a matrix of trade determinants. In early specifications, this matrix included only distance and incomes. In later contributions, a number of other country-specific factors have been added, becoming standard in empirical applications, such as the countries' population (augmented gravity), land areas, and per capita incomes, and country pair variables capturing cultural affinity (common language), geography (common border), and political factors (preferential trade agreements, common currency, common colonizer or former colonial relationship).

The intercept and the slopes in equation (5.1) are restricted to be the same across all country pairs, that is to say $a_{ij} = 0$ and $B_{ijt} = B_t$, and the model is estimated over a cross-sectional dimension. More recently, however, the gravity model has been estimated using panel data,[8] by imposing the further restriction of identical slopes across years, that is to say $B_t = B$. Hence, equation (5.1) becomes:

$$\log(X_{ijt}) = a_0 + a_t + BG_{ijt} + \varepsilon_{ijt}, \quad \text{with } t = 1, \ldots, T, \qquad (5.2)$$

where the intercept is further allowed to vary over time using dummies for year controls. More recently, a number of papers (see Mátyás

1997a, 1997b) have suggested the use of country dummies in order to account for unobserved country components. Anderson and van Wijncoop (2003, 2004), in particular, have sustained the importance of including *multilateral trade resistance* terms by using dummies referring to the country as an exporter and to the country as an importer.[9]

Hence, we may write equation (5.2) in the following form:

$$\log(X_{ij}) = a_0 + a_1 Z_i^X + a_2 Z_j^M + B_1 G_{ij} + B_2 D_t + \varepsilon_{ij}, \qquad (5.3)$$

where Z_i^X denotes a dummy for the exporting country, and Z_j^M a dummy for the exporting country, and D_t is a matrix of T-1 time dummies. Equation (5.3) is then generally estimated by OLS.[10]

In this empirical exercise, we consider equation (5.3) as the most general specification (we also use equation 5.2 with time dummies as a preliminary regression, see discussion below) and use it to investigate intra-EU-MeFTA trade. In particular, on the road to the Free Trade Area, it seems important to estimate the extent of overall integration between the future FTA members, but also the extent of trade inter- and intra- the geographical blocs. After all, the Barcelona Process envisaged the building of the Euro-Mediterranean partnership in a number of steps beginning with bilateral and multilateral agreements (such as the Agadir Agreement). Hence, as a first step in our analysis, we try to estimate the geographical patterns of intra-EUMeFTA trade. As discussed in the previous section, the sample is divided into three main areas presented in Table 5.2: the non-Mediterranean coastal countries from the EU (Northern Europe, NE), Mediterranean coastal EU members (Southern Europe, SE), and non-EU Mediterranean Sea coastal countries which will take part in the Free Trade Area (Middle East and North Africa, MENA). The European countries are then grouped into the fifteen European Union members who signed the Barcelona Conference Declaration (EU-15). Clearly, since these countries have been in an explicit preferential trade agreement for most of the period under observation,[11] this dummy is essentially equivalent to the Free Trade Area dummy present in most gravity studies. Furthermore, we try to estimate the extent of inter-bloc trade, that is to say trade for all bilateral pairs belonging to two different blocs (but excluding intra-bloc bilateral trade). This is possible by introducing separate dummies for North European and South European countries' trade with the MENA countries. Hence, as a first step we investigate trade blocs by using the above equation (5.3) specification and progressively adding the trade bloc variables, TB_{ij}:

$$\log(X_{ij}) = a_0 + a_1 Z_i^X + a_2 Z_j^M + B_1 G_{ij} + B_2 D_t + \delta TB_{ij} + \varepsilon_{ij}, \qquad (5.4)$$

Secondly, we try to estimate whether the patterns of trade between these blocs have been changing over the period considered by looking at the interaction between trade blocs and the time dummies. Finally, we estimate again the most general version of the gravity model (equation (5.3)) and use it to derive the trade potential between each country pair.

5 Data

The data set consists of annual observations from 1980 to 2004 of trade between EU-MeFTA (see the data appendix for a full description of data sources and variables transformations). The data on FOB bilateral exports, X_{ij}, are taken from the IMF's *Direction of Trade Statistics* (DTS, 2006).[12] They are expressed in US dollars and converted into constant dollars using the US Consumer Price Index. Both the GDP and Population series are taken from the IMF's *International Financial Statistics* (2006). The GDP series have been converted into US dollars and divided by the US consumer price index. Land areas are taken from the *World Development Indicators* (2005) of the World Bank. The computation of distance relies on the arc-geometry formula between the two most populous cities. In the general model, where we include a large set of conditioning variables, a set of dummies serve to identify whether two trading partners use the same currency, whether they have been in a colonial relationship post-1945, and whether they speak the same language. This last variable is obtained from Melitz (2008),[13] who calculates a continuous indicator with values going from 0 to 1 rather than a 0/1 dummy.[14] Landlocked/Island are two variables taking a value of one if one of the countries in the pair is Landlocked/Island and two when both are. A summary of the statistics and the correlation matrix are reported in the data appendix.

6 Results

6.1 Trade blocs

As a preliminary step, a general version of the gravity model is estimated with all of the traditional gravity variables (and time dummies) – but without the Anderson and van Wijncoop (2003) multilateral trade resistance terms. Progressively, trade bloc dummies are included. The results from these regressions are presented in Table 5.3. In order to check the validity of the specification, we report in the first column the basic model without bloc dummies. All of the estimates are statistically significant and correctly signed, providing support for our gravity model specification. Adding the EU-15 dummy – almost equivalent here to the traditional FTA dummy – yields the expected large effect of the free trade area on bilateral trade. In columns 2 and 3 the EU-15 dummy is broken into a dummy for the Northern and Central countries and one for the Southern ones. Interestingly, only the NE dummy remains statistically significant and positive, indicating that most of the trade-creating effect of the EU is felt in Central and Northern Europe. The EU Mediterranean coastal countries do not seem to trade more than average. Table 5.3 shows similar results in column 5 for the intra-MENA trade, which is always significant, but below average. Column 8 reports on the inclusion of both the EU-15 and the MENA dummies, summarizing and confirming the above results. Column 9 regression controls for intra-EU-15 trade, intra-MENA trade, North–South trade (NEMENA), and South–South trade (SEMENA). Again, the only statistically significant dummies are the ones of European trade (positive) and MENA (negative) trade. No significant effect can be detected for the North–South and the South–South trade.

In the regressions reported in Table 5.4, we repeat the same analysis but now control for multilateral trade resistance (Anderson and van Wijncoop 2003). Again, inspection of column 1 validates our gravity specification, except for the lost significance of the log product of land areas. This, however, is not too surprising given that the multilateral trade resistance terms capture most of the time invariant country characteristics. As before, in columns 2 to 9 we have progressively included the bloc dummies. Similarly, some of the variables with lower time variability lose their significance, depending on the introduction of a particular bloc dummy. The introduction of the country dummies has also modified the significance and/or sign of some of the dummy coefficients. Clearly, there must be some form of interaction between the country dummies and association to a particular trade bloc, which can itself be considered as a trade resistance factor. However, in the most complete specification presented in column 9 the punch line is the same as in Table 5.3: the EU-15 trade more than average, the MENA countries trade less and, importantly, North–South and South–South trade are not significantly above or below the rest of the sample.

6.2 Time effects

As discussed above, in order to monitor the evolution of the trade blocs, in particular with respect to the introduction of the euro, and its trade-creating/diverting effect on European trade with the non-EU partners, particularly interesting is the time analysis of trade relationships in the

Table 3.3 Regressions without country dummies

	(1)	(2)	(3)	(4)	(5)	(6)	(7)	(8)	(9)
log(Dij)	-1.13***	-0.74***	-1.16***	-0.81***	-1.27***	-1.11***	-1.16***	-0.91***	-0.89***
	(0.105)	(0.093)	(0.104)	(0.092)	(0.096)	(0.112)	(0.102)	(0.080)	(0.084)
log(Yi*Yj)	0.247***	0.245***	0.267***	0.065***	0.196***	0.246***	0.263***	-0.018	-0.015
	(0.017)	(0.015)	(0.018)	(0.019)	(0.017)	(0.020)	(0.017)	(0.017)	(0.019)
log(POPi*POPj)	0.775***	0.865***	0.756***	0.978***	0.809***	0.774***	0.781***	1.049***	1.056***
	(0.073)	(0.061)	(0.072)	(0.060)	(0.068)	(0.075)	(0.068)	(0.054)	(0.057)
log(Ai*Aj)	-0.306***	-0.250***	-0.297***	-0.277***	-0.266***	-0.314***	-0.293***	-0.230***	-0.240***
	(0.052)	(0.050)	(0.052)	(0.048)	(0.051)	(0.053)	(0.050)	(0.046)	(0.049)
Landlocked	-0.590***	-0.733***	-0.584***	-0.558***	-0.580***	-0.530***	-0.705***	-0.590***	-0.600***
	(0.183)	(0.160)	(0.184)	(0.153)	(0.180)	(0.184)	(0.182)	(0.144)	(0.147)
Island	-0.655**	0.262	-0.524*	-1.408***	-0.806***	-0.804***	-0.532*	-1.586***	-1.638***
	(0.258)	(0.258)	(0.285)	(0.219)	(0.259)	(0.269)	(0.249)	(0.213)	(0.237)
Colonial Rel	1.516***	1.459***	1.476***	1.393***	1.241***	1.472***	2.071***	1.042***	1.094***
	(0.306)	(0.262)	(0.301)	(0.239)	(0.326)	(0.318)	(0.298)	(0.227)	(0.253)
Language	0.409*	0.512***	0.435**	0.510***	0.479**	0.419*	0.417**	0.597***	0.609***
	(0.218)	(0.181)	(0.219)	(0.180)	(0.202)	(0.218)	(0.202)	(0.159)	(0.158)
EMU	0.759***								
	(0.139)								
NE		2.109***							
		(0.138)							
SE			-0.476						
			(0.298)						
Intra EU15				2.353***				2.489***	2.142***
				(0.142)				(0.134)	(0.363)
MENA					-1.801***			-2.176***	-2.490***
					(0.233)			(0.216)	(0.394)
NEMENA						-0.196			-0.332
						(0.183)			(0.375)
SEMENA							-1.364***		-0.430
							(0.147)		(0.364)
Time dummies	Yes	Yes	Yes	Yes	Yes	Yes	Yes	Yes	Yes
Country dummies	No	No	No	No	No	No	No	No	No
Observations	13328	13328	13328	13328	13328	13328	13328	13328	13328
R²	0.67	0.73	0.67	0.75	0.69	0.67	0.69	0.78	0.78

In parentheses robust standard errors corrected for clustering by country pair; constant and year dummies are omitted; * significant at 10%; ** significant at 5%; *** significant at 1%

Table 5.4 Regressions with country dummies

	(1)	(2)	(3)	(4)	(5)	(6)	(7)	(8)	(9)
log(Dij)	-0.87***	-0.77***	-0.89***	-0.82***	-0.82***	-0.77***	-0.89***	-0.82***	-0.80***
	(0.064)	(0.072)	(0.064)	(0.066)	(0.066)	(0.072)	(0.064)	(0.066)	(0.074)
log(Yi*Yj)	0.427***	0.418***	0.415***	0.419***	0.419***	0.419***	0.415***	0.419***	0.419***
	(0.072)	(0.073)	(0.073)	(0.073)	(0.073)	(0.072)	(0.073)	(0.073)	(0.072)
log(POPi*POPj)	0.497*	0.303	0.298	0.238	0.238	0.270	0.304	0.238	0.245
	(0.269)	(0.258)	(0.258)	(0.260)	(0.260)	(0.258)	(0.258)	(0.260)	(0.260)
log(Ai*Aj)	-0.144	0.081	0.611***	-0.119	0.637***	0.621***	-0.039	-0.187**	-0.011
	(0.157)	(0.142)	(0.150)	(0.125)	(0.150)	(0.150)	(0.151)	(0.082)	(0.092)
Landlocked	-1.302***	-0.062	1.553**	-1.177***	1.360*	1.576**	-1.270***	-1.597***	-1.630***
	(0.324)	(0.376)	(0.782)	(0.373)	(0.785)	(0.784)	(0.329)	(0.334)	(0.334)
Island	0.144	1.466***	4.381***	-1.834***	4.236***	4.313***	-0.169	-2.403***	-2.443***
	(0.492)	(0.520)	(1.028)	(0.573)	(1.037)	(1.040)	(0.476)	(0.375)	(0.353)
Colonial Rel.	1.182***	1.128***	1.251***	1.260***	1.260***	1.104***	1.179***	1.260***	1.151***
	(0.152)	(0.157)	(0.156)	(0.146)	(0.146)	(0.151)	(0.161)	(0.146)	(0.152)
Language	0.655***	0.634***	0.630***	0.619***	0.619***	0.645***	0.648***	0.619***	0.616***
	(0.140)	(0.141)	(0.137)	(0.136)	(0.136)	(0.144)	(0.141)	(0.136)	(0.140)
EMU	0.355***								
	(0.080)								
NE		0.627***							
		(0.122)							
SE			0.317*						
			(0.163)						
EU15				0.712***				1.227***	2.533***
				(0.202)				(0.263)	(0.465)
MENA					0.712***			-0.515	-1.501***
					(0.202)			(0.340)	(0.504)
NEMENA						-0.434***			0.058
						(0.105)			(0.305)
SEMENA							0.023		0.381
							(0.112)		(0.295)
Observations	13328	13328	13328	13328	13328	13328	13328	13328	13328
R²	0.88	0.88	0.88	0.88	0.88	0.88	0.88	0.88	0.88

In parentheses robust standard errors corrected for clustering by country pair; constant, country and year dummies are omitted; * significant at 10%; ** significant at 5%; *** significant at 1%

Table 5.5   The effect of EMU

	(1)	(2)
log(Dij)	−0.878***	−0.878***
	(0.064)	(0.064)
log(Yi*Yj)	0.427***	0.428***
	(0.072)	(0.072)
log(POPi*POPj)	0.497*	0.497*
	(0.269)	(0.269)
log(Ai*Aj)	−0.144	0.511***
	(0.157)	(0.154)
Landlocked	−1.302***	2.026**
	(0.324)	(0.801)
Island	0.144	5.106***
	(0.492)	(1.055)
Colonial Rel.	1.182***	1.182***
	(0.152)	(0.152)
Language	0.655***	0.655***
	(0.140)	(0.140)
EMU	0.355***	
	(0.080)	
EMU in 1999		0.395***
		(0.077)
EMU in 2000		0.341***
		(0.080)
EMU in 2001		0.391***
		(0.084)
EMU in 2002		0.303***
		(0.085)
EMU in 2003		0.365***
		(0.086)
EMU in 2004		0.333***
		(0.091)
Time dummies	Yes	Yes
Country dummies	Yes	Yes
Observations	13328	13328
R^2	0.88	0.88

In parentheses robust standard errors corrected for clustering by
country pair; constant, country and year dummies are omitted;
* significant at 10%; ** significant at 5%; *** significant at 1%

region. Table 5.5 presents a first set of regressions for a quick and dirty
assessment of the overall impact of the introduction of the euro on the
EU-MeFTA trade. Column 2 in the table shows the results of regressions
where the common currency dummy is interacted with the year effects.
These results seem to suggest that in each year EMU has had an increasing

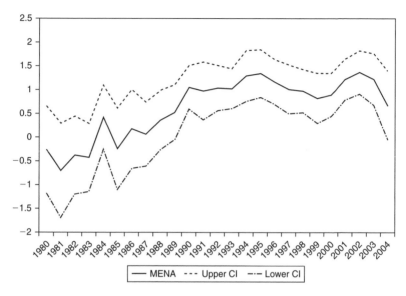

Figure 5.1   Intra-MENA trade (estimated time dummies and 95% confidence interval)

effect on trade.[15] Overall the increase is steady and always statistically significant at the 1 per cent confidence level.

In order to investigate the patterns of trade over time, we have run a set of regressions where we have used the most general representation (with multilateral trade resistance and time dummies) of the gravity model and have added a set of dummies, where the trade blocs are interacted with the time effects. These specifications allow us to extract the time patterns over and above the general effect of time (for example globalization) on the same bloc and the other blocs. Given that we are mostly interested in the time evolution of each specific bloc of trade partners, we do not report here the full set of regressions, but simply plot the dummy variables estimates with the respective confidence intervals.

The results presented in Figures 5.1 to 5.3 paint a clear picture. Intra-MENA trade has been increasing from negative to significantly positive values at the beginning of the 1990s. At the introduction of the euro in 1999, intra-MENA trade has increased significantly until 2001 and then experiences a large fall towards insignificance. Figures 5.2 and 5.3 show an interesting pattern of European trade with MENA. Trade along the South–South axis has undergone a decrease from the beginning of

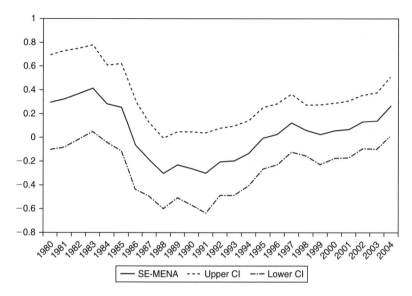

Figure 5.2 Trade between Southern Europe and MENA (estimated time dummies and 95% confidence interval)

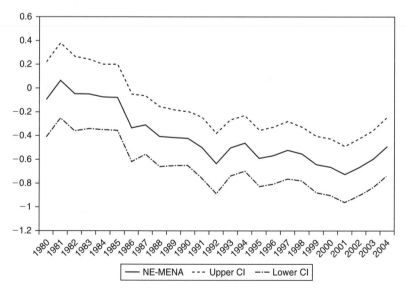

Figure 5.3 Trade between Northern Europe and MENA (estimated time dummies and 95% confidence interval)

the period till the end of the 1980s. From the 1990s onwards, trade has started to pick up with time coefficients becoming positive, though still insignificant, from the middle of the 1990s (interestingly, since the Barcelona Conference). Just like South–South trade, North–South trade has been decreasing since the beginning of the 1980s. This trend is, interestingly, unmodified by the Barcelona Process post-1995. The euro effect from 1999 onwards on European trade with MENA is the opposite. The euro boosts Southern Europe trade with MENA, but decreases (at least in 1999 and 2000) Northern European trade with MENA. This evidence seems to point towards the possible development of diverging trade blocs within the future Free Trade Area, with the Mediterranean countries probably benefiting more from the trade liberalization than the Northern and Central European ones.

7   Conclusion

Further trade integration is important to build peace and shared prosperity in the Euro-Mediterranean region. The introduction of the European single currency represents an epochal event for the entire region. A few years after the introduction of the euro and from the institution of the Euro-Mediterranean Free Trade Area, we ran an empirical investigation into the nature of trade between the future FTA members. In particular, we used a gravity model specification to identify and monitor the existence of trade blocs along different geographical directions. The evidence presented seems to suggest that within the Euro-Mediterranean Partnership, EU trade is clearly dominant. Within European trade, North European trade dominates. Southern Mediterranean trade is still below average, and there is little North–South interdependence (that is to say Centre and North European and Southern European trade with the Southern Mediterranean). By monitoring these blocs over time, we find mixed evidence on the impact of the euro on trade interdependence in the area. Middle East North African trade has been showing a positive trend since the beginning of the 1990s (although there is also evidence of a drop post-2001, possibly due to the impact of the events following 2001). Interestingly, differing patterns can be detected between Southern Europe–Southern Mediterranean trade (falling until the mid-1980s and recovering afterwards, especially after the Barcelona Conference) and Northern Europe–Southern Mediterranean trade (falling steadily for the full period). These trends are particularly evident at the introduction of the euro in 1999, when the Southern European and Northern European trade with MENA takes diverging paths.

Strengthening the policies in favour of the Euro-Mediterranean Partnership becomes crucial in determining the future of trade interdependence and international relations in the area. These policies should clearly aim at removing the still remaining frictions to further integration, such as the missing infrastructures, institutions and the remaining trade policy frictions still constraining goods and factor mobility in the area. Removal of these limitations represents the critical and necessary step to strengthen the dialogue, promote further integration, and create the potential for future monetary co-operation in the area.

7.1 Data appendix

The data set includes all the future members of the Euro-Mediterranean Free Trade Area. The Palestinian Authority and Lebanon were excluded because of a lack of data.

15 EU member states in 1995:

Austria (122, NE), Belgium (124, NE), Denmark (128, NE), Germany (134, NE), Spain (184, SE), Finland (172, NE), France (132, SE), Greece (174, SE), Ireland (178, NE), Italy (136, SE), Luxembourg (137, NE), Netherlands (138, NE), Portugal (182, NE), United Kingdom (112, NE), Sweden (144, NE).

10 governments from the wider Mediterranean region:

Algeria (612, NA), Cyprus (432, SE), Egypt (469, NA), Israel (436, ME), Jordan (439, ME), Malta (181, SE), Morocco (686, NA), Syria (463, ME), Tunisia (744, NA), and Turkey (186, ME).

Variables definitions

X_{ij}: Average between Bilateral Exports Fob of country i to country j and Imports cif of country j from country i (Source: IMF *Directions of Trade Statistics*, DTS 2006), expressed in US\$ and scaled by the US Consumer Price Index (CPI), taken from the IMF *International Financial Statistics* (2006) line 64.

Distance$_{ij}$: Great circle distances are calculated using the arc-geometry formula on the latitude and longitude co-ordinates of the most populous city.

Y: Gross Domestic Product of country in current US\$ divided by the US CPI series. Both series are taken from the IMF *International Financial Statistics* (2006).

Population: Population taken from the IMF *International Financial Statistics* (2006).

Table AI   Summary statistics

Variable	Observations	Mean	Std. Dev.	Min	Max
$Log(X_{ij})$	14911	0.126	2.860	−10.091	6.609
$Log(D_{ij})$	15052	7.416	0.717	4.444	8.321
$Log(Y_i{}^*Y_j)$	13425	35.215	4.589	24.074	50.062
$Log(P_i{}^*P_j)$	15052	18.608	1.946	11.984	22.515
$Log(A_iA_j)$	15052	23.233	2.583	13.613	28.494
Landlocked	15052	0.1068	0.312	0	2
Island	15052	0.1581	0.373	0	2
Colonial Rel.	15052	0.0232	0.150	0	1
Language	15052	0.1131	0.316	0	1
Currency Union	15052	0.0511	0.220	0	1

Table AII   Correlation matrix

	$Log(D_{ij})$	$Log(Y_i * Y_j)$	$Log(P_i * P_j)$	$Log(A_iA_j)$	LL	*Island*	COL	L
$Log(D_{ij})$	1							
$Log(Y_i{}^*Y_j)$	−0.164	1						
$Log(P_i{}^*P_j)$	−0.069	0.531	1					
$Log(A_iA_j)$	0.068	0.309	0.829	1				
Landlocked (LL)	−0.10	0.105	−0.186	−0.164	1			
Island	0.027	−0.431	−0.662	−0.690	−0.073	1		
Colonial Rel (COL)	0.072	−0.055	0.062	0.039	−0.056	0.052	1	
Language (L)	−0.207	−0.05	−0.155	−0.167	0.244	−0.010	0.246	1
Currency Union	−0.146	0.3	0.027	−0.025	0.173	−0.107	−0.039	0.086

Common Language: See Mélitz (2008).

Ex-Colonial Relationship: *Source*: CIA *World Factbook* (2005).

France, Algeria, Morocco, and Tunisia; **Italy** and Libya; **United Kingdom**, Cyprus, and Malta (in bold the ex-colonizers).

European Monetary Union (since 1999)
Austria, Belgium, Germany, Spain, Finland, France, Greece (since 2000), Ireland, Italy, Luxembourg, Netherlands, Portugal.

Notes

1. A similar result is achieved by Mihov and Rose (2007) with respect of most monetary arrangements and inflation targeting in particular.

2. The European Commission dedicates around 1 billion euros a year in favour of the Euro-Mediterranean Partnership through MEDA, its second biggest external relations programme, and other programmes.
3. The ENP includes the EU member states, Algeria, Armenia, Azerbaijan, Belarus, Egypt, Georgia, Israel, Jordan, Lebanon, Libya, Moldova, Morocco, Syria, Tunisia, Ukraine, and the Palestinian Authority.
4. We refer the reader to Harrigan (2003) and Cheung and Wall (2005) for a literature review on gravity and trade.
5. For example, to estimate the relationship between trade and growth see Frankel and Romer (1999); for the importance of currency unions to boost trade see Rose (2000).
6. In his controversial paper on the effects of currency unions, Andrew Rose (2000) notes ironically that this is one of those cases where attempts have been made to prove that a model works not only in practice, but also in theory.
7. See, for example, Bergstrand (1985, 1989) and Deardorff (1998).
8. See, for example, Glick and Rose (2002).
9. See Fazio et al. (2008), for a further discussion.
10. A number of complications arise when zero trade is present in the sample. Tobit rather than OLS estimation is often suggested as a quick solution. Other authors have suggested alternative estimation techniques. Santos Silva and Tenreyro (2006) suggest the use of a pseudo-Poisson model; Helpman et al. (2004) suggest a two-step Heckman estimation, dealing with the zero trade issue in the first regression. In our case, all trade is greater than zero. Hence, we rely on the traditional OLS methodology.
11. EC/EEA/EFTA/EU trade agreements include Belgium, Bel-Lux, Denmark, France, Germany, Ireland, Italy, Luxembourg, Netherlands, UK, Norway, Switzerland, Malta, OCTs (Greenland, New Caledonia, French Polynesia, St Pierre and Miquelon, Aruba, New Antilles, Falklands, St. Helena which are not considered here); Austria (since 1995), Finland (since 1995), Sweden (since 1995), Greece (since 1981), Portugal (since 1986), Spain (since 1986).
12. In order to account for potential data discrepancies in the direction in which trade is reported and to average the CIF costs, we use the average of the X_{ij} and M_{ji} directions.
13. I am greatly indebted to Jacques Mélitz for making available his data and formulas to compute the language variable.
14. Given the dominance of European countries in our data set, we use Mélitz's Open Circuit Communication variable.
15. In the rounds of 140% (that is to say $100 \cdot (e^{\approx 0.35} - 1)$).

References

Al-Atreash, H. M. and Yousef, T. (1999), 'Intra-Arab trade: is it too little?', IMF Working Paper WP/00/10.

Anderson, J. and van Wijncoop, E. (2003), 'Gravity with gravitas: solution to the border problem', *American Economic Review*, 93: 170–92.

Anderson, J. and van Wijncoop, E. (2004), 'Trade costs', *Journal of Economic Literature*, 42: 691–751.

Baldwin, R. (2006), 'The euro's trade effects', ECB Working Paper, no. 594.

Bayoumi, T., Fazio, G., Kumar, M. and MacDonald, R. (2007), 'Fatal attraction: using distance to measure contagion in good times as well as bad', *Review of Financial Economics*, 16(3): 259–73.

Bergstrand, J. (1985), 'The gravity equation in international trade: some microeconomic foundations and empirical evidence', *Review of Economics and Statistics*, 67: 474–81.

Bergstrand, J. (1989), 'The generalized gravity equation, monopolistic competition, and the factors-proportions theory in international trade', *Review of Economics and Statistics*, 71: 143–53.

Cheng, I.-Hui and Wall, H. (2005), 'Controlling for heterogeneity in gravity models of trade and integration', *Review of the Federal Reserve Bank of St. Louis*, 87(1): 49–63.

Deardorff, A. V. (1998), 'Determinants of bilateral trade: does gravity work in a neoclassical world?' in J. A. Frankel (ed.), *The Regionalization of the World Economy*, Chicago: University of Chicago Press.

Eichengreen, B. and Irwin, D. (1997), 'The role of history in bilateral flows', in J. Frankel (ed.), *The Regionalization of the World Economy*, Chicago: University of Chicago Press, 33–57.

Fazio, G., MacDonald, R. and Mélitz, J. (2008), 'Trade costs, trade balances and current accounts: an application of gravity to multilateral trade', *Open Economies Review*, forthcoming.

Frankel, J. A. and Romer, D. (1999), 'Does trade cause growth?', *American Economic Review*, 89(3) (June): 379–99.

Glick, R. and Rose, A. K. (2002), 'Does a currency union affect trade? The time series evidence', *European Economic Review*, 46 (June): 1125–51.

Harrigan, J. (2003), 'Specialization and the volume of trade: do the data obey the laws?', in K. Choi and J. Harrigan (eds), *The Handbook of International Trade*, New York: Basil Blackwell.

Helpman, E., Mélitz, J. and Yeaple, S. R. (2004), 'Export versus FDI with heterogeneous firms', *American Economic Review*, 94(1) (March): 300–16.

Honohan, P. and Lane, P. R. (2000), 'Will the euro trigger more monetary unions in Africa?', World Bank Policy Research Working Paper, no. 2393.

Masson, P. (2007), 'Currency unions in Africa: is the trade effect substantial enough to justify their formation?', *World Economy*, doi: 10.1111/j.1467-9701.01028.x, 1–15.

Mátyás, L. (1997a), 'Proper econometric specification of the gravity model', *World Economy*, 20(3): 363–8.

Mátyás, L. (1997b), 'The gravity model: some econometric considerations', *World Economy*, 21(3): 397–401.

Mélitz, J. (2008), 'Language and foreign trade', *European Economic Review*, forthcoming.

Mihov, I. and Rose, A. K. (2007), 'Is old money better than new? Duration and monetary regimes', Economics Discussion Paper, no. 2007–25. http://www.economics-ejournal.org/economics/discussionpapers/2007-25

Polachek, S. W. and Seigle, C. (2006), 'Trade, peace and democracy: an analysis of dyadic disputes', IZA Discussion Paper, no. 2170.

Rose, A. K. (2000), 'One money, one market: estimating the effect of common currencies on trade', *Economic Policy*, 30: 7–45.

Santos Silva, J. M. C. and Tenreyro, S. (2006), 'The log of gravity', *Review of Economics and Statistics*, 88: 641–58.

Subramanian, A. and Tamirisa, N. T. (2003), 'Is Africa integrated in the global economy?', *IMF Staff Papers*, 50: 352–72.

Tinbergen, J. (1962), 'Shaping the world economy', New York: Twentieth Century Fund.

Tsangarides, C. G., Ewenczyk, P. and Hulej, M. (2006), 'Stylized facts on bilateral trade and currency unions', IMF Working Paper, no. WP/06/31.

6
In and Out of Monetary Unions: Lessons From, and Risks For the EMU. An Alternative Approach to Monetary Unions[1]

Antimo Verde

1 Introduction

Barry Eichengren (2008) maintains that the European Monetary Union (EMU) is an unprecedented experiment. Indeed, its very distinguishing feature is to be a monetary union without being a political one. Thus, the EMU experience is dominated by the overwhelming role of the member states. In particular, France and Germany have guided every step in the European economic and monetary integration process. We have full evidence of this. To limit ourselves to a few examples: the so-called Werner plan was launched in 1970 by Willy Brandt, Chancellor of the German Federal Republic.[2] Two years later, Germany, safeguarding its industry's interests, imposed the so-called European Monetary Snake on the other EEC member states.[3] In 1979, German and French economic interests pushed Helmut Schmidt and Giscard d'Estaing towards a new Exchange Rate Mechanism (ERM) binding all EEC currencies to prevent any competitiveness gains against the Deutschmark and to protect French farmers' interests.[4] The third stage of monetary union witnessed an unexpected and impressive speeding up in Madrid in 1995, thanks to France and Germany. Finally, in November 2003 the ECOFIN, i.e. the member states, decided – in opposition to the Commission – to hold the Stability Growth Pact (SGP) sanctions and the Excessive Deficit Procedure in abeyance against France and Germany whose fiscal deficits breached the ceiling of 3 per cent of GDP twice. After this incident, in September 2004 the European Commission hastened to propose a more flexible SGP, as it realized, after a long opposition to any change to the European fiscal rules, that the member states were the union's bosses.[5]

In his book *The Birth of the Euro*, Otmar Issing (2008), former ECB chief economist, points out that 'the euro is historically unprecedented and while countries have surrendered control of lower interest rates to Frankfurt-based ECB, they have retained considerable autonomy in other economic policy areas. It is no coincidence, therefore, that observers speak of an experiment ... whose outcome seems likely to remain uncertain for a considerable time to come' (*Financial Times*, 16 April 2008: 2).

Concerning whether the EMU should be enlarged to more than 27 countries, many believe that 'the group dynamics do not function at 27. Six is really a good number – you can sit round a dinner table. Fifteen is just about OK, you can see each other. But 27 is more like a parliament' (*Financial Times*, 1 May 2008: 11). In such a context, words like 'disintegration' or 'two-speed union' have become relatively frequent after the EU enlargement.

However, the optimal currency area (OCA) theory has nothing to say on this point, in particular because it overlooks the decision-making process boosting states either to join a monetary union or to leave it.

A monetary union, once established, lives for ever. Most of the literature on monetary union usually tries to explain why two or more countries could be induced to join it, but there is less discussion of the decision to quit it. Thus, if we look at the future of EMU, which is in the member states' hands, the OCA theory would be a very poor guide, just as it was when the EMU was established. Yet, the traditional OCA theory's criteria and 'costs and benefits' of the single currency really matter and they cannot be ignored.

The aim of this chapter is twofold:

1. to suggest a very simple conceptual scheme, whereby member states assume the crucial role in deciding the destiny of monetary unions;
2. to clarify the interaction between states' policies and the main OCA theory concepts, such as the effects (cost/benefits) of single currency and the OCA criteria.

This scheme appears to be an alternative approach to the theory of optimum currency areas, but it utilizes definitions and concepts of the OCA theory to include them in a single theoretical model.

Indeed, the search for an alternative approach to the OCA theory is justified by its unsatisfactory state, in spite of the growing numbers of contributions on this topic. In particular, this theory has nothing to say about the reasons urging states to leave the monetary union. In more general terms, the OCA theory appears completely inadequate to tackle the problems of a monetary union which is not a political one.

Putting the states at the centre of our analysis, we will try to focus on the reasons for the establishment and disruption of monetary unions. The conceptual scheme presented in this chapter deals mostly with the decision-making process leading countries either to join or to quit a monetary union, while it inevitably overlooks many other important issues.

In particular, we will have little to say about political factors[6] and the adjustment problems which still dominate the economics of monetary union. A full debate on the consequences of a monetary union would have to consider the problems of a generalized process of specialization, as suggested by Krugman (1993), and whether we should hope for a growing synchronization of national business cycles, as maintained by the Commission (1990) and Frankel and Rose (1998). These issues are crucial, capable of decisively influencing results of any analysis, but they are not included in our analysis.

For our purposes, we simply suppose that the integration policies – which include both economic and institutional ones – are capable of making *all* the OCA criteria endogenous, thus reducing the risk and costs of asymmetric shocks and the costs of monetary union.

Finally, we leave aside all considerations about the characteristics – economic, political, cultural – of the member states of a monetary union, even if some mechanisms of our scheme – institutional and legal harmonization criteria, endogeneity, solidarity – suggest that they should not be too 'different'.

This chapter is organized as follows. In section 2 we look at the evolution of the OCA theory since the seminal work by Robert Mundell. The aim of this analysis is to show the unsatisfactory state of the theory, from our point of view, and the opportunity to proceed in new directions. Section 3 is completely devoted to the hypotheses of the theoretical scheme suggested in this chapter. The theoretical model is described in section 4. It is then used in section 5 for a simulation regarding the hypothesis of a 'two-speed EMU' after and because of the EU enlargement. Section 6 concludes.

2   The evolution of the OCA theory

A brief reconstruction of the evolution of the optimum currency area theory, starting from Mundell's 1961 seminal contribution, is given here in order to verify its inadequacy and to introduce the theoretical basis of the suggested model. Table 6.1 highlights the main characteristics of its different approaches.

The traditional approach to OCA stresses, above all, the costs deriving from joining a currency area, i.e. the relinquishment of the exchange rate. The traditional approach aims at identifying the conditions, or criteria, under which the loss of an instrument of economic policy, the exchange rate, believed to be a very important device to withstand asymmetric shocks, can be sustainable. Criteria could include wage and price flexibility, reducing the probability of asymmetric shocks or making their absorption easy. Some economists[7] have stressed, still in this traditional approach, how differences between countries can hamper monetary integration, in particular differences in national legal systems, in financial and labour markets as well as differences concerning the choice between inflation and unemployment. This approach was updated in 1975, when Ishyama (1975) emphasized the role of benefits in joining a monetary union: costs are important, but what really matters is the balance between benefits and costs.

The predominant role of the New Classical Macroeconomics (NCM) led to important consequences also for the OCA theory. The Keynesian framework is substituted by a neo-classical one which looks at the exchange rate as a source of concern, instead of being a mechanism that allows countries to adjust better to asymmetric shocks. McKinnon (2004) and De Grauwe (2007) include Mundell II in this approach. In a paper written in 1970 and published in 1973, Mundell reversed his previous pessimism about monetary union, to argue that a monetary union can be an efficient instrument for organizing an insurance system (currency reserves pooling) to cope with asymmetric shocks. Moreover he emphasized the fact that exchange rate is not a useful policy instrument, but a 'policy problem'. For this reason, McKinnon and De Grauwe refer to this 'new' Mundell as Mundell II. In this approach we find the time inconsistency or credibility issue: monetary union is seen as a way of 'tying the politicians' hands', hampering them from engineering surprise devaluations.

A real shake-up to the OCA theory follows with Frankel and Rose's (1998) thesis of the endogeneity of the OCA criteria. According to this contribution, the single currency can significantly raise international linkages which would result in more closely correlated business cycles across countries, i.e. a higher symmetry in the movements of output between states to form a monetary union which, for this reason, becomes an OCA. Therefore, countries joining a monetary union may satisfy OCA criteria ex post, even if they do not ex ante. Indeed, in principle, closer international links with the other members of the union could result in more specialized economies, each exploiting comparative advantage,

Table 6.1 The evolution of the OCA theory

	Approaches	Characteristic features	Theoretical scheme	Outcome	References
A	**Traditional**			Is the relinquishment of exchange rate costly?	
1	Criteria	Costs	Keynesian	Costly	Mundell (1961) McKinnon (1963) Kenen (1969)
2	Updating	Costs: differences between countries	Neo-classical and Keynesian	Costly	Corden (1972) Baldwin and Wysplosz (2006) De Grauwe (2007)
3	Updating	Comparison between costs and benefits	Keynesian	Depends on the benefits, not only on the costs	Ishyama (1975)
B	**Neo-classical critique**				
4	Mundell II	Insurance mechanism		Financial integration	Mundell (1973) McKinnon (2004)
5	Neo-classical macroeconomics	Differences in the preferences	Neo-classical macroeconomics	Benefits > costs	Tavlas (1993)
6	Credibility	Economic policy ineffectiveness Time inconsistency	Neo-classical macroeconomics Lucas (1973) Barro and Gordon (1983)	States' benefits > costs	
C	**Endogeneity/ specialization**				
7	Business-cycle synchronization	Single currency: higher trade intensity, higher synchron. Criteria met ex post	Keynesian and growth theory Barro & Sala-i-Martin (1995)	Benefits > costs	Frankel and Rose (1998) European Commission (1990)
8	Specialization	Inter-trade specialization	Keynesian	Costly	Krugman (1993)
D	**Empirical**				
	Econometric analysis	Various	Shock and financial structures similarity		Various
E	**Alternative**				
9	Maastricht	Convergence criteria	Neo-classical	Benefits higher than expected according to the OCA theory	EU Commission (1990)

and in more asymmetric shocks (Krugman 1993). However, Frankel and Rose (1998) and Rose (2000) show that empirical results strongly support the hypothesis that closer international links result in more correlated business cycles across countries.

In recent years an empirical approach has emerged which includes recent estimates referring broadly to benefits and costs from EMU (Mongelli 2008). The benefits identified include: the effects of the euro in the area of trade deepening and financial integration (Micco et al. 2003); euro and foreign direct investments and cross-border mergers and acquisitions (Petroulas 2007; Coeurdacier and Martin 2007); benefits stemming from the international role of the euro (ECB 2005); and the effects of the euro on labour markets (Boeri 2005).

Finally, it is possible to identify an alternative approach: the 'Maastricht approach' based on specific 'Maastricht criteria' (Artis 2003: 299), i.e. those actually applied in the establishment of EMU. In these terms, the union was born only because its member states overlooked the OCA theory's criteria and prescriptions.

What can we conclude from this brief reconstruction of the evolution of the OCA theory? Firstly, the traditional approach is unconvincing. The criteria are often conflicting (Ishyama 1975); and they could be time inconsistent (Tavlas 1993). The principle of a single optimizing criterion is inadequate to explain a very complex phenomenon. Thus, it is not surprising that the OCA theory was for years consigned to intellectual limbo. At the end of the 1960s, Johnson (1969) argued that the OCA theory was no longer of any value.

Secondly, the neo-classical approach stresses new important benefits to the member states stemming from monetary union, such as policy credibility and monetary stability, and states enter the analysis as important actors, but the emphasis is put on the quality of national policies, while the decision-making regarding the integration process, its beginning and end, is left out completely.

Thirdly, the endogeneity approach of Frankel and Rose, by itself, eradicates any predictive ability and explanatory power of the OCA theory: even if the OCA criteria are not met when a monetary union is established, they could be satisfied ex post. But 'a currency area may sub-optimise over time because a spatial division of labour evolves that makes it more susceptible to idiosyncratic shocks. The paradoxical conclusion is that member states may have qualified for higher optimality ranking before EMU than after forming EMU. This may lead one to the conclusion that OCA theory is inherently inapplicable to any existing currency union' (Schelkle 2007: 2).

Finally, the alternative approach based on the Maastricht criteria shows that the OCA theory is defective on both theoretical and operational grounds and strengthens our opinion that the states' choices are crucial, irrespective of the economic conditions or criteria.

Summing up: the OCA theory's approaches appear inadequate because they do not explain the considerations whereby one state decides either to join a monetary union or to leave it. As we have already argued, these approaches are unable to cope with the problems of a monetary, but not a political, union.

3   A new conceptual scheme: the basic steps

Let us now focus on the new suggested conceptual scheme of OCA according to the following points:

1. the role of (member) states and the redefinition of the phases of the economic and monetary integration process;
2. the states' objectives and their integration policies and the interaction with the OCA effects and criteria;
3. the states' costs and benefits and their explanatory variables.

3.1   States and phases of the economic and monetary integration process

One important missing link in the OCA theory is the lack of explicit reference to the states. We are talking about the *economic* theory of the optimum currency area, not the political one. Some years ago, McCallum (1995) emphasized the crucial role of national borders and the related home bias. These factors hamper the constitution of a single market, making the adjustment process within the union more complex. Furthermore, recent papers on monetary unions revalue the harmonization of national institutional and legal systems as a useful device to establish a monetary union. Both national boundaries and harmonization policies suggest that states play an important role in making the monetary integration process easier or more difficult. However, despite these insights, states are not included in the theory.

Moreover, the OCA theory overlooks the fact that a monetary union is one phase of a more complex and lasting integration process. Balassa's (1961) paper, published in the same year as Mundell's seminal work, identifies five phases of this process: (a) free trade; (b) customs unions; (c) common market; (d) monetary union; (e) complete market integration. The main phases of the European economic and monetary integration are easily identifiable from this list.

In the conceptual scheme suggested in this chapter, the different phases are important as they interact with costs and benefits. In other words, each phase has its costs and benefits and, conversely, if either costs or benefits change dramatically, we enter a 'new' phase.

Given this definition and making reference to the European integration process, we should add to the previous list at least two other phases: the European Monetary System (EMS) and the EU enlargement, giving a total of seven phases:

1. Free trade, from 1957 until 1968;
2. Customs union, since 1968;
3. European Monetary System, from 1979 to 1998;
4. Common market, since 1993;
5. Monetary union, since 1999;
6. EU enlargement, the current moment;
7. Complete market integration.

Quite often, in joining a particular phase of the integration process, states aim to reap the expected benefits of the following phases. For instance, in 1979, the Italian government decided to join the European Monetary System, even though this accession was very costly, taking into account the future economic benefits of the European integration process, and the political risks of being left outside.

3.2 States' objectives, integration policies, effects of single currency and OCA criteria

The 'core' of our conceptual scheme is represented by the link between national economic and institutional policies, on the one hand, and the effects of single currency along with the OCA criteria, on the other.

Each phase of the integration process has its own goals. Balassa (1961) suggests that the final goal of each phase is the 'increase in national welfare'; Collignon (2001: 33) hints at 'community's utility function'.

In this chapter we prefer to define these final goals of each integration phase, for the 'representative' state i, as the increase in a composite index of its current and potential growth.[8]

The 'representative' state is needed because it allows us to avoid taking into consideration the N different national situations. To reach its objective in a monetary union, the representative state i and the 'union' (or federal 'government') can count on economic policies (P) as well as the harmonization and institutional policies (H).

The economic policies P can be divided in short-run or demand policies – monetary and fiscal policies, P_1 – and long-run or structural policies, P_2. We can reasonably suppose that the current growth is affected mainly by P_1, while the potential growth is mostly linked to P_2, as well as to the harmonization and institutional policies, H.

Thus, we can write the relation between the final goal of monetary union for state i, Ψ_i, and the above-mentioned policies in the following 'reduced form':

$$\Psi_i = g(P_1, P_2, H) \tag{1}$$

where Ψ_i = objective (current/potential growth) of the monetary union for the state i; P_1 = short-run economic policy; P_2 = long-run economic policy; and H = harmonization and institutional policy.

Equation (1) requires a short preliminary explanation. In the first place, we shall underline the relation between Ψ_i and P_1. The neo-classical theoretical scheme denies any link, even in the short term, between current growth and demand policies, if these are anticipated by the economic agents. However, we can suppose the reduced form (1) to be consistent with a structural neo-Keynesian model, in which prices and wages stickiness makes demand policy effective.

Indeed, this policy's effectiveness seems to be confirmed by the EMU experience. According to Demertzis et al. (2000), fiscal policy is not only effective, but a good part of the symmetry observed in the shocks experienced by the European Union economies is due to policy interventions; they seem to be held together by policy-makers, rather than by any natural symmetry in the underlying economies.

If we denote P_1 with P, and P_2 and H simply with H, we can rewrite the relation between economic targets Ψ and policies, P and H, in the following 'reduced form':

$$\Psi_i = P^\alpha H^\tau \tag{1'}$$

where subscript i shows that economic targets refer to country i; if α, $\tau > 0$ then the higher the value of P and H, the higher the level of ψ_i.

Secondly, we can suppose that the reactivity of Ψ_i to P and H also depends on the context in which these policies work. In a monetary union, the two elasticities α and τ could be a function of the traditional *net* benefits of the single currency: reduced uncertainty and risks, as well as disappeared transaction costs, on the one hand, and the relinquishment of the exchange rate, on the other. It is reasonable to suppose that α and τ are affected by these factors stemming from the traditional OCA theory, because the impact of both policies on Ψ_i increases as the net benefits of single currency are revealed.

More complex is the relationship between Ψ_i and H, the institutional and harmonization policies, which also include the long-term economic policies P_2 which can be summarized by 'structural reforms'. By 'structural reforms' we mean all long-term policies increasing the overall union's flexibility.

By 'institutional and harmonization policies' we mean 'policy decisions taken by two or more governments of countries belonging to the same geographical area in order to promote co-operation in terms of deepening and/or widening the spheres of co-ordination under the terms of an agreed pact. Pacts may vary widely in form, ranging from intergovernmental agreements on sectoral co-operation to economic and monetary unions with transfer of sovereignty to supranational institutions (Mongelli et al. 2005: 4).

Verde (2003) stressed the role of harmonization and institutional policies in making the adjustment and integration processes easier. According to Dorrucci et al. (2004) economic integration is led by institutional integration: it is a confirmation of the crucial role of the harmonization measures. They have the task of reducing the differences in the national legal and regulatory systems, and in the national labour markets; they make national boundaries less pervasive, reducing obstacles to the creation of the single market programme.

At the moment, the institutional and harmonization policies have assumed an important role, but the channel through which they are able to affect the objectives of integration is not absolutely clear.

In this regard, useful reference points are the endogeneity issue and the OCA criteria. Criteria can be defined as the particular conditions which reduce, or avoid, the costs stemming from the relinquishment of the exchange rate because they allow countering possible asymmetric shocks: labour mobility, openness or trade intensity, business cycle synchronization, and private transfers through integrated financial markets.[9]

As we have seen, according to Frankel and Rose (1998), a monetary union can evolve into an optimal monetary area, because a single currency leads to an increase in trade intensity, which would produce more intra-industry trade and then more synchronized national business cycles.

In contrast, in our scheme the OCA criteria are endogenous, thanks to (credible) policies supporting the single currency: harmonization and institutional and long-term economic policies (H). In other words, the institutional and harmonization policies and structural reforms (H) work through the endogeneity channels, i.e. they endogenously directly improve the conditions or criteria, already cited and identified by the OCA theory.

In turn, higher labour mobility, and/or higher cycle synchronization and/or public transfers, make asymmetric shocks less probable or their absorption easier, thus indirectly again modifying α and τ, and in this way positively affecting the final goals Ψ_i.

If we denote the net effects of the single currency and OCA criteria as NBC we can write:

$$\alpha = \alpha(NBC) \quad \tau = \tau(NBC) \tag{2}$$

By substituting (2) for (1') we introduce net benefits and OCA criteria into our scheme.

Summing up: the short-term economic policies (P), on the one hand, and the long-term economic policies (or structural reforms) and harmonization and institutional policies (H), on the other, have different fields of action and effects, according to their 'comparative advantages'. The short-term economic policy is mainly devoted to macroeconomic goals – current economic growth, inflation and employment – while structural reforms and harmonization reforms have a direct impact on the economic flexibility and on institutional, legal and regulatory context.

The positive impact of P and H on the potential and current economic growth is directly and significantly affected by the *net* benefits of the single currency. Moreover, the OCA criteria are endogenously created by the harmonization policies and the long-term economic policies (H), reducing the probability of asymmetric shocks and providing an indirect support to the current and potential growth. Both the net benefits of the single currency and the OCA criteria change the key parameters α and τ, i.e. the reactivity of the states' policy objectives.

Turning to the 'reduced form' (1'), we can conclude that both P and H have a positive impact on the final goals, i.e. on Ψ: higher values of P and H give rise to higher levels of Ψ, i.e. of current and potential growth.

With α and $\tau > 0$, partial derivatives with respect to Ψ are positive: $\delta\Psi/\delta P > 0$ e $\delta\Psi/\delta H > 0$.

Therefore a key characteristic of our theoretical scheme is given by the original link between the monetary union's objectives and the policies carried out to achieve them, on the one hand, and the net benefits of the single currency and the OCA criteria on the other.

3.3   The monetary union's costs and benefits: explanatory variables

According to Ishyama (1975: 346) a monetary union is established 'if the pros outweigh the cons from the point of view of national self-interest and welfare, rather than of global welfare'. Thus, states will decide to join a monetary union if the perceived expected benefits to them exceed the perceived expected costs.

In the OCA theory the monetary union's costs and benefits are linked to the single currency, while in our scheme, benefits and costs refer to the member states, or the representative state i and, as we have seen, they are linked to the final goals of the phases of the integration process.

In a monetary union, we have supposed that, in a first approximation, these final goals may be summed up in the maximization of non-inflationary current and potential economic growth. These final goals Ψi are the economic 'benefits' to the member states, and to achieve them states and the 'union' will undertake the appropriate economic and institutional policies.

Thus, for the representative state i, its benefits depend on policies P and H, whose impact on Ψi is measured by parameters α and τ which are in turn affected by the traditional OCA benefits and criteria, as shown in equation (2).

On the other hand, the representative state i is aware of the costs, related to the integration policies, which it will incur in a monetary union when, for instance, monetary policies are inconsistent with price stability, or because of unsustainable fiscal deficits and debt or short-term costs of structural reforms.

Therefore, in a first approximation, the representative state's function costs are analogous to the benefits' costs, as costs depend on P and H according to two parameters α_2 and τ_2 measuring the reactivity of costs to policies.

The representative state's benefits and costs functions can be completed by including other specific costs and benefits stemming from the monetary union. In particular, in our scheme we have supposed that both benefits and costs depend on the union's dimension, N, that is on the number of member states.

In our model, N has a particular meaning: net benefits are positive when N is relatively small, and negative when it exceeds a critical value, N*. Indeed, benefits stemming from a monetary union react positively to its dimension as more states use the single currency: the curve showing the relationship between the benefits and the union's dimension is upward-sloping.

More complex is the link between the costs and the dimension: when the number of states of the monetary union exceeds a critical value, N*, new costs are bound to emerge.

We may suppose that *diversity* increases when the union size increases. And diversity matters for economic and political reasons because it

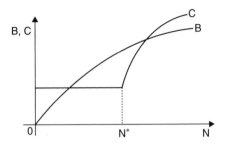

Figure 6.1   Cost (C), benefits (B) and union size: the general case

translates into asymmetric shocks (Baldwin and Wyplosz 2006) and makes the problems related to collective action more serious (Alesina et al. 1999).

Before the critical value N* is reached, costs are exclusively related to P and H, but after N* new costs emerge and they could gradually exceed the benefits, reversing the sign of net benefits and creating the conditions for a changed attitude towards the economic and monetary integration process.

These negative factors, linked to a number of countries N higher than N*, enter directly in the state's function of costs: unlike the OCA criteria and single currency effects, N does not directly affect policies, P and H, but has important effects on the optimal policy mix and therefore on the state's welfare.[10] Thus, in general terms, the evolution of benefits and costs reflects the union's size, N, as shown in Figure 6.1.

Finally, among the explanatory variables of costs and benefits we cannot overlook 'solidarity' which plays an important role in the integration process. To a certain degree, it is tied to the union's dimension, but it has quite a distinct role. Indeed a lack of solidarity can also be a problem in a very small monetary union and economists and policy-makers believe that they have several confirmations of this factor. Eichengreen (2006), for instance, concludes that the prospect of an Asian monetary union is very dim because of the lack of the solidarity which characterizes the European experience.

'Solidarity' is a variable entering both the benefits and costs equations. It is a cost because it usually implies, by definition, a loss of or costly support to other member states[11] and, at the same time, it is a benefit for the whole monetary union, i.e. it is a political goal believed worthy of preservation by the states showing it.

Summing up: we can write, *in general terms*, the benefits and costs stemming from joining a monetary union for a representative state i, as follows:

$$B_i = B_i(P, H, N, S) \tag{3}$$

$$C_i = C_i(P, H, N, S) \tag{4}$$

where B = benefits of a monetary union; C = costs of a monetary union; N = dimension, number of member states, of the monetary union; and S = solidarity.

The representative state i, will decide to join the monetary union if $Bi \geq Ci$. In this case, we define the monetary union as 'optimal'.

The next two figures refer to the logic of the theoretical scheme suggested in this chapter (Figure 6.2) and the logic of the OCA theory (Figure 6.3).

4 The model

We have expounded the main assumptions of our scheme. They yield the following system of equations:

$$\Psi_i = P^\alpha H^\tau \, \alpha, \tau > 0 \tag{5}$$

$$B_i = B_i(P, H, N, S) \tag{6}$$

$$C_i = C_i(P, H, N, S) \tag{7}$$

where $P = P_1$ and $H = \{P_2, \ H\}$, N = number of member states; S = solidarity.

We shall now demonstrate the *modus operandi* of the model by:

1. explaining the underlying game structure (section 4.1);
2. showing the general scheme (section 4.2);
3. analysing a specific formulation of the model (5)–(7) which will lead us to a diagrammatic specification closer to that utilized in the literature on monetary unions (section 4.3).

In section 4.5, we show two simulations of the model, regarding the two-speed EMU hypothesis and the impact of solidarity.

The specific formulation of the model (5)–(7) is obtained by replacing its general form with log-linear equations as follows:

$$\Psi_i = P^{\alpha_1} H^{(1-\alpha_1)} \tag{5'}$$

$$B_i = B_i(P^{\alpha_1} H^{(1-\alpha_1)} N^\beta S^\gamma) \tag{6'}$$

$$C_i = C_i(P^{\alpha_2} H^{(1-\alpha_2)} N^\delta S^\tau) \tag{7'}$$

where, for the sake of simplicity, $\alpha = \alpha_1$ and $\tau = 1 - \alpha_1$.

124

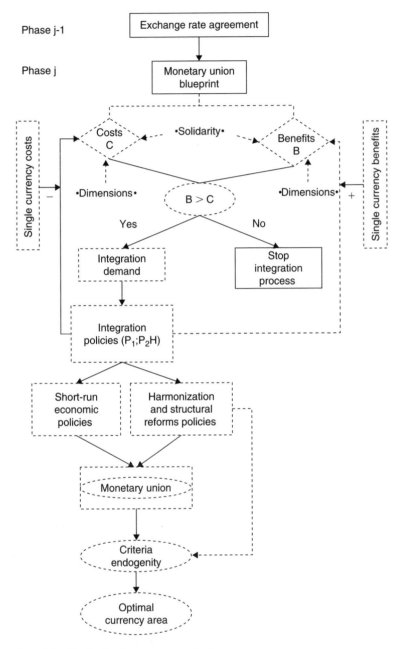

Figure 6.2 The logic of our conceptual scheme

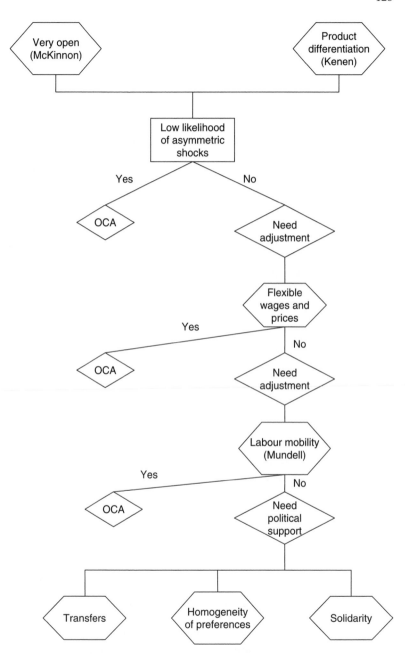

Figure 6.3 The logic of the OCA theory
Source: Baldwin and Wyplosz (2004: 370).

4.1 The 'game' structure

In our conceptual scheme we have two 'players': the 'representative' member state *i* and the 'union'.[12]

We observe that in EMU – i.e. our reference experience – there are different levels of government, 'national' and 'federal', and both are responsible for the integration policies carried out in the union.

As regards P_1, monetary policy is centralized; fiscal policy is decentralized at national level, but it is co-ordinated by the 'union' through the fiscal rules of the Stability and Growth Pact (SGP). The long-term economic policies P_2 are assigned to member states, but formally co-ordinated within the EMU's Broad Economic Policy Guidelines (BEPGs). Finally, the harmonization and institutional policies are strictly co-ordinated by the 'union'.

Thus, our 'game' is organized as follows: the 'union' or its 'government' carries out the economic and institutional policies needed to reach the monetary union's objectives; it chooses the values of P and H for all the countries, i.e. for our 'representative' state *i*, which decides, after having compared the expected benefits and costs produced, directly or indirectly, by these policies, to join the monetary union or, if it is in the union already, to leave it.

Therefore, even if policies are carried out by the 'union', member states play the crucial role in deciding the union's destiny. Thus in the previous and in the following equations, the integration policies do have not the subscript *i* because they are carried out by the union.

4.2 The model: the general scheme

We can now start from the union's policies, observing that in order to implement a monetary union it is necessary that the level of those policies exceeds certain minimum values. Or, better, it must be:

$$P_{min} \leq P \leq P_{max} \tag{8}$$

$$H_{min} \leq H \leq H_{max} \tag{9}$$

where H_{min} and P_{min}, and P_{max} and H_{max} are, respectively, the minimum and the maximum values of the two variables, H and P. The first is the level needed for the establishment (or survival) of a monetary union and the second is the level beyond which P and H cannot go for technical and/or political reasons.[13]

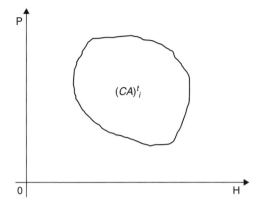

Figure 6.4 The monetary union acceptability area for state *i*

Joining a monetary union, at time t, the representative member state *i* gets benefits B_i^t and costs C_i^t which, as we know from equations (6) and (7) depend, beyond H and P, on the union's dimension and solidarity:

$$B_i^t = B_i^t(H, P, N^t, S_i^t) \tag{10}$$

$$C_i^t = C_i^t(H, P, N^t, S_i^t) \tag{11}$$

At each instant t, for the member state *i*, it must be the case that:

$$B_i^t \geq C_i^t$$

This constraint identifies in the first quadrant ($H \geq 0$, $P \geq 0$) an area $(CA)_{it}$ we can call 'the monetary union acceptability area' for state *i* (Figure 6.4).

The meaning of Figure 6.4 is clear cut: if the values (H,P) regarding the integration policies carried out by the union fall in the 'acceptability area', i.e. if $(H,P) \in (CA)_i^t$, the state *i* will believe it expedient to join the monetary union. In other words, the perceived expected benefits exceed the perceived expected costs.

This reasoning may be generalized, repeating it for all N states that are candidates to join the monetary union. In this case, we can obtain an area given by the junction of the N sets $(CA)_i^t$:

$$(OCA)^t = \bigcap_{i=1}^{N} (CA)_i^t \tag{12}$$

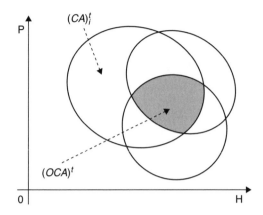

Figure 6.5   The OCA zone

Equation (12) and Figure 6.5 define our OCA zone. It is the set of all the integration policies (H,P) for all states where the expected benefits are not lower than the expected costs.

The decision problem

The decision problem completes our scheme. Over time, the acceptability areas and then the OCA zone may change. This can happen if the coefficient in the previous equations or union size, N, or the solidarity S change. In particular, if in equations (10) and (11) some coefficients and/or variables change, the OCA zone will be modified and one or more states could fall in the non-OCA zone.

In this case, we say that there is a decision problem. This means that the union must identify a new equilibrium point of the representative state, always meeting the constraint $B_i^t \geq C_i^t$. In general, these goals can be represented by a welfare function for *all* member states to be maximized, $W(H,P)$ $\left(\frac{\partial W}{\partial H} > 0, \frac{\partial W}{\partial P} > 0\right)$, or by a distance function $D(H,P)$ to be minimized. In the following analysis we will consider the latter case: the distance from the previous equilibrium point is to be minimized, as it was an accepted compromise for the states.

At time t' the representative state i (or the union) is in equilibrium in $E^* \in (OCA)^{t'}$ with coordinates ($H=H^*$, $P=P^*$); at time $t>t'$ $(OCA)^{t'}$ changes in *(OCA)*.

Then it can happen either that:

- the point E* is in the new OCA zone;
- the point E* is outside the new OCA zone.

In the first case the usual constraints $B_i^t \geq C_i^t$ ∀i are satisfied: things are unchanged. In the second case E* is not an 'acceptable' point, i.e. there exists at least one country i for which the condition $B_{it} \geq C_{it}$ is not met.

The union must then move from one point towards a new equilibrium point E, in the new OCA zone. As we have already said, the union will try to move as little as possible from E*, because $E^* = (H^*, P^*)$ represents a satisfactory compromise for all the states. Therefore the union will try to minimize the distance function:

$$D(H,P) \geq 0 \, \forall(H,P), D(H^*,P^*) = 0, \text{growing in} |H - H^*| \text{and} |P - P^*|,$$

such as:

$$D(H,P) = a \cdot (H - H^*)^2 + b \cdot (P - P^*)^2 con \ a > 0, b > 0$$

The new policy (H, P) carried out by the union will be the solution (if there exists one) of the following constrained optimization problem:

$$Min \quad D(H,P)$$

s.t.

$$(H,P) \in (OCA)^t$$

$$H \geq 0, P \geq 0$$

If a solution does not exist, i.e. $(OCA)_t = \Phi$, the monetary union can find itself in trouble. Moreover, let us remember that H and P are the deviations from their minimum values H_{min} and P_{min}. Therefore the solutions with H or P near 0 imply a crisis scenario.

4.3 The model: a specific formulation

We can deepen the *modus operandi* of our model by choosing log-linear functions for our general equations concerning benefits and costs of a monetary union. This specific formulation of the model is useful to us, because it allows a diagrammatic representation of the model similar to that utilized in the recent literature on monetary unions.

The specific form of equations (6′) and (7′) regarding benefits can be written as follows:

$$B_i^t = B_{0i}^t \cdot P^{\alpha_{1i}^t} \cdot H^{(1-\alpha_{1i}^t)} \cdot (N^t)^{\beta_i} \cdot (S_i^t)^{\lambda_i}$$
$$C_i^t = C_{0i}^t \cdot P^{\alpha_{2i}^t} \cdot H^{(1-\alpha_{2i}^t)} \cdot (N^t)^{\delta_i} \cdot (S_i^t)^{\mu_i}$$

with $0 < \alpha^t_{1i}, \alpha^t_{2i} < 1$, $\alpha^t_{1i} \neq \alpha^t_{2i}$ e $\beta_i, \delta_i, \lambda_i, \mu_i \geq 0$ and the variables having the usual meaning.

To make notations lighter, we drop apex t and index i:

$$B = B_0 P^{\alpha_1} H^{1-\alpha_1} N^\beta S^\lambda \tag{13}$$

$$C = C_0 P^{\alpha_2} H^{1-\alpha_2} N^\delta S^\mu \tag{14}$$

Thus the condition $B \geq C$ becomes:

$$B_0 P^{\alpha_1} H^{1-\alpha_1} N^\beta S^\lambda \geq C_0 P^{\alpha_2} H^{1-\alpha_2} N^\delta S^\mu$$

That is:

$$\frac{P^{\alpha_1}}{P^{\alpha_2}} \geq \frac{C_0 N^\delta S^\mu H^{1-\alpha_2}}{B_0 N^\beta S^\lambda H^{1-\alpha_1}}$$

Letting:

$$R = \left(\frac{C_0 N^\delta S^\mu}{B_0 N^\beta S^\lambda} \right)^{\frac{1}{\alpha_1 - \alpha_2}}$$

we can write:

$$P^{\alpha_1 - \alpha_2} \geq R_i^{\alpha_1 - \alpha_2} H^{\alpha_1 - \alpha_2}$$

where, to remember that we are considering the member state i, we wrote R_i.

Finally, we have:

$$P \geq R_i H \quad \text{if } \alpha_1 > \alpha_2 \tag{15}$$

$$P < R_i H \quad \text{if } \alpha_1 < \alpha_2 \tag{16}$$

Equations (15) and (16) define the 'acceptability area' $(CA)_{it}$ for the member state i at time t in both cases and we find out that the position of the OCA zone depends crucially on the reactivity of benefits and costs to the integration policies P and H (Figure 6.6).

As before, we can obtain the OCA zone repeating the previous reasoning for all the N states. Thus in this specific formulation of our general scheme, the OCA zone can be written mathematically as equation (12) $(OCA)^t = \bigcap_{i=1}^{N} (CA)_i^t$ and graphically as the area in first quadrant included between the H-axis and the line of the equation, with its origin in O, $P = RH$ where $R = \min\{R_i | i = 1, 2, \ldots N\}$, i.e. R is the line of the marginal state, the one whose OCA zone is the smallest.

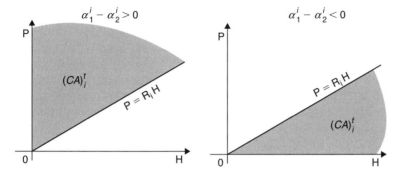

Figure 6.6 The acceptability areas for state i

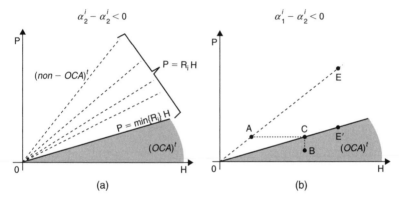

Figure 6.7 The OCA zone in the specific formulation

Once the 'union' knows the OCA zone, it can choose the values of (H, P) within the area. Figure 6.7 refers to the OCA zone in the specific formulation of our general scheme when $\alpha_1 < \alpha_2$.[14]

A couple of points are suggested by Figure 6.7(b). Firstly, once the OCA zone is identified, the union can choose a couple of values of P and H allowing the states included in it to reach the final goal of the monetary union, as they meet the constraint $B_{it} \geq C_{it}$. The function of final goals – which did not explicitly appear in our general case – is given by Equation (5').

Secondly, within the OCA zone, B is not an optimal point because, given the 'input' of harmonization and structural reforms (H), it is possible to reach point C on the R_i of the marginal state, which is superior to B, thanks to a higher level of P, always meeting $B_{it} \geq C_{it}$.

Point A is outside the OCA zone and so costs exceed benefits. P is higher than its optimal value. From A, it is possible to reach an equilibrium point in C, thanks to a higher level of structural reforms and harmonization policies, to get more benefits, such as gains in flexibility, efficiency and transparency.

We must remember that P is not the absolute level, but the difference $(P-P_{min})$, where P_{min} is the level of P needed for the establishment or survival of the monetary union. Thus in A the difference between P and P_{min} could indicate an excessive deficit, or an excess of monetary stabilization, responsible for prices and wages increases.

According to equation (5′) the higher the levels of P and H, the higher is the level of welfare. In other words, the optimal policy mix (P* and H*) will be on the line R_i of the marginal state and that marks the boundary of the OCA zone.

Furthermore, if in Figure 6.7(b) we overlap it with a new OCA zone larger than the first one, the new equilibrium point E is preferable to point E* as, according to equation (5′), higher levels of P and H imply higher levels of expected objectives and welfare. Moreover, E, in general, is superior to A.

We can reasonably suppose that a monetary union's long-term gains exceed short-term pains and then we can imagine, in the long-run, a shift from E* to E. However, we must remember that both P and H cannot exceed their maximum values determined by technical and political reasons. Thus, in Figure 6.7(b) there are limits to the variables on the right side of the R_i line.

The decision problem in the specific case

Also in this specific case, an optimization problem emerges when coefficients and/or variables change. The hypothesis we have in mind is a change of N, that is, the number of the union's member states, because of the accession of new countries.

Let us suppose that at time t′ the union is in the equilibrium point E*, whose coordinates are H* and P* in the $(OCA)_t$ zone defined by the line $P = R_{t'} H$.

Let us also suppose that, at time $t > t'$, as a result of changes of parameters α_1, α_2, β or of variables N or S, the slope of the OCA line becomes $R < R_{t'}$.

If $P^* > R H^*$ it means that point $E_{t'}$ is outside the OCA zone: $E^{t'} \notin (OCA)^t$.

Then the union must move from point $E_{t'}$ towards a new equilibrium point $E^t \notin (OCA)^t$ and, also in this case, it will try to move E_t as little as possible from E*, because $E^* = (H^*, P^*)$ represented a satisfactory compromise for all the states. Therefore the union will try to minimize the distance function D(H, P), subject to the constraint $B \geq C$:

$$\begin{cases} Min\ D(H,P) = a \cdot (H - H^*)^2 + b \cdot (P - P^*)^2 \\ \qquad\qquad t \cdot c \cdot p = R \cdot H \\ \qquad\qquad P \geq 0, \quad H \geq 0 \end{cases} \qquad (17)$$

$$(a > 0\ e\ b > 0)$$

The Lagrange function is:

$$F(H, P, \lambda) = a(H - H^*)^2 + b(P - P^*)^2 + \lambda(P - RH)$$

Differentiating $F(H, P, \lambda)$ and putting equal the partial derivatives to 0, we have:

$$\frac{\partial F}{\partial H} = 2a(H - H^*) - \lambda R = 0$$

$$\frac{\partial F}{\partial P} = 2b(P - P^*) + \lambda = 0$$

$$\frac{\partial F}{\partial \lambda} = P - RH = 0$$

We obtain the new optimal values of H and P, i.e. the coordinates of the equilibrium point E:

$$H = \frac{aH^* + RbP^*}{a + R^2b}$$

$$P = R\frac{aH^* + RbP^*}{a + R^2b}$$

We can calculate now the changes of H and P when the 'union' moves to the new equilibrium point:

$$\Delta H = H - H^* = \frac{aH^* + RbP^*}{a + R^2b} - H^* = Rb\frac{P^* - RH^*}{a + R^2b}$$

$$\Delta P = P - P^* = \frac{a}{bR}\Delta H$$

That is:

$$\Delta H > 0$$

$$\Delta P < 0$$

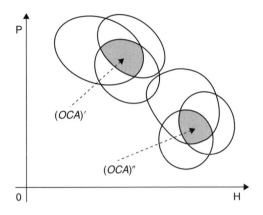

Figure 6.8   The two-speed European Monetary Union hypothesis: the general case

as $P^* > R\,H^*$ by hypothesis. In other words, the new equilibrium position is obtained increasing H and reducing P.

5   The model simulations: the two-speed Europe

We can utilize our model for a first simulation: a 'two-speed Europe' materialized after and because of the EU enlargement (Figure 6.8). In 2007 the EU grew from 15 to 27 countries. Economists and policy-makers believe that such an increase is likely to lead to disintegration. As we know, the final outcome depends more on the states' will than on the national characteristics, as suggested by the traditional OCA theory.

5.1   The general case solution

In general terms, the two-speed Europe hypothesis can be easily visualized. Let us go back to Figure 6.5 and imagine now that $(OCA)_t = \emptyset$, i.e. the OCA zone is an empty set. This means that the establishment of the monetary union will not occur or, if it already existed, it has disintegrated.

However, it is also possible to have different OCA zones, stemming from different overlapping states' acceptability areas, as depicted in Figure 6.8. As we know, the two OCA zones are characterized by two policy mixes (H, P) and, then, by two levels of welfare. We can write:

$$(H^1, P^1) \in (OCA)' \text{ and } (H^2, P^2) \in (OCA)'' \text{ as } (OCA)' \cap (OCA)'' = \emptyset$$

5.2   The specific case solution

We can deepen the 'two-speed Europe' problem making use of the 'specific' version of the model. In section 3.3 we have dealt with the costs to member states due to the union size; now we deal with the same problem making reference to the EU experience, and in this case the difference between the 'old' and the 'new' EU (or 'newcomers') member states is useful.

Let us take Figure 6.1, depicting the relationship between states' costs and benefits and union size, as our starting point. Then, we must refer to equations (5′) and (6′) in which a crucial role is assumed by the N's parameters β and δ, because the evolution of the benefits and costs will depend on their values. Thus, to complete our model, some reasonable assumptions about these values are needed. We already know that both β and δ are positive and for $N < N^*$, costs, for the representative state i, are exclusively related to the integration policies, P and H.

Moreover, the experience concerning the EU enlargement clearly suggests that 'new' costs emerge when the *expected* union size exceeds a critical value, in our case symbolized by N^*, which is given by the EMU member states and the EU 'newcomers', the future EMU member states.

In this case, according to the EU experience and to the discussion in section 3.3, we expect that the costs to the 'old' member states should *increase* more than benefits. Economic and social problems boost a perceived general diversity between 'old' countries and 'newcomers' which produces rising costs, related to:

(a) the perceived weakening of the common purpose among countries;
(b) a perceived reduction of ownership of the integration process by the 'old' member states;
(c) a perceived reduction in security from crime;
(d) a growing fear of job losses because of the invasion of unskilled manpower from the newcomer states.

These points seem to support the (reasonable) idea of growing *marginal* costs, for the representative (of the 'old' members) state i, with respect to the union size, when $N > N^*$.

This idea and the general feature of the model discussed in section 3.3 are consistent with the following values of δ: $\delta = 0$, for $N < N^*$ and $\delta > 1$ for $N > N^*$, while $\beta < 1$ is always valid.

Thus, the relationship between costs and benefits for the 'old' member states and union size is depicted in Figure 6.9 where both benefits and

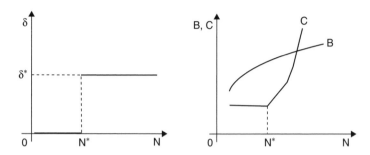

Figure 6.9 Costs and benefits for the 'old' member states and the union size according our scheme

costs are rising, while marginal costs are increasing and marginal benefits decreasing.

Now, we must move from the 'old' union size to the 'new' one, in which we include the EU newcomers, i.e. the future member states of the European Monetary Union.

Our starting point is Figure 6.7(b). Let us suppose that new states joining the 'union' lead, in the short term, to its number N exceeding the critical level N*. After the accession of the 'newcomers', the union must obviously redefine the acceptability areas and, then, the new OCA zone.

In our model, as we know, the dimension of the union *directly* affects net benefits and *indirectly* the *policy mix*, through the change of the OCA zone; and in changing the OCA zone the union's welfare also changes. This result stems from the model, from the link between net benefits, policies and union dimensions established by it and analysed in the previous pages.

As N changes the 'union' faces an optimization problem. The new equilibrium point is identified, as we know, by minimizing the distance with the previous one.

All in all, it is important for us to obtain a *new* OCA zone referring to *all* member states (old and newcomers) and to show that it will be smaller than the pre-accession zone, as in Figure 6.10.

It is easy to prove that when N soars beyond the critical value N*, the marginal state R_i line is now nearer the H-axis than before, i.e. after the EU enlargement the new OCA zone (Figure 6.10(b)) is smaller than the previous one.

Let us remember that the OCA, or R_i line, when net benefits are zero, i.e. $P = R \cdot H$, can be written as follows:

$$R = \left(\frac{C_0 N^\delta S^\mu}{B_0 N^\beta S^\lambda} \right)^{\frac{1}{\alpha_1 - \alpha_2}} = \left(\frac{C_0}{B_0} S^{\mu - \lambda} \right)^{\frac{1}{\alpha_1 - \alpha_2}} \cdot \frac{\delta - \beta}{N^{\alpha_1 - \alpha_2}}$$

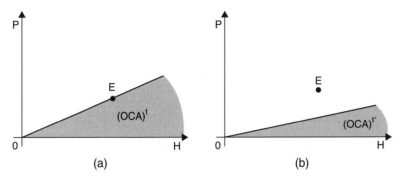

Figure 6.10   The OCA zone: (a) before and (b) after the EU enlargement

Letting:

$$R_0 = \left(\frac{C_0}{B_0} S^{\mu - \lambda} \right)^{\frac{1}{\alpha_1 - \alpha_2}}$$

we have:

$$R = R_0 \cdot N^{\frac{\delta - \beta}{\alpha_1 - \alpha_2}}$$

The value R defines, as we know, the slope of the OCA line, the boundary of the OCA zone. Calculating the derivative of R with respect to N, we have:

$$\frac{dR}{dN} = R_0 \cdot \frac{\delta - \beta}{\alpha_1 - \alpha_2} \cdot N^{\frac{\delta - \beta}{\alpha_1 - \alpha_2} - 1}$$

The sign of $\frac{dR}{dN}$ is given by $\frac{\delta - \beta}{\alpha_1 - \alpha_2}$ because, by hypothesis, $\alpha_1 - \alpha_2 < 0$ we can write:

$$\left| \frac{\partial R}{\partial N} > 0 \text{ if } \delta < \beta \right.$$

$$N > N^* : \left| \begin{array}{ll} \frac{\partial R}{\partial N} = 0 & \text{if } \delta = \beta \\[2mm] \frac{\partial R}{\partial N} < 0 & \text{if } \delta > \beta \end{array} \right.$$

$$N \leq N^* : \left| \frac{\partial R}{\partial N} > 0 \right.$$

The case in which we are interested is when $\delta > \beta$, i.e. when, after the EU enlargement, costs are more responsive than benefits to the union size.

The accession of new member states and the related higher costs for a part of them, the 'old' ones, lead to a smaller OCA zone. Thus the union is forced to choose policies within a smaller space (Figure 6.10(b)). In this case, the former equilibrium point E is now in the 'non-OCA zone'.

Compared with the previous equilibrium point E, the new E* is consistent with lower values of P and H and then with a lower level of welfare. This result stems from the model and its structure but it is also based on the assumptions concerning the economic and social problems perceived in many 'old' EU countries, after the enlargement.

If the 'old' member states are not prepared to accept the loss of the expected welfare, the conditions for a two-speed monetary union are destined to emerge. They could claim the pre-accession net benefit, and this would be attainable only by leaving the newcomers outside the union.

5.3 The solidarity hypothesis

The 'two-speed union' is not the only solution when N exceeds the critical value N^*. It is possible that 'old' countries could behave expressing solidarity, in such a way as to fill up the negative gap between costs and benefits. In this case we can proceed as follows.

The benefits line $P = R \cdot H$ delimiting the OCA zone is:

$$R = \left(\frac{C_0 N^\delta S^\mu}{B_0 N^\beta S^\lambda} \right)^{\frac{1}{\alpha_1 - \alpha_2}} = \left(\frac{C_0}{B_0} N^{\delta - \beta} \right)^{\frac{1}{\alpha_1 - \alpha_2}} \cdot \frac{\mu - \lambda}{S^{\alpha_1 - \alpha_2}}$$

where S stands for solidarity.

Letting:

$$R_1 = \left(\frac{C_0}{B_0} N^{\delta - \beta} \right)^{\frac{1}{\alpha_1 - \alpha_2}}$$

we have

$$R = R_1 \cdot S^{\frac{\mu - \lambda}{\alpha_1 - \alpha_2}}$$

R defines the slope of the benefits line; then it is the R derivative with respect to S

$$\frac{dR}{dS} = R_1 \cdot \frac{\mu - \lambda}{\alpha_1 - \alpha_2} \cdot N^{\frac{\mu - \lambda}{\alpha_1 - \alpha_2} - 1}$$

The sign of $\frac{dR}{dS}$ is given by $\frac{\mu - \lambda}{\alpha_1 - \alpha_2}$ and we can say that the OCA zone increases with S, when the elasticity of costs with respect to S is lower than that of benefits, i.e. if $\mu < \lambda$.

Thus the pre-accession situation is restored, and the $N > N^*$ member states can go ahead together.

6   Concluding remarks: the future of EMU and the OCA theory

Four years after the European Union threw open its doors to ten new member states, mostly former communist countries, the future of EMU appears seriously at risk. The 'No' vote in the referendum in France and the Netherlands in 2005 on the EU constitutional treaty and the Euro-barometer opinion polls show a majority in several states clearly against the EU enlargement. A growing opposition is also perceived against new accessions of other Balkan countries, such as Serbia, Bosnia and Albania. It is not only a question of (dramatic) changes to the EMU institutions. The enlargement has produced a large gridlock in the process of monetary integration because the majority or perhaps all the old member states fear mass migration from East to West as well as unfair competition from the low-wage and low-tax economies in the East (*Financial Times*, 1 May 2008: 11).

After the enlargement the prospect of a 'two-speed EMU' has become the centre of an animated debate, and it is a realistic outcome of the current situation. However, the OCA theory has little or nothing to say on this matter.

De Grauwe (2007: 97–101) tries to deal with the 'challenge of enlargement of EMU' using exclusively the traditional concepts of openness and asymmetry of shocks, but his results are unconvincing because: (a) they depend strictly on the concepts used and we do not know how to weigh one against the other; (b) more importantly, he completely overlooks the (cited) problems which could make the two-speed EMU probable, while using concepts which will never capture the actual decision-making process regarding this occurrence.

The OCA theory has been a very poor guide to European monetary integration, just as it is in predicting its future. It is completely inadequate to cope with the problems of a monetary union which is not a political one.

This conclusion represents the starting point of our very simple conceptual scheme. We have identified the decision-making processes urging member states either to join a monetary union or to leave it, focusing on their objectives and policies in reaching a decision. At the same time, the model suggested borrows from the OCA theory the traditional criteria and effects of single currency, capable of affecting policy effectiveness and macroeconomic results.

We have used the model to simulate the event of a two-speed EMU. Our results suggest that EU enlargement to 27 will imply

- higher economic as well as social costs;
- a lower level of economic welfare for the 'old' member states;
- most probably, a delay in the achievement of the European political union, as already maintained (De Grauwe 2007), because of the enlargement-related losses in terms of common purpose and ownership after the accession of the new Eastern European countries.

Thus, old states could claim that a two-speed monetary union is to be expected. However, this is not the only solution, because the old states could close the gap between costs and benefits thanks to their solidarity.

To sum up: states decide to form or to join a monetary union if its expected benefits are higher than its costs. The union defines the OCA zone, in which it can choose policy mix (P^*, H^*) consistent with the constraint $B > C$. Over time benefits and costs to all member states may change. The union redefines the OCA zone and some or all member states decide to remain in the union or to leave it. In our scheme 'solidarity' means that one or more countries may opt to remain in the union, even if its economic benefits are lower than its costs.

Notes

1. I thank Mario Latorre, Simona Talani, Filippo Cesarano and Paolo Biraschi for valuable comments and criticisms. The usual disclaimers apply.
2. Giavazzi and Giovannini (1989: 25, 27) discuss the 'active role played by Chancellor Brandt at the Hague Summit – he officially put forward the plan for monetary unification – [which] probably also reflected the special interest of Germany in a harmonized European revaluation vis à-vis the dollar' as well as 'the fear of possible damage to Germany's competitiveness'.
3. According to Carli (1993) the European Monetary Snake de facto was an expedient to escape the Deutschmark's revaluation vis-à-vis the dollar and other European currencies.
4. Cf. De Cecco (1994) and Verde (1999).
5. Cf. Verde (2003).
6. For a political analysis of the European economic integration process, see Talani (2004).
7. Cf. De Grauwe (2007: ch. 2).

8. Thus we are hypothesizing that current and potential growth are not correlated, contra Fitoussi and Saraceno (2004).
9. Indeed, public transfers (or fiscal federalism) – another OCA criterion – imply a functional form of political union.
10. We will return to this issue and to Figure 6.1 in section 5.2 when we will consider the EU experience.
11. According to Eichengreen (2006: 432), 'Defending a system of currency pegs in the presence of high capital mobility requires the close convergence of policies and the maintenance of confidence. If either precondition is disturbed, a country will require extensive financial support in order to defend its peg or to undertake an orderly realignment. In practice, Asian countries possess neither the willingness to subordinate other policies to these imperatives nor the *solidarity* needed to receive other extensive financial support.'
12. In this context, the words 'game' and 'players' have nothing to do with game theory.
13. From here onwards, writing H and P we mean respectively (H-H_{min}) and (P-P_{min}); then $H \geq 0$ means $H \geq H_{min}$ and the same for P; both within the maximum levels P_{max} and H_{max}.
14. Things do not change if we consider the opposite case $\alpha_1 > \alpha_2$.

References

Alesina, A., Baqir, R. and Easterly, W. (1999), 'Public goods and ethnic divisions', *Quarterly Journal of Economics*, 114 (1999): 1243–84.
Artis, M. (2003), 'Reflections on the optimal currency area (OCA) criteria in the light of EMU', *International Journal of Finance and Economics*, 8(4): 297–307.
Baldwin, R. and Wyplosz, C. (2004), *The Economics of European Integration*, 1st edn, New York: McGraw-Hill.
Balassa, B. (1961), *The Theory of Economic Integration: Limits and Prospects*, London: Allen & Unwin.
Barro, R. and Gordon, D. (1983), 'Rules, discretion and reputation in a model of monetary policy', *Journal of Monetary Economics*, 12: 101–21.
Barro, R. and Sala-i-Martin, X. (1995), *Economic Growth*, New York: McGraw-Hill.
Boeri, T. (2005), 'Reforming labor and product markets: some lessons from two decades of experiments in Europe', IMF Working Paper, no. 05/97.
Carli, G. (1993), *Cinquant' Anni di Vita Italiana*, Rome: Laterza.
Coeurdacier, N. and Martin, P. (2007), 'The geography of asset trade and the euro: insiders and outsiders', CEPR Discussion Paper, no. 6032.
Collignon, S. (2001), 'Economic policy coordination in EMU: institutional and political requirements', mimeo.
Corden M. (1972), 'Monetary integration', *Essays in International Finance*, 93, Princeton.
De Cecco, M. (1994), 'L'Italia e il sistema monetario Europeo', in R. Pizzuti (ed.), *L'economia italiana dagli anni '70 agli anni '90: pragmatismo, disciplina e saggezza convenzionale*, Milan: McGraw-Hill.
De Grauwe, P. (2007), *Economics of Monetary Union*, Oxford: Oxford University Press.

Demertzis, M., Hughes, A. and Rummel, O. (2000), 'Is the European Union a natural currency area, or is it held together by policy makers?', *Weltwirtschaftliches Archiv*, 136(4): 657–79.

Dorrucci, E., Fratzscher, M. and Mongelli, F. P. (2004), 'The link between institutional and economic integration: insights for Latin America from the European experience', *Open Economies Review*, 15: 239–60.

ECB (2005), *Review of the International Role of the Euro*, Frankfurt: European Central Bank.

Eichengreen, B. (2006), 'The parallel-currency approach to Asian monetary integration', *American Economic Review*, 96(2): 432–6.

Eichengreen, B. (2008), 'Sui generis EMU', Economic Paper, no. 303, Brussels: European Commission.

European Commission (1990), 'One market, one money', *European Economy*, 44, Brussels.

Fitoussi, J. P. and Saraceno, F. (2004), 'The Brussels–Frankfurt–Washington consensus: old and new tradeoffs in economics', mimeo.

Frankel, J. and Rose, A. (1998), 'The endogeneity of the optimum currency area criteria', *Economic Journal*, 108(449): 1009–25.

Giavazzi, F. and Giovannini, A. (1989), 'Can the EMS be exported? Lessons from ten years of monetary policy coordination in Europe', CEPR Discussion Paper, no. 285.

Ishyama, Y. (1975), 'The theory of optimum currency areas: a survey', *IMF Staff Papers*, 22 (July): 344–83.

Issing, O. (2008), *The Birth of the Euro*, Cambridge: Cambridge University Press.

Johnson, H. G. (1969), 'The "problems" approach to monetary reform', in R. Mundell and A. Swoboda (eds), *Monetary Problems of the International Economy*, Chicago: University of Chicago Press.

Kenen, P. (1969), 'The optimum currency area: an eclectic view', in R. Mundell and A. Swoboda (eds), *Monetary Problems of the International Economy*, Chicago: University of Chicago Press.

Krugman, P. (1993), 'Lessons of Massachussets for EMU', in F. Torres and F. Giavazzi (eds), *Adjustment and Growth in the European Monetary Union*, Cambridge: Cambridge University Press.

Lucas, R. (1973), 'Some international evidence on the output-inflation tradeoffs', *American Economic Review*, 63(3): 326–34.

McCallum, J. (1995), 'National borders matter: Canada–US regional trade patterns', *American Economic Review*, 85(3).

McKinnon, R. (1963), 'Optimum currency areas', *American Economic Review*, 53: 717–25.

McKinnon, R. (2004), 'Optimum currency areas and key currencies: Mundell I versus Mundell II', *Journal of Common Market Studies*, 42(4): 689–715.

Micco, A., Ordonez, G. and Stein, E. (2003), 'The currency union effects on trade: early evidence on trade', *Economic Policy*, 18(37): 315–56.

Mongelli, F. P. (2008), 'European economic and monetary integration and the optimum currency area theory', *Economic Papers*, 302, Brussels: European Commission.

Mongelli, F. P., Dorrucci, E. and Agur, I. (2005), 'What does the institutional integration tell us about trade integration?', mimeo.

Mundell, R. (1961), 'A theory of optimum currency areas', *American Economic Review*, 51: 657–64.

Mundell, R. (1973), 'Uncommon arguments for common currencies', in H. G. Johnson and A. Swoboda (eds), *The Economics of Common Currencies*, Cambridge, MA: Harvard University Press.

Petroulas, P. (2007), 'The effect of the euro on foreign direct investment', *European Economic Review*, 51(6): 1468–91.

Rose, A. K. (2000), 'One money, one market: estimating the effect of common currencies on trade', *Economic Policy*, 30: 7–46.

Schelkle, W. (2007), 'EMU: what did we think we know, what do we know and what should we know?', mimeo.

Talani, L. S. (2004), *European Political Economy: Political Science Perspectives*, London: Ashgate.

Tavlas, G. S. (1993), 'The "new" theory of optimum currency areas', *World Economy*, 16: 663–85.

Verde, A. (1999), *Economia Internazionale Monetaria*, Bari: Cacucci Editore.

Verde, A. (2003), 'E'l'UEM un'area valutaria ottimale? Riflessioni e spunti per un approccio alternativo alle unioni monetary', *Rivista Economica del Mezzogiorno*, 3.

7
EMU and the Quest for Competitiveness

Leila Simona Talani

1 Introduction

Standard lectures on costs and benefits of EMU cannot avoid touching upon the issue of whether the adoption of a single European currency, with the related loss of the exchange rate tool, has modified the competitiveness of the euro-area member states and in which way. Optimum currency area (OCA) and sustainable currency area (SCA) theories deal precisely with this question (see Chapters 1 and 3). This chapter addresses the problem of European competitiveness from a political science perspective focusing on the way in which the main socio-economic sectors within the most important EU member states have used the process of European monetary integration to enhance their competitive position not only in the European arena, but also in the global context.

This chapter will study from a historical perspective the phases of the quest for competitiveness of the European member states and their leading socio-economic sectors. It will start with a general overview of the theoretical context in which to analyse the issue. It will then proceed by evaluating the first phase in the quest for competitiveness represented by the ECB's monetary policy and exchange rate policy of 'benign neglect' vis-à-vis the devaluation of the exchange rate and the overshooting of the monetary targets. In the second phase, from 2002 onwards, given the unlikelihood that the ECB could reverse or even slow down the depreciation of the dollar, the imperative of competitiveness produced new attention towards structural reforms and the flexibility of the labour markets. The chapter will highlight the relation between EMU, unemployment and structural reforms and their importance for the leading European socio-economic sectors. Finally this contribution will stress how the most powerful member states, namely Germany and France, sought to obtain a relaxation of the macroeconomic policy framework, much needed by their economic domestic actors, by loosening the grip of the SGP.

2 The quest for competitiveness in theory

Colin Crouch (2002) provides an analysis of how the quest for competitiveness by the European socio-economic sectors has influenced European states' attitudes towards EMU, the euro and the Stability and Growth Pact (SGP). The focus of his contribution is on the way in which national governments react to the lack of competitiveness of their industrial sectors in terms of the lack of the instrument of competitive devaluations. In particular, the author identifies three phases in the development of an EU industrial relations system as a consequence of the establishment of EMU: short-term, medium-term and long-term. Leaving aside the long term in which the possibility of the creation of a transnational, European collective bargaining system is envisaged (Crouch 2002: 297), this chapter is concerned particularly with the short and the medium term. In the short term, the devaluation of the euro is considered as the means by which nation-states have generally addressed the lack of competitiveness of their industrial sectors (see below). In this context, the policy of benign neglect towards the devaluation of the euro, implemented by the ECB in the first years of its activity, should be regarded as a short-term surrogate for the national competitive devaluations lost with the establishment of EMU. As such, it was more than welcome by the socio-economic sectors of the main members of the euro-zone hoping for an export-orientated growth of their economies (Crouch 2002: 282). It is important to note that according to Crouch this policy was perfectly in line with the previous behaviour of Germany, which had relied on a weak although stable currency for most of the 1970s (Crouch 1994; Streeck 1994). It is also consistent with the intergovernmentalist view that Germany decided to enter EMU to guarantee a stable but slightly less strong currency to its industrial sector (Moravcik 1998).

In Crouch's opinion, however, the euro-devaluation strategy could not be sustained for too long, and would be substituted in the medium term by social pacts and labour market reforms. What is particularly important here is that, according to Crouch, structural reform in the euro-zone member states would happen in a neo-corporatist fashion (for similar arguments see Marsden 1992; Pochet 1998; Boyer 2000). Neo-corporatism is defined more as action co-ordination amongst social partners, than institutionalization of corporatist practices. It can take various forms, including organized decentralization, which is defined as 'a shift away from centralised bargaining managed by employers' organisations and trade unions' (Crouch 2002: 293). In turn, the relation of the government with the social partners is one of mutual dependence, as the government needs the consensus of the social partners to ensure smooth acceptance by the electorate of the structural welfare policy reform, while social partners, particularly trade unions, need neo-corporatism to keep them involved in the decision-making process (Crouch 2002: 285). This is true, according to Crouch, for the great majority of Western European cases, excluding only the UK. Also according to Rhodes (2002), the reform of the labour markets and of the welfare state would not happen in a deregulatory fashion, but through a neo-corporatist strategy, or better, as he calls it, 'competitive corporatism' (Rhodes 1997). Paradoxically, EMU, instead of decreasing the power of social partners, increases their role in the welfare and wage bargaining processes. For our purposes it is important to note that these neo-corporatist practices entail that structural reforms need to rely on the consensus of the social partners. The necessity of achieving such consensus led to the relaxation of the German and French commitment to the SGP, not to EMU, whose foundations have not been undermined either by the crisis of the SGP or by the social struggles provoked by the necessity to implement structural reforms.

2.1 The quest for competitiveness phase one: the ECB, monetary targets and the devaluation of the euro in the first years of EMU

There were many worries concerning the performance of the ECB on the eve of its establishment, given the unprecedented nature of its tasks as the institution responsible for the implementation of a European common monetary policy and the management of a European common currency in a situation lacking full political integration. These concerns ranged from the lack of credibility of the ECB monetary stance to its lack of flexibility, from the need to increase its democratic accountability to that of ensuring its independence from the governments of the member states. At this point it is worth noting that the European Central Bank is the most independent of all central banks.[1] Indeed, its independence is guaranteed by its very statute in order to ensure as its exclusive goal the achievement of monetary stability, defined as a level of inflation rates below 2 per cent. Independence from political constraints, both national and supranational, on the one hand created further preoccupation over the democratic deficit of the European institutional setting, but on the other hand allowed central bankers to concentrate theoretically only on monetary variables, leaving aside the performance of the real economic indicators, namely growth and employment rates.

The reality of the first years of implementation of a single monetary policy in the euro-area, however, demonstrates that monetary policy considerations have not been separated from the performance of real economies.

According to the CEPR,[2] from its inception the ECB displayed more flexibility than expected regarding asymmetries within the euro-zone. This result was possible thanks to the adoption of a so-called 'two-pillar' monetary strategy at the expense of transparency. Given the goal of price stability, defined as a harmonized index of consumer prices (HICP) between 0 and 2 per cent, the two pillars of monetary policy are, on the one hand, a money growth reference target and, on the other hand, a number of unspecified indicators including the exchange rates and asset prices.

The first issue to address is the importance attributed by the ECB to output growth in euro-land (and in some member countries in particular) relative to inflation.

Since the establishment of EMU, in 1999, the economic outlook recorded a marked slow-down in all OECD countries for the first time since the 1970s. Whereas the Japanese economy had been in recession for some time, in 2001 the US economy experienced its first substantial fall of the business cycle in a decade. Also, the euro-zone, with a lag of some months with respect to the US, slowed significantly in 2001 (Figure 7.1). It is important to notice that this had a major impact especially on the most important European economies, namely Italy, France and Germany (Figure 7.2).

Theoretically, as underlined in many speeches and documents,[3] the ECB would pay little attention to the short-run output developments, and this also to avoid the threat of losing credibility in its anti-inflationary stance in the eyes of the financial markets.

Despite this, even from a superficial analysis it is easy to see that the 30 point cut of interest rates to 3 per cent on 1 January 1999 was associated with deflationary risks in the wake of the Asian crisis. Furthermore, the April 1999 cut to 2.5 per cent coincided with declining output in important euro-land members (notably Germany). Finally, the cut in the minimum bid rate on the euro-system's main refinancing operation by 50 points to 3.75 on 17 September 2001 clearly reflects a similar decision taken by the US Federal Reserve in the aftermath of the terrorist attacks of 11 September and their recessive consequences (ECB, *Monthly Bulletin*, various issues).

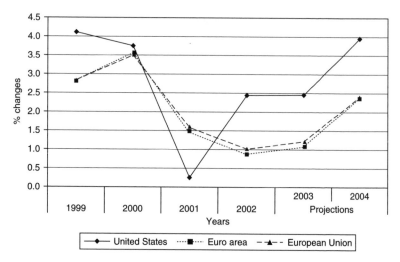

Figure 7.1   Real GDP % changes, 1999–2004
Source: OECD.

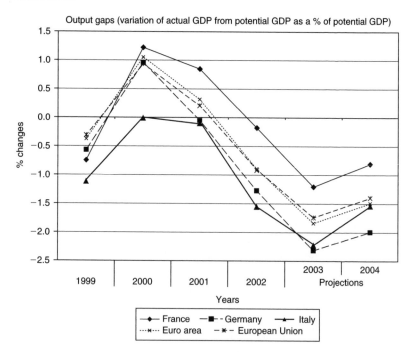

Figure 7.2   Output gaps
Source: OECD.

More sophisticated analyses clearly show that the ECB's monetary policy, and, in particular, the timing and frequency of interest rate changes, reflected its aim to engage in some output stabilization and not only to control prices, though leading central bank personalities constantly denied it (CEPR 2002).

If the output level was never officially recognized as a point of reference in the monetary policy-making of the ECB, but was certainly taken into consideration, the opposite happened with monetary targets. Indeed, the 'two-pillar' strategy theoretically rests on the prominence of the target for M3 growth as the main official indicator for ECB monetary policy decisions. However, on many occasions, when the target was overshot, the ECB did not react accordingly. For example, despite the fact that the target had been publicly set at 4.5 per cent for 1999, no measures were taken by the ECB when it became clear that the target would not be achieved by the end of the year. On the contrary, the ECB cut the interest rates and engaged in sophisticated explanations over why the departure from the reference M3 growth rate did not represent any rupture with the 'two-pillar' monetary strategy.

As the outlook for inflation turned upward by the end of 1999, the ECB did promptly intervene by increasing the interest rate by 50 basis points. Of course, given the parallel increase in the M3 growth, this seemed to be consistent with the monetary strategy declared by the ECB, while the final divorce between the ECB changes in the interest rates and the M3 growth rate appears justified by the necessity of keeping the HICP within the 2 per cent limit.

In any case, the experts' suspicion that the M3 target was never really given the importance implicit in the adoption of the 'two-pillar' strategy, and was often subordinated to pragmatic considerations about the level of output, was never abandoned. Indeed, reacting to the many criticisms levelled against the first pillar, the ECB effected some modifications of the M3 series, by first removing non-resident holdings of money market funds from the definition of euro-zone M3 and then purging non-resident holdings of liquid money, market paper and securities.

However, this adjustment was no more than a cosmetic change and has not improved the reliability of the monetary pillar. If anything, Figure 7.3 shows that M3 percentage changes and interest rate decisions by the ECB, in its first years of activity, went in opposite directions.

Even more obscure is the role attributed by the ECB to the exchange rates within the two-pillar monetary strategy.[4] Indeed, the second pillar of the strategy makes explicit reference to a series of indicators influencing the ECB's monetary decisions amongst which are the exchange

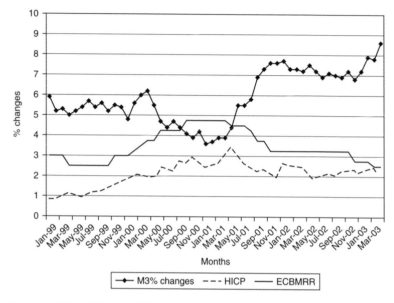

Figure 7.3   M3, HICP and ECB main refinancing rate % changes, 1999–2003
Source: OECD.

rates of the euro. However, looking at the performance of the newly born currency in the first months of its existence raises spontaneously the suspicion that the Bank had adopted an attitude of 'benign neglect' vis-à-vis the exchange rate of the euro.[5]

Indeed, the euro lost around 15 per cent of its value vis-à-vis the dollar between August 1999 and August 2000, while the parity with the dollar was already lost in January 2000. Also the effective nominal and real exchange rate of the euro experienced a marked decrease (−11.3 and −10.1 respectively between August 1999 and August 2000) (see Figure 7.4).

Of course the ECB has always underlined that the performance of a currency must be assessed in the long run. And indeed in the long run the euro/dollar exchange rate has witnessed a reversal of its previous performance with a marked appreciation of the euro, though it might be better to talk about a strong depreciation of the dollar (Chapter 2).

However, the substantial lack of concern about the fall of the euro on the part of the European monetary authorities provoked further doubts about the real scope of the two-pillar strategy.[6] In short, the emphasis on the performance of the monetary aggregates (M3) as the first pillar of the ECB monetary strategy seems to conceal the desire by the ECB to trade-off

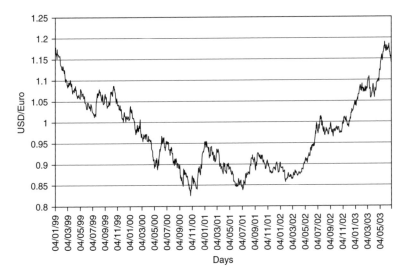

Figure 7.4 US$/euro exchange rates, 1999–2004
Source: ECB.

some of the transparency that the adoption of an alternative monetary strategy would imply (such as targeting the inflation rate, for example), in exchange for more flexibility. In turn, this flexibility has been used to pursue output objectives that would not be acceptable otherwise within the strict anti-inflationary mandate of the ECB.[7]

Similarly, the attitude of the ECB towards the performance of the exchange rate, particularly in the first two years of its activity (an attitude that economists fail to fully understand[8]) acquires a completely different meaning in the light of the analysis of the manufacturing export performance of the euro-zone and, in particular, of some of the euro-zone countries (Talani 2005). The export-oriented manufacturing sectors gained the most from a devalued currency.

Focusing on changes in the balance of trade in goods with the US between 1995 and 2001 the data indicate that the countries recording the highest improvements of their trade balances with the US[9] were Italy (from 0.7 per cent to 1.2 per cent), France (from −0.3 per cent to 0.55 per cent) and Germany (from 0.6 per cent to 1.5 per cent) (Talani 2005). Therefore, the countries heavily relying on the performance of the export-oriented manufacturing sector, like Italy, Germany and France, had a vested interest in adopting a policy of 'laissez-faire' with respect to the depreciation of the euro.

Things drastically changed, however, when the dollar started depreciating leaving countries of the euro-zone with the long-lasting problem of how to increase their economic competitiveness, especially in the wake of increased globalization of the world economy.

One way to increase competitiveness is indeed to reduce the costs of labour by adopting supply-side measures to increase the flexibility of the labour markets. The expression 'flexibility of labour markets' as used by the scholars of industrial relations (Rhodes 1997) refers to three forms of flexibility:

- internal (or functional) flexibility in the workplace;
- external (or numerical) flexibility vis-à-vis the wider labour market;
- greater pay flexibility at local levels.

Is there a relation between the EU discourse on structural interventions to increase the flexibility of the labour markets and the implementation of EMU? This is what we will discover in the next section.

2.2   The quest for competitiveness phase two: EMU and unemployment, the flexibility of labour markets and structural reforms

EMU should be read as a major institutional undertaking whose economic outcomes are not only constrained, but also defined by its institutional framework. This is to say that the economic consequences of EMU are specific to the way in which this particular currency union has been devised and this, in turn, is the product of a unique historical process.

From an institutional point of view, the Maastricht Treaty and its protocols solved the long-lasting controversy between the 'monetarist' and the 'economist'[10] approaches to monetary union. This was possible on the one hand by establishing a rigid institutional framework with a clear-cut economic objective (that of pursuing price stability) and a three-stage timetable to achieve EMU (cf. Gros and Thygesen 1998), and on the other hand by devising a set of convergence requirements that applying member states had to respect before entering. These requirements included permanence in the 'new' ERM (within 15 per cent bands) for at least two years; inflation rates no more than 1.5 per cent higher than the average of the three most virtuous member states; interest rates no more than 2 per cent higher than the average of the three most virtuous member states; a debt-to-GDP ratio not exceeding 60 per cent, subject to conditions; and, most importantly, a deficit-to-GDP ratio not exceeding 3 per cent (TEU Art. 104(c) and Art. 109(j)).

The economic viability and the political (or political economy) rationale of the Maastricht criteria has been the subject of a number of studies from many academic points of view, and will not be pursued here. What is important to underline, however, is that their strict anti-inflationary aim was further strengthened by the adoption of the Stability and Growth Pact (Talani and Casey 2008). The first version of the Pact[11] confirmed the objective of a deficit-to-GDP ratio not exceeding 3 per cent and commits EMU member states to a medium-term budgetary stance close to balance or in surplus. It also defined the terms and sanctions of the excessive deficit procedure (EDP) (Gros and Thygesen 1998: 341).

The major questions to answer at this point is how, if at all, the implementation of this particular kind of currency union did influence EMU member states' performances in terms of unemployment and what were the consequences of the SGP. There are two ways of tackling the first issue. One is to assess to what extent this particular form of currency union contains a recessive bias, thus reducing the level of output ceteris paribus. The other way is to see how the establishment of EMU has been linked in theory and in practice to the flexibility of labour markets. These two streams of reasoning might have opposite outcomes. Indeed, while the former would point to an increase in the level of unemployment, the second could lead to its decrease. However, the tricky aspect lies in the fact that the first way of reasoning might be used to further the second, thus adding to its economic rationale and fostering its political feasibility.

The first stream of economic reasoning assesses the overall recessive effects of the implementation of the Maastricht fiscal criteria and/or of the SGP. Some authors have argued that the effort brought about by the implementation of the Maastricht criteria, and in particular of the fiscal ones, as well as the determination to stick to the ERM in a period of high interest rate policy, can explain the upsurge of European unemployment in the 1990s (Artis 1998). Of course, economic analyses are far from agreeing on the issue. Indeed, the counter-arguments tend to underline the necessity of fiscal consolidation and anti-inflationary policies. Others point out that the time period over which unemployment has been growing in Europe is too long to be easily explained in macroeconomic terms (Nickell 1997). However, deflationary policies implicit in the implementation of the Maastricht way to EMU seem to have eventually worsened the level of European unemployment, at least by increasing the equilibrium rate of unemployment (a phenomenon called hysteresis in the literature) (Cameron 1997, 1998, 1999; Artis 1998).

Moreover, some econometric simulations show that the implementation of the SGP from 1974 until 1995 in four European countries (namely, Italy, France, Germany and the UK) resulted in limited economic growth by reducing the annual growth rate (Eichengreen and Wyplosz 1998: 93). This would lead to cumulated output losses of around 5 per cent in France and the UK, and of 9 per cent in Italy. The economic theory rationale of these results is, of course, that the SGP constraints would limit (and will limit, in the future) the use of automatic stabilizers to counter recessive waves, thus increasing the severity of recessions. This, however, will happen only if member states are not able to achieve a balanced or surplus budgetary position allowing them to use automatic stabilizers during mild recessive periods in the appropriate way without breaching the Maastricht/SGP threshold.

There is the counter-argument that the SGP gives credibility to the ECB's anti-inflationary stances, thus reducing the level of interest rates required to maintain the inflation rate below 2 per cent and boosting the economy. Finally, even if the recessive bias of the fiscal criteria and the SGP were proved, this would not necessarily lead to a higher unemployment level (Artis and Winkler 1997; Buti et al. 1997).

However, there is another way in which the Maastricht criteria and the SGP might affect unemployment, a more indirect way, which is the basis to justify a neo-functionalist automatic spillover leading from EMU to labour market flexibility. This is related to how member states should react to possibly arising asymmetric shocks. By definition, autonomous monetary policy and exchange rate policies are not available to react to idiosyncratic shocks in a currency union. At the same time, common monetary and exchange rate policies should be used with caution since they can have mixed results in the event of the other members of the Union experiencing an opposite business cycle situation. Thus, economic theory leaves few options: fiscal policy, labour mobility and relative price flexibility.

Indeed, a country could react to an asymmetric shock by using national fiscal policy, both as a counter-cyclical tool, through the action of automatic stabilizers, and in the form of fiscal transfers to solve more long-term economic disparities (as in the case of Italian Mezzogiorno). However, in the special kind of monetary union analysed in this chapter, the Maastricht criteria and, to an even greater extent, the requirements of the SGP constrain substantially the ability of member states to resort to national fiscal policy to tackle asymmetric shocks.

Alternatively, some authors suggest the redistributive and stabilizing functions of fiscal policy should be performed at the European level. Proposals range from the increase in the size of the European budget, to the pooling of national fiscal policies, to the establishment of a common fiscal body, which would act as a counterbalance to the ECB (Obstfeld and Peri 1998). However, the feasibility of similar proposals looks dubious in the light of the difficulties EU member states encounter in finding some agreement on the much less challenging task of tax harmonization (Overbeek 2003). Moreover, any discussion about fiscal policy inevitably triggers a discussion on the loss of national sovereignty and a related one on political unification whose outcomes are still far from being unanimous. Overall, there does not seem to be a compelling will on the part of EU member states to reach an agreement on the creation of a common fiscal policy nor to find some way to increase the size of the EU budget so as to introduce a stabilization function.

Given the difficulties in using national fiscal policy to tackle asymmetric shocks, and the lack of any substantial fiscal power at the European level, economists suggest the option of resorting to labour mobility. The EU does indeed provide an institutional framework in which labour mobility should be enhanced. The Treaty's articles regarding the free movement of workers, the single market programme, and the provisions about migration of course represent this. However, economic analyses show little evidence of mass migration in response to asymmetric shocks in the EU (unlike in some respects the US) (Obstfeld and Peri 1998). Indeed, few European policy-makers, if any, would seriously endorse temporary mass migration as a credible way to react to national economic strains, for obvious political as well as social considerations.

There thus remains only one policy option for national policy-makers to tackle the problems arising from asymmetric shocks, that is, increasing the flexibility of labour markets so that 'regions or states affected by adverse shocks can recover by cutting wages, reducing relative prices and taking market shares from the others' (Blanchard 1998: 249). Not only this. Since reform of the labour market is clearly a structural intervention, it will help to eliminate also the structural component of unemployment, apart from the cyclical one, if it is still possible to distinguish between the two (Artis 1998).

Indeed, the employment rhetoric and strategy officially adopted by EU institutions in the last few years shows clearly that the European Union has chosen to give priority to labour flexibility and structural reforms as 'the' means to tackle the problem of unemployment in Europe (Talani 2008; Chapter 8, this volume). However, the implementation of structural reforms is a costly endeavour which produces social unrest and requires the co-operation of domestic constituencies and actors. Is this effort going to disrupt economic and monetary union and put strains on the process of European integration as a whole? What is the future of EMU?

3   Conclusion: the future of EMU, structural reforms and the crisis of the SGP

Some answers about the disruptive potential of the implementation of structural reforms on EMU and European integration have already been given with the crisis and reform of the Stability and Growth Pact.

'Refrigerated', 'hospitalized', 'dead': these were the adjectives the press used to describe the SGP on the eve of the historical ECOFIN decision not to impose sanctions on the delinquent French and German fiscal stances.[12] The fate of the SGP was settled in the early hours of 25 November 2003 in what was a true institutional crisis between the European Commission and the ECB on one side, demanding that the rules be applied, and the intergovernmentalist ensemble of the euro-zone finance ministers rejecting the application of sanctions to the leading EU member states on the other.[13]

The most amazing thing was that, throughout the crisis, the euro remained stronger than ever and the markets did not even think about speculating on the lack of credibility of a post-SGP EMU (Talani and Casey 2008). Here a fundamental paradox arises: how can a currency remain as strong as ever in the midst of a serious crisis of the fiscal rule? The answer will be sought in the evolution of the quest for competitiveness of the most relevant socio-economic sectors of the leading euro-zone's member states.

Following Crouch we have analysed how the socio-economic sectors have pursued their quest for competitiveness by first relying on the devaluation of the euro. In Crouch's opinion, however, the euro-devaluation strategy could not be sustained for long, and would be substituted in the medium term by social pacts and labour market reforms within the context of the EES, which, in turn, had to be supported by the social partners. Indeed, as Dyson points out (2002: 182), Shroeder, his economic adviser Klaus Gretschmann, finance minister Hans Eichel, economics minister Werner Muller and labour and social affairs minister Walter Riester all agreed that the way forward for Germany to improve its competitiveness was 'managed capitalism'. Managed capitalism revolved around co-operation, co-ordination in wage bargaining, dialogue with the social partners and consensus in managing supply-side reforms (Chapter 8). Consensus was indeed the main principle of managed capitalism and was deeply entrenched in both the political and economic German systems (Dyson 2002). By the same token, France's recipe to combat the loss of competitiveness attached to globalization implied a short-term reliance on competitive devaluation and a medium-term consensus by the social partners over the pension reform (Crouch 2002). It is true that, since Mitterand's decision to keep the franc in the ERM in 1983, the process of European monetary integration had been seen as a tool to reinforce domestic economic reform. But, particularly after German reunification, the constraints of EMU were increasingly blamed for the French economic crisis (Howarth 2002). However, the substantial decline of the euro in relation to the dollar and the yen suited the French preferences. Throughout the 1990s the French government had argued that European currencies were overvalued in relation to the dollar (Howarth 2002).

Therefore, both in Germany and in France consensus over structural reform as a reaction to the impossibility of sustaining the short-term strategy of a devaluation of the euro, would mean relaxing the adherence to the SGP budgetary constraints.

In other words, the economic interests of the French and German business sectors aimed at increasing their competitiveness, after relying for a short time on the devaluation of the euro, with the reversal of this trend, focused on a reduction of taxes and on the implementation of the structural reforms (Crouch 2002). In turn, the adoption of structural reform in a neo-corporatist system had still to rely on the consensus of the trade unions. This means that when the external, international conditions could not be modified by their previous institutional referents, such as the ECB, socio-economic groups and the governments supporting their interests modified their policy preferences and decided to target other referents, in this case the ECOFIN. On the basis of similar considerations it is possible to explain why, from 2002 onwards, given the unlikelihood that the ECB could reverse or even slow down the depreciation of the dollar, the most powerful member states, namely Germany and France, sought to obtain a relaxation of the macroeconomic policy framework, much needed by their economic domestic actors, by loosening the grip of the SGP. The exact timing of the crisis, in turn, was defined by the political needs of Germany, which was involved in November/December 2003 in the final stages of a tough negotiation with both the opposition and the trade unions for the approval of a package of structural reforms called Agenda 2010 (Talani and Casey 2008).

As underlined above, however, the demise of the SGP did not signify an abandonment of the EMU project, but only a short-term contingent shift of the economic interests of the most powerful euro-zone states. Therefore the credibility of their commitment to EMU remained intact, and the markets did not feel the need to attack the euro in the aftermath of the abandonment of the fiscal rule or to bet against the stability of EMU by asking for higher yields. In brief, the future of EMU was safe, the credibility of the EMU project was still rooted in structural considerations, while the decision to relax the fiscal rule was justified by a change of macroeconomic preferences by the leading socio-economic groups in their quest for competitiveness.

Notes

1. For a similar interpretation see Berger et al. (2000); see also Cukierman et al. (1992).
2. See CEPR (2000).
3. For some quotations see CEPR (2002).
4. See CEPR (2000), for a similar interpretation.
5. Intervention of the central banks in favour of the euro in the summer 2000.
6. Doubts on the behaviour of the euro exchange rates have been expressed by many economists. See, for example, Koen (2000); Artis (2003).
7. About the effective mandate of the ECB there is a huge debate within the academic community. See, for example, CEPR (2002).
8. See Artis (2003).
9. The figures for Ireland are very high but have to be related to the overall incredible improvement of the country's economic performance in the same period.
10. The distinction between 'monetarists' and 'economists' emerged in the course of the discussions over the Werner Plan and referred to the strategy to be adopted during the transitional period. The 'monetarists' stressed the importance of achieving exchange rate stability through European institutional arrangements, while the 'economists' pointed out the necessity of policy co-ordination and, ultimately, convergence before agreeing on the adoption of a European fixed exchange rate regime or a currency union. For more details see Tsoukalis (1997).
11. In November 2003 the SGP was suspended to be reformed in March 2005. For more details see Talani and Casey (2008). See also below in this chapter.
12. See Parker (2003).
13. See Heipertz and Verdun (2004).

References

Artis, M. (1998), 'The unemployment problem', *Oxford Review of Economic Policy*, 14(3).

Artis, M. (2003), 'EMU: four years on', EUI: unpublished manuscript.

Artis, M. and Winkler, B. (1997), 'The stability pact: safeguarding the credibility of the European Central Bank', CEPR Discussion Paper, no. 1688.

Berger, H., de Haan, J. and Eijffinger, S. (2000), 'Central bank independence: an update of theory and evidence', CEPR Discussion Paper, no. 2353.

Blanchard, O. J. (1998), Discussion of 'Regional non-adjustment and fiscal policy', *Economic Policy*, 26 (April): 249.

Boyer, R. (2000), 'The unanticipated fall out of the European Monetary Union: the political and institutional deficit of the euro', in C. Crouch (ed.), *After the Euro: Shaping Institutions for Governance in the Wake of European Monetary Union*, Oxford: Oxford University Press.

Buti, M., Franco, D. and Ongena, H. (1997), 'Budgetary policies during recessions: retrospective application of the Stability and Growth Pact to the post-war period', *Economic Paper*, no 121, Brussels: European Commission.

Cameron, D. (1997), 'Economic and monetary union: underlying imperatives and third-stage dilemmas', *Journal of European Public Policy*, 4: 455–85.

Cameron, D. (1998), 'EMU after 1999: the implications and dilemmas of the third stage', *Columbia Journal of European Law*, 4: 425–46.

Cameron, D. (1999), 'Unemployment in the new Europe: the contours of the problem', *EUI Working Papers*, RSC, no. 99/35.

CEPR (2000), *One Money, Many Countries: Monitoring the European Central Bank 2*, London: CEPR.

CEPR (2002), *Surviving the Slow-down, Monitoring the European Central Bank 4*, London: CEPR.

Crouch, C. (1994), 'Incomes policies, institutions and markets: an overview of recent developments, in R. Dore, R. Boyer and Z. Mars (eds), *The Return to Incomes Policies*, London: Pinter.

Crouch, C. (2002), 'The euro, labour markets and wage policies', in K. Dyson (ed.), *European States and the Euro*, Oxford: Oxford University Press.

Cukierman, A., Webb, S. B. and Neyapti, B. (1992), 'Measuring the independence of central banks and its effects on policy outcomes', *World Bank Review*, 6: 353–98.

Dyson, K. (2002), 'Germany and the euro: redefining EMU, handling paradox and managing uncertainty and contingency', in K. Dyson (ed), *European States and the Euro*, Oxford: Oxford University Press.

Eichengreen, B. and Wyplosz, C. (1998), 'The Stability Pact: more than a minor nuisance?' *Economic Policy*, 26 (April).

Gros, D. and Thygesen, N. (1998), *European Monetary Integration*, London: Longman.

Howarth, D. (2002), 'The French state in the euro-zone: modernization and legitimising dirigisme', in K. Dyson (ed), *European States and the Euro*, Oxford: Oxford University Press.

Koen, V. (2000), 'EMU: one year on', *OECD Observer*, March, Paris: OECD.

Marsden, D. (1992), 'Incomes policy for Europe? Or will pay bargaining destroy the single European market?', *British Journal of Industrial Relations*, 30: 587–604.

Moravcsik, A. (1998) *The Choice for Europe: Social Purpose and State Power from Messina to Maastricht*, Ithaca, NY: Cornell University Press.

Nickell, S. (1997), 'Unemployment and labour market rigidities: Europe vs North America', *Journal of Economic Perspectives*, 11: 55–74.

Obstfeld, M. and Peri, G. (1998), 'Regional non-adjustment and fiscal policy', *Economic Policy*, 26 (April).

Overbeek, H. (ed.) (2003), *The Political Economy of European Unemployment*, London: Routledge.

Parker, G. (2003), 'Europe's Stability Pact: ministers conduct late-night burial for EU fiscal framework', *Financial Times*, 26 November.

Pochet, P. (1998), 'The social consequences of EMU: an overview of national debates', in P. Pochet and B. Vanhercke (eds), *Social Challenges of Economic and Monetary Union*, Brussels: European Interuniversity Press.

Rhodes, M. (1997), 'Globalisation, labour markets and welfare states: a future of "competitive corporatism?"', EUI Working Papers, no. 97/36.

Rhodes, M. (2002), 'Why EMU is, or may be, good for European welfare states', in K. Dyson (ed), *European States and the Euro*, Oxford: Oxford University Press.

Streeck, W. (1994), 'Pay restraints without incomes policies', in R. Dore, R. Boyer and Z. Mars (eds), *The Return to Incomes Policies*, London: Pinter.

Talani, L. S. (2005), 'The European Central Bank: between growth and stability', *Comparative European Politics*, 3: 204–31.

Talani L. S. (2008), 'The Maastricht way to the European Employment Strategy', in S. Baroncelli, C. Spagnolo and L. S. Talani, *Back to Maastricht*, CSP.

Talani, L. S. and Casey, B. (2008), *Between Growth and Stability: the Demise and Reform of the Stability and Growth Pact*, Cheltenham: Edward Elgar.

Tsoukalis, L. (1997), *The New European Economy Revisited*, Oxford: Oxford University Press.

8
The Lisbon Strategy, Macroeconomic Stability and the Dilemma of Governance with Governments (Or Why Europe Is Not Becoming the World's Most Dynamic Economy)

Stefan Collignon

1 Introduction

In March 2000 at the Lisbon European Council, the heads of states and governments promised to make the EU by 2010 'the most dynamic and competitive knowledge-based economy in the world, capable of sustainable economic growth with more and better jobs and greater social cohesion, and respect for the environment'. If this statement was meant to inspire enthusiasm, it has failed. Over-commitment and unachievable goals have ridiculed European policy-makers. Despite desirable objectives, national compliance with the Lisbon Strategy remains poor. The European Commission (2005a: 4) has explained this underperformance by 'a policy agenda, which has become overloaded, failing coordination and sometimes conflicting priorities'. Yet, the official mid-term review did not explain the reasons for this co-ordination failure. It has exhorted governments 'to do more reforms', but few member states seem capable of achieving them and when they do so, the results are not as expected.

In 2005, five years after Lisbon and midway to the goal, the Commission proclaimed a 'new departure' by focusing on a limited number of 'key actions that promise the highest and most immediate dividends' (Barroso 2005), namely investment, innovation and jobs. The new focus was primarily on the supply-side. Ironically, as soon as this was declared, a mix of favourable demand for exports and domestic demand due to higher wages and improved consumer confidence after the German elections pulled the euro-area out of its stagnation (European Commission 2006). The question is whether the growth spurt will be sustainable and for how long. Economic reforms under the 'new' Lisbon Strategy are intended to improve research and development, labour market flexibility and capital market integration. No doubt this would improve Europe's productive capacities. However, the past has shown that, contrary to the American experience under Clinton, a favourable macroeconomic environment is usually short-lived in the EU. Two noticeable holes in the 'new' Strategy may endanger the recent growth performance: the absence of a macroeconomic policy strategy and the issue of governance. In fact, the new Lisbon Strategy is 'less, of the same'. It is *less*, because macroeconomic management and social cohesion have been dropped from the agenda. It is the *same*, because it does not address Europe's institutional imbalances. I will show that the EU's disappointing performance is due to a collective action problem, which applies to both supply-side reforms and macroeconomic management. Europe's economic difficulties cannot be separated from constitutional questions. The problem is 'governing without government' (Rosenau 1992; Rhodes 1996), or more precisely 'governance with many governments'. I will first examine where the Lisbon Strategy is failing in its present arrangement, and then focus on the flawed macroeconomic framework, which requires constitutional reforms.

2   Where the Lisbon Strategy is failing

The Lisbon Strategy must be seen in its political context, which has dramatically changed since its inception and has shifted the emphasis on to economic supply-side reforms. But even these reforms are not forthcoming because of collective action problems. The result is a disappointing performance.

2.1   The political context

Europe's Lisbon Strategy was inspired by the strong economic growth in the United States in the late 1990s. The Clinton administration had followed advice from the Federal Reserve Bank and consolidated public finances to bring interest rates down. The longest economic upswing in US history followed. The investment share in US GDP rose from 16 per cent in 1992 to 21 per cent in 2000 and unemployment fell to 4 per cent, the lowest level since the 1960s. New investment incorporated technological innovation in ITC industries raising productivity after a long period of stagnation. This was the envied model of America's 'new economy'. By contrast, in Europe growth and investment were low, unemployment high. The investment share, which stood at 27 per cent in the 1960s and early 1970s, had fallen to 20 per cent by 1996. Because investment was low, technological progress was not incorporated to the same degree as in the USA and human capital seemed to be deficient. In the late 1990s a sense of stagnation was all-pervasive.

The shift to a 'new' economy in America reflected a policy choice. Before 1992, the 'old' US economy had also been stagnating, with growth of real investment negative between 1985 and 1992 and widespread criticism of the American economic model.[1] The US economy was deregulated in the early 1980s, but economic growth only came in the 1990s after macroeconomic policies changed. The Republican administrations of Reagan and Bush maintained high fiscal deficits and interest rates; under Clinton, both came down – with the deficit even turning into a surplus. US real long-term interest rates were one percentage point higher in 1985–91 than the synthetic interest rate for euro-land, but over 1992–2004 they were 19 base points lower. This change in macroeconomic policy was instrumental in turning the US economy around.

The EU's unsatisfactory performance is not usually explained in terms of policy choices, but by structural factors, particularly in the labour market. It has often been affirmed that *Eurosclerosis* due to protective national regulation and the insufficient integration of markets have been impeding economic growth in the EU. Yet, the rapid reversal of fortunes in the US indicates that Europe's problems may depend more on policies than on institutions and structures. The single market has already removed many obstacles and was largely completed by the early 1990s. Nevertheless, the following decade was marked by stagnation and unemployment remained stubbornly high.

In response to this situation, different European Councils have doubled up on structural reforms by setting up so-called reform 'processes' without addressing the difficulty of conducting macroeconomic policy in the euro area. The Luxembourg process set an agenda for labour market reforms in 1997. Procedures for the complete unification of the goods and capital market were put into place in Cardiff in 1998. Only in 1999 at the Cologne Council did macroeconomics appear on the European agenda by setting up a dialogue on the policy mix between wage bargainers, finance ministers and the European Central Bank (ECB). But these 'processes' did not produce the expected results. In fact, they were called *processes* because the European heads of states and governments could not agree on substantial policies (Talani 2004).

The Lisbon Strategy in 2000 was an attempt to overcome these difficulties. No longer a 'process', it was meant 'to load substance into the empty lorries of Cardiff, Luxembourg and Cologne'.[2] The Lisbon Strategy sought to match supply-side reforms with responsible demand management in order to increase growth. Higher welfare necessitated higher productivity and therefore innovation and knowledge to improve potential output. Formally, the Strategy addressed four policy areas:

1. Reforms to create a knowledge society, intended to help Europe catch up with the 'new economy' and improve productivity.
2. Optimal macroeconomic policies to ensure that the higher potential output would effectively be absorbed by demand in product markets without creating inflationary tensions.
3. Completing the integration of Europe's capital market to increase investment, especially by raising venture capital for innovation in small and medium-sized companies.
4. Reformulating the European social model, not by dismantling the welfare state, but by putting social inclusion first and empowering governments to deal with the challenges of globalization and an ageing society.

The Lisbon agenda reflected the dominance of centre-left governments in Europe at the time and their commitment to macroeconomic policy. Portugal's Prime Minister Antonio Guterres had first designed its basic objectives in a working group of the European Socialist Party (ESP) aimed at reducing unemployment (Kulahci 2002). A year later he used the EU presidency to put it into practice.

The focus of the Lisbon Strategy was economic growth. The creation of a 'knowledge society' aimed at improving the supply-side. But given that job creation requires actual GDP to grow faster than productivity (Collignon 2002), macroeconomic policy was considered indispensable for creating higher employment, consolidating public finances and releasing resources for Europe's social model. The European Commission had previously calculated that the EU would reach full employment if GDP grew at 3 per cent for one decade. The Portuguese EU presidency now proposed the idea of setting a 3 per cent growth rate as a numerical policy target for euro-land. Given that the ECB had defined price stability as a rate of inflation 'below, but close to 2 per cent' it seems reasonable that the European Council could also set its growth target numerically. This approach was justified by the Treaty on European Union. The ECB was committed to price stability as its 'primary objective' (Art. 105.2), but according to Art. 2 of the Treaty on European Union, it also was obliged 'to promote throughout the Community a harmonious, balanced and sustainable development of economic activities, a high level of employment and of social protection, equality between men and women, sustainable and non-inflationary growth, a high degree of competitiveness and convergence of economic performance', provided price stability was assured.

Thus, by specifying the numerical content of the Treaty's Art. 2, the European Council would define clearly what kind of growth rate the ECB ought to support when price stability was achieved. For example, the ECB should have taken the more ambitious growth objective of 3 per cent, rather than 2.5 per cent, when setting the reference values for monetary aggregates. The numerical target for economic growth would also have strengthened the voice of finance ministers at the informal meetings of the euro-group and improved the democratic legitimacy of European policy making. It might even have prevented some of the ECB-bashers in later years. Furthermore with growth at 3 per cent and inflation at 2 per cent, and with budget deficits capped at a maximal 3 per cent, the debt/GDP ratio would have stabilized below 60 per cent, ensuring the long-run sustainability of public finance. But in the end the option of fixing a numerical growth target was not adopted at Lisbon, because a member from an opt-out country insisted that more ambitious objectives would unleash entrepreneurial creativity. The 3 per cent target was replaced by the goal of becoming 'the world's most dynamic and competitive economy'. This formulation effectively prevented the institutional anchoring of macroeconomic policy into the Lisbon Strategy.

In the following years, right-wing governments swept back into power. The emphasis on macroeconomic policy and social inclusion was lost and a more narrow supply-side approach became dominant. With the growing political heterogeneity in the Council, agreement on binding policies became even more difficult. The Lisbon Strategy had to rely on the 'open method of co-ordination' with best-practice comparisons and peer pressure as instruments.[3] With this method it was not possible to conduct a coherent set of structural supply-side reforms and a growth-supporting macroeconomic framework. Not surprisingly, the Lisbon Strategy never really took off.

2.2 The 'open method of co-ordination' and the collective action problem

The repeated co-ordination failure in economic policy has institutional causes. It is a consequence of collective action problems, which emerge when autonomous governments seek to maximize collective utilities in isolated constituencies. Governments are constrained by national debates and by the partial interests articulated within their home constituencies.[4] In order to get (re-)elected, political leaders and parties must attempt to maximize the utility of their national constituency. As long as a European government does not exist, there is no European constituency and therefore no European-wide deliberation on collective policy preferences. Factional interests of national constituencies will then prevent the realization of the collective utility optimum, as Madison had already shown more than 200 years ago.[5] This is exactly the problem in the EU. Policies are shaped by negotiations in a 'two-level-game' (Putnam 1988), where governments take the preferences within their constituency as given and negotiate compromises at the lowest common denominator in the European Council. The resulting Nash-equilibrium does not optimize welfare. This is different from a 'normal' democracy, where formulating common policy preferences requires a deliberation process, which takes into account the interests of all European citizens and not only those of national factions. In the EU such democratic deliberation is institutionally impossible. The idea of 'policy processes' and the 'open method of co-ordination', etc. therefore expressed the less ambitious objective of going through a deliberation process amongst policy-making elites, so that governments would ultimately find solutions acceptable to all. However, this idea has underestimated the importance of vested interests articulated in national politics. Changing policy preferences through bureaucratic deliberation only works for technocratic issues, such as setting technical regulations for the single market. In areas of high politics, which are submitted to universal suffrage in national constituencies, the emergence of consensual policy preferences can take a very long time.[6] Europe's economic governance therefore has become a mix of cheap talk about reforms and gridlock in decision-making.

In essence, the failure of the Lisbon Strategy is due to a collective action problem: countries find it in their national interest *not* to stick to policies which would maximize the overall collective European welfare, as long as everyone else pursued them. But because everyone has the same incentives, no one will make the efforts necessary for achieving the common interest.[7] Why would national governments agree to European policies that might constrain their actions at home? The somewhat naïve Europhile answer is that the existence of positive policy externalities creates incentives to co-operate. As the Kok report (2004) formulated it:

> Actions by any one Member State ... would be all the more effective if all other Member States acted in concert; a jointly created economic

tide would be even more powerful in its capacity to lift every European boat. The more the EU could develop its knowledge and market opening initiatives in tandem, the stronger and more competitive each Member State's economy would be.

Along these lines, the European Commission has also been propagating for years the view that 'massive potential gains' were to be reaped from wider and deeper integration, while 'non-Europe' was a costly waste of resources. But the question remains: why are these gains not realized despite such obvious advantages for all? The answer is not simply lack of focus or insufficient support, as the Commission (2005a: 5) claims. It is rooted in the structure of political incentives.

The theory of collective action has clearly established that the existence of potential positive spillover effects is not enough to ensure co-operative behaviour (Olson 1971). Collective action problems are caused by externalities that provide incentives for non-cooperative behaviour. If the costs and benefits of actions are not properly matched for individual actors, co-operation failure is the result. These externalities can be linked to different types of public goods. *Inclusive public goods*, sometimes called club goods, are characterized by positive externalities as more members participate in a group. Because one can impose restrictions on access to the club, every individual member can be obliged to make the necessary efforts for the realization of the common benefits. Thus, inclusive goods provide incentives for successful voluntary co-operation between independent utility maximizing actors. It is, however, possible that asymmetric information could lock partners into suboptimal equilibria (the prisoner dilemma). Procedures for improving the information flow are then required, possibly in the form of an independent and impartial authority. The 'regulatory mechanism' by which public goods are provided without formal and central authority is therefore dependent on the nature of externalities. A policy regime that allows the efficient provisions of inclusive public goods on the basis of voluntary co-operation has been called 'governance without government' (Rosenau 1992; Rhodes 1996).

For a long time, European integration has thrived in the domain of inclusive public goods. The existence of the European Commission has ensured that information asymmetries were overcome so that everyone knew what action was required. For example, successful political co-operation has created the single market in order to engender economies of scale. Network projects like the Galileo satellite navigation system or the Airbus project provide high benefits from co-operation and the possibility of reaping them is clearly allocated to each contributing participant.[8] Another typical club good phenomenon is participation in European Monetary Union (EMU), which induced the convergence of macroeconomic policies, clearly a public good. The Maastricht criteria helped create low inflation, because (nearly) everyone wanted to share in the benefits from monetary union and the possibility of being excluded made governments comply. Convergence policies were therefore 'owned' by member states. The role of the Commission consisted in monitoring the process and overcoming information asymmetries to prevent blockages. Hence, the logic of inclusive public goods makes successful voluntary co-operation among governments possible, while the Commission has to provide formal procedures to facilitate the flow of information.

With the successful convergence to the Maastricht criteria as a model, the designers of the Lisbon Strategy thought that a list of structural indicators with clear goals and objectives for each member state would accelerate reforms, release synergies and ameliorate the EU's performance. However, the logic of self-sustained policy convergence does not work for *exclusive public goods*, which are also called common resource goods. Here it is impossible to prevent access to the consumption of the collective goods by any member of the group and therefore it is hard, if not impossible, to make them pay for the cost of producing them. Exclusive public goods therefore create incentives for free-riding.[9] A single member could benefit by deviating from the strategy pursued by everyone else. As a consequence, nobody will wish to conform and voluntary co-operation cannot provide exclusive public goods optimally. The resulting collective action problem is known as 'the tragedy of the commons' (Hardin 1968). It can explain many aspects of the disappointing performance of the Lisbon process, because the intergovernmental governance with many national actors has no mechanism for co-ordinating the co-operative behaviour needed to provide exclusive goods.

As European integration has deepened in recent decades, the range of exclusive public goods has increased. In a monetary union, most macroeconomic policy variables, such as inflation, nominal and real interest rates, exchange rates, economic growth and employment policies have become exclusive public goods. All members consume these goods collectively, but Europe's *governance with many governments* creates incentives for individual member states to free-ride on others. It can be shown that the incentive problems caused by the exclusive nature of public goods increase with the size of the EU.[10] The free-riding problem applies to supply-side reforms as well as to macroeconomic policy.

For example, member states are frequently criticized for not implementing EU legislation.[11] The reason for the implementation failure can be a collective action problem: although integrated production structures and supply chains would improve Europe's competitiveness in the world and are therefore in the interest of all member states, deviating behaviour by individual governments may yield partially higher benefits. If everyone else is liberalizing markets, it may be advantageous for individual countries to keep restrictions in place at least temporarily when this allows gaining uncontested market power in the larger single market.[12] Thus, each country has an incentive to wait with its own reforms, while pushing others to do them soon.

The problem is even more severe for macroeconomic policy because of flawed institutional arrangements. Fiscal policy is permanently hampered by co-ordination failure, because capital funds in EMU are a common resource good and interest rates are their scarcity price. Given that it must maintain price stability, the ECB has to restrain the provision of liquidity, which is the 'common resource' in the financial system. But access to liquidity in the capital market is free for all. Higher structural public deficits will therefore, ceteris paribus, increase equilibrium interest rates and appreciate exchanges. This will lower economic growth. Recognizing this problem, the Stability and Growth Pact (SGP) demands the balancing of cyclically adjusted budgets. Interest rates would then be low, but at low rates it is advantageous for each member state to borrow money rather than to incur the political cost of fiscal consolidation. Hence, there exists an incentive for individual governments not to respect the Pact, while publicly insisting that everyone else should. Not surprisingly, structural deficits are not 'in balance' (they are above 2 per cent of GDP for the whole of euro-land and even above 3 per cent for France, Germany, Italy, Portugal and Greece). After the aggressive consolidation before 1999, structural deficits deteriorated until 2002, while long-term interest rates remained high – despite the negative growth shocks in 2001 and 2002. Thus, consolidation fatigue rather than excessively tight monetary policy has kept interest rates from falling more than they did. I will discuss this claim in greater depth in the second part of this chapter.

The correct policy response would be either hard and constraining binding rules or policy delegation to a European institution in order to ensure a coherent and unified policy in the interest of the Union. Especially when there is some need for discretionary policies, exclusive public goods require the governance of a government (Collignon 2003b). But delegating macroeconomic competences to a European institution poses a problem of legitimacy. Modern democracies are founded on the principle of 'No taxation without representation'. This must imply that citizens have some control over fiscal policy through elections. But if they cannot elect a European government, they only have the national channel for control. Hence fiscal policy is confronted by a dilemma: either national parliaments make budgets and are tempted by free-riding on others, or European rules are imposed on national policies, thereby hollowing out democratic processes. Decentralizing decision-making to the nation-state according to the subsidiarity principle reduces output-legitimacy; more centralization to increase technocratic efficiency reduces input-legitimacy. The only solution is more democracy at the European level, so that the input by citizens determines the output they prefer.

It is now increasingly recognized that the economic governance of the EU has remained sub-optimal due to inefficiencies, lack of credibility and eroding legitimacy. Unfortunately the logic underlying this failure is not clear. In its Communication to the Spring European Council, the Commission (2005a) emphasized the need to create 'political ownership' for the Lisbon goals. But once more, this was cheap talk. Ownership is not established by 'streamlining existing guidelines' and by appointing 'Mr or Ms Lisbon'. Ownership implies property rights. Who is to be the owner of European policies? Governments or the citizens? Ownership means rights to limit access and exclude non-performers. This is precisely how a modern democracy works: it gives citizens the right to select and reject governments as their agents. Ownership for Lisbon would imply the sovereignty of citizens and a proper European democracy. Europe's economic governance needs to be rethought.

2.3   A disappointing performance: comparing euro-land to the USA

Has the Lisbon Strategy made a difference? Progress should be measured against the headline objective of a 'dynamic economy'.[13] The result is disappointing as shown by per capita income growth in Figure 8.1. Instead of increasing in the six years following the Lisbon Council compared to the performance over the previous six years, it actually fell. Only in the six less developed new member states and Greece was it higher. This is the opposite of what Lisbon sought to achieve. Although growth has also slowed down in the United States under George W. Bush, in 16 EU countries out of 25 – including some of the biggest member states – per capita growth was less than in the US. Only Sweden, Finland, Poland, Luxembourg, Ireland and Cyprus experienced higher growth. Interestingly, the EU-25 as a whole does not perform dramatically different from

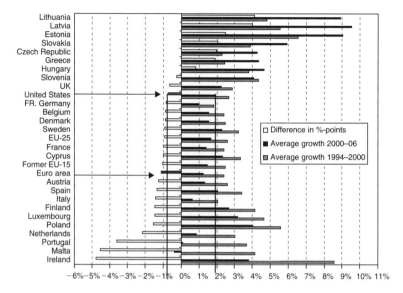

Figure 8.1 Average per capita growth rates and differentials
Source: EUROSTAT.

the US; the problem is the euro-area, where growth has been lagging significantly behind the American economy. The US growth rate is nearly 50 per cent higher than euro-land's.

How can the slow growth in euro-land be explained? Standard theory tells us that it can be decomposed into the growth rates for employment and for labour productivity. Given that the Lisbon Strategy seeks structural improvements, we are less interested in the short-term fluctuations and focus on the long-term trends. Figure 8.2 therefore shows employment growth trends in the euro-area and the US smoothed by a Hodrick-Prescott filter. Employment growth in America has had a downward trend since the 1970s, falling by more than half from over 2.1 to 0.9 per cent. In Europe, we notice the low growth rate in the 1960s and 1980s,[14] a clear increase in the second half of the 1990s and stabilization above 1 per cent since then. Yet, in recent years the contribution from employment to growth has been higher in Europe than in the US. This is surprising, given that the labour market is often blamed for Europe's bad performance.

The main reason for the better US income performance is therefore essentially due to the higher growth in labour productivity. As Figure 8.3 shows, labour productivity improved from the 1980s on, while it first

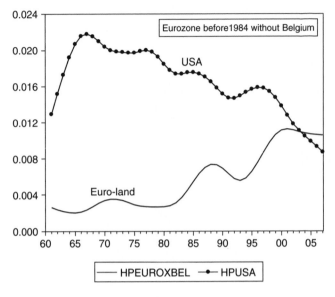

Figure 8.2   Employment growth trends

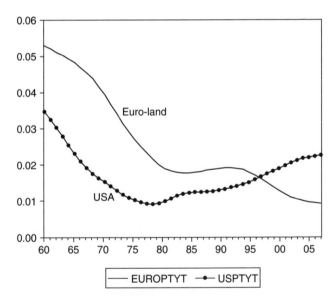

Figure 8.3   Labour productivity trends

stagnated in euro-land and then deteriorated after 1990. Only since 1997 has the growth trend for labour productivity been higher in the United States than in Europe.

Explaining labour productivity is not uncontroversial, but we know that it can be further decomposed into:

1. Human and capital investment per unit of labour, that is to say the capital intensity of production (also called capital deepening);
2. Output produced per unit of human and capital investment, that is to say total factor productivity (TFP).

Total factor productivity in the USA slowed down in the 1960s and 1970s, but has gradually improved since the early 1990s. In Europe it accelerated in the 1980s when the single market was put in place, but it fell back again in the 1990s (see Figure 8.4). There are no indications that the Lisbon Council has made any difference to this development, although it may have slowed down the deceleration.

As is well known, growth in total factor productivity represents output growth not accounted for by changes in inputs. It is therefore dependent on a wide range of qualitative factors, such as technological innovation, learning, social regulation, etc. Europe's low performance is usually attributed to these factors and this is where the supply-side agenda of Lisbon has a role to play. For example, Kok (2004: 12) argues that the US were leaders in technical innovation, accounting for 74 per cent of the top 300 IT companies and 46 per cent of the top 300 firms ranked by R&D spending, while Europe was falling behind. However, while there is truth in this claim, as it would appear from Figure 8.4, one must not forget that innovation, knowledge, technology and skills must be incorporated into the stock of human and physical capital. Without investment, modern technology remains an abstract dream.

Figure 8.5 shows the trend performance of capital deepening. Here we find the most dramatic difference between euro-land and the United States. The US economy has gone through a process of rapid capital deepening since the early 1990s, beating all historic records; in Europe it is falling. Thus, Europe's problem is low investment.

The differences between Europe and America are striking. On both continents investment growth fell dramatically in the 1970s, but in the US it stabilized in mid-decade, while it nearly collapsed in Europe amidst the monetary chaos following the breakdown of Bretton Woods (Collignon 2002). Investment recuperated in Europe in the mid-1980s, but it remained at fairly low levels. In the US, however, investment per unit of

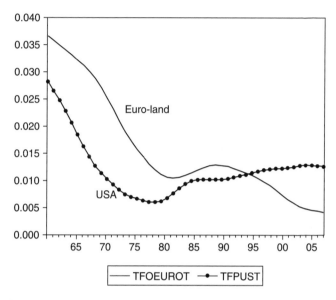

Figure 8.4   Total factor productivity growth trends

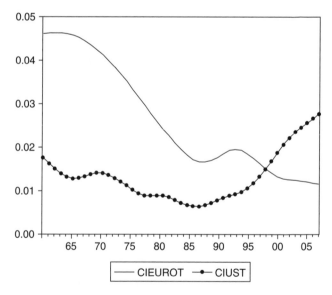

Figure 8.5   Capital deepening trends

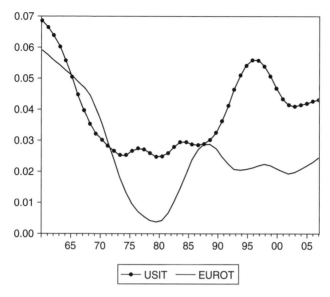

Figure 8.6 Gross investment trend growth

output accelerated at an unexpected rate during the Clinton/Greenspan years and seems to have settled at a permanently higher rate than in the euro-area (Figure 8.6).

The question is then: why is the rate of investment so low in euroland? While microeconomic factors are surely important at the firm level, aggregate investment must be related to the profits entrepreneurs expect to make in their different markets. This is where aggregate demand – and therefore macroeconomics – matter.

3   The flawed macroeconomic and institutional framework

If Europe wants to become 'one of the most dynamic economies in the world', it will have to improve its macroeconomic management. The policy debate on macroeconomics frequently focuses on short-term micro-management, particularly the role of monetary and fiscal policy in minimizing output volatility and stabilizing the business cycle. However, the fiscal and monetary policy mix also has important implications for long-term economic growth. Critics have often accused the European Central Bank of being too restrictive and thereby impeding investment and growth. I will show that this argument misses the more important co-ordination failure resulting from the flawed institutional set-up for fiscal policy. An improved macroeconomic framework would require substantial institutional reforms in Europe.

3.1   Macroeconomic stability and investment

How should we measure the impact of the monetary/fiscal policy mix on the growth rate? Conventional econometric models of regressing monetary and fiscal variables on output have produced ambivalent evidence.[15] In particular, disentangling short-term and long-term effects is difficult. I will therefore attempt a different approach.

Supply-side reforms and macroeconomic management are the two major factors determining investment. Structural reforms can improve labour productivity and the elasticity of labour supply, thereby improving the potential rate of growth. But actual growth will only accelerate if aggregate demand stimulates investment. Firms create jobs when they see opportunities for profit. Lowering labour costs and implementing structural reforms may be necessary for the competitiveness in international trade, but domestic demand remains the key to the overall economic performance. Take the UK. While supply-side reforms under Thatcher and Major have revolutionized British society, GDP in Britain increased on average 2.08 per cent between 1979 and 1996, hardly more than in Mitterrand's socialist France, where it grew at 2.05 per cent per annum. With Labour's new macroeconomic framework introduced in 1996, UK GDP increased on average by 2.68 per cent after 1997, compared to 2.08 per cent in France. The reason was hardly that France reformed the supply-side less than Britain; between 1999 and 2006, domestic demand contributed 3.1 per cent to UK growth and 1.8 per cent in France; foreign trade subtracted 0.5 per cent in the UK, and only 0.3 per cent in France. Investment contributed 0.55 per cent in Britain and 0.69 per cent in France. Or look at Germany. Under the Schröder government, an aggressive reform agenda has reduced unit labour costs by 10 percentage points below the euro-land average, far below any other country, but growth has remained elusive. While German exports exceeded those of all other countries in the world, GDP grew only by 1.1 per cent p.a. from 1999 to 2006, and 1.3 per cent p.a. in the seven years before. Under Schröder domestic demand contributed only 0.46 per cent to growth, foreign trade 0.76.[16] Economic growth returned after consumer confidence was established after the German elections and wage settlements became more accommodating.

A widely believed proposition asserts that macroeconomic management no longer works in the age of globalization. This is wrong. After all, the US and the UK also live in a globalized world. The share of the EU-15 non-tradable value added is still above 43 per cent and may be even larger.[17] Hence, there is a significant part of Europe's economy where profits depend exclusively on domestic demand. Comparing the two biggest economies in the world, domestic demand has contributed 3.5 per cent to growth in the US, but only 1.9 per cent in euro-land. Furthermore, macroeconomic management may also influence foreign demand through the exchange rate. What is needed to stimulate investment is therefore a policy where the interaction of monetary, fiscal and wage developments creates the incentive for firms to exploit profitable market opportunities. These incentives require returns on real investment that are higher than interest rates and a framework of stability that reduces the risk premium on investment due to uncertain expectations.

During the 1970s, 1980s and 1990s, Europe has suffered from monetary instability that followed the breakdown of the Bretton Woods international system. With the creation of monetary union, euro-land has regained monetary stability, but it is still uncertain whether it can achieve a policy mix capable of sustaining accelerated capital accumulation, growth and higher employment. The first few years of EMU achieved a positive policy mix with historically unprecedented job creation (2.3 million in 1999, 2.4 million in 2000, 1.9 million in 2001, but only 280,000 in 2003), although the experience was too short to make a significant impact on unemployment rates. We need to understand why. There are two possibilities:

1. High volatility due to macroeconomic instability had deterred investment and created excess savings.
2. The steady macroeconomic environment had not encouraged investment because equilibrium interest rates are too high when compared to achievable rates of return on investment.

In this section we focus on instability, in the next on the steady state.

When macroeconomic policy fails to stabilize shocks, the increased uncertainty will lead economic actors to ask for higher risk premiums on the return on capital and this will lower investment. Therefore, stability of the macroeconomic environment matters for investment. If macroeconomic uncertainty can be modelled as the volatility (that is to say the conditional variance) of the growth rate of investment, we would expect a negative relation between uncertainty and the growth rate of investment (Collignon 2002; Aghion and Howitt 2005). The expected rate of investment would be a decreasing function of the conditional variance

Table 8.1   ARCH-M model for US and euro-land investment

Estimation Equation:
=====================
Investment = C(1)*GARCH + C(2)
GARCH = C(3) + C(4)*RESID(-1)^2 + C(5)*GARCH(-1)
The RESID(-1)^2 term describes news about volatility from the previous period, measured as the lag of the squared residual from the mean equation
The GARCH(-1) term is last period's forecast variance

Estimated Coefficients for euro-land:
EUROinvest = −0.272*GARCH + 0.0079
GARCH = 0.0001 + 0.438*RESID(-1)^2 + 0.326* RESID(-2)^2

Estimated Coefficients for USA:
USinvest = −0.342*GARCH + 0.019
GARCH = −1.31E-07 + 0.281*RESID(-1)^2 − 0.563
Resid(-2)12 − 0.159 Resid(-3)12 + 0.935*GARCH(-1)

---

and the coefficient would measure the sensitivity of aggregate real investment to uncertainty. The time-varying equilibrium investment rate can be measured by an ARCH-M model (Enders 2004), where the expected growth rate of the capital stock depends on the volatility of investment, measured by the weighted sum of past squared surprises. In other words, firms feel uncertain about investment prospects to the degree that shocks in previous periods affect this period's market conditions and on their experience of how much they have misinterpreted market conditions in the past. Table 8.1 gives the results for euro-land and the United States.[18]

As expected, macroeconomic uncertainty (GARCH) reduces autonomous investment C(2). The rate of investment responds negatively to macroeconomic instability in both economies. Interestingly, the coefficient that measures the elasticity of this response is not dramatically different between the American and euro-economy. It is −0.34 for the US, −0.27 for euro-land. However, the dynamics of uncertainty are different. In Europe uncertainty is strongly affected by cumulative expectation surprises in the last two quarters. Europeans seem to believe that when things are bad, they will get even worse. By contrast, in the US, past surprises partially compensate each other. This may reflect optimism under conditions of more 'flexible' market structures or more activist macro-policies in the US. However, the net effect of these expectation errors is long-lasting in its impact on today's uncertainty. Thus, greater macroeconomic stability is likely to have a more persistent positive impact on investment. This may in part explain the remarkable performance of the US economy during the Greenspan years.

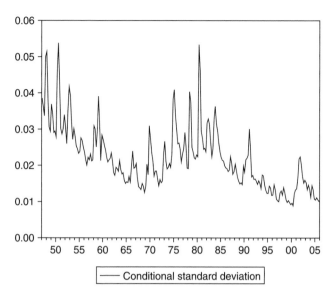

Figure 8.7   US: volatility in the growth of capital stock

But it is an interesting fact that whatever causes uncertainty in economic expectations, the reaction by firms undertaking real investment is fairly similar on either side of the Atlantic, with Europeans being slightly less responsive than Americans.

In general, real investment is more volatile in the US than in the euro-area (Figure 8.7). Our time series for the US starts before 1950 and shows a period of diminishing volatility until the mid-1960s (during the Golden Age). A dramatic increase in uncertainty occurs during the break-up years of Bretton Woods and then a long period of returning to high economic stability during the Greenspan years. This trend is interrupted by the two Bush presidencies.

For euro-land (Figure 8.8), our data series is shorter. After the set-up of the European monetary system, a higher degree of stability prevails at first, but is low in the second half of the 1980s. The 1990s are shocked by the ERM crisis in 1992/3 and financial instability in the mid-1990s. With the creation of the euro a high degree of macroeconomic stability has been restored. This is an interesting result. It shows that European Monetary Union has attained its objective: stability. But why has the improved macroenvironment environment not translated into higher growth? The answer is found in the low steady state investment growth in euro-land. Autonomous investment growth is more than twice as high

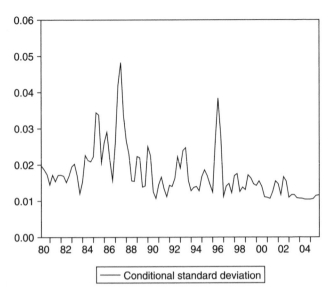

Figure 8.8   Euro-land: volatility in the growth of capital stock

in the US (1.9 per cent) than in Europe (0.8 per cent). An explanation for this difference may be found in the long-term policy mix.

3.2 It's the deficit, stupid!

In a large and fairly closed economy, the key to active demand management is the interaction between budget and monetary policy. This interaction may matter from a short-term perspective when excess savings prevent potential output from being absorbed by effective demand or from a growth perspective in the steady state. The short-term effect occurs when individuals will not hold real capital unless its yield exceeds some minimum required return. Keynesian policies seek to reduce interest rates to make real investment more attractive relative to financial assets or to increase the government deficit to provide demand for the resources that would not otherwise be used. Such policies are adequate to tackle the problem of excess savings, but they do not solve the problems with low steady state growth, which is Europe's problem. As Feldstein (1980) has shown a long time ago, in an environment of low inflation and reasonable stability of savings, *budget deficits will lower the accumulation of capital in the steady state.* One therefore has to distinguish between

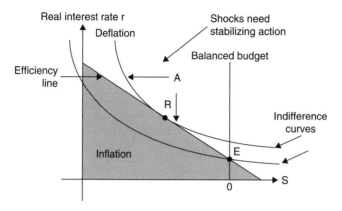

Figure 8.9   The optimal policy mix

the short-term effects for the fiscal-monetary policy mix, which are supposed to restore overall macroeconomic stability after shocks, and the
long-term growth effects of different steady-state policy mixes.

From a theoretical point of view, the interaction between fiscal and
monetary policy should have a negative trade-off if the economy is in
equilibrium. This is evident from Figure 8.9. The downward-sloping efficiency line represents the set of all efficient policy mix points where the
economy is in equilibrium, without inflation or rising unemployment.
In other words, it reflects a zero output gap. Above the line, say at point
A, the combination between fiscal and monetary policy is too tight and
the economy is in a deflationary position with rising unemployment.
Below the line, the mix is too loose and inflationary pressures occur. For
simplicity we will assume that the efficiency-line is stable.[19] The argument for a negative slope of the efficiency line can be made in terms
of long-term interest rates in the government bond market (Feldstein
1980), or in terms of monetary policy adjustments in the short-term
money market (Collignon 2003a: Annex 3).

A loosening of fiscal policy, that is to say higher deficits, would then
imply tighter monetary policy, that is to say higher interests rates, to
keep inflation at bay. Tighter fiscal policies should cause rates to come
down. The specific combination along the trade-off curve represents a
specific policy mix. For example, the Reagan/Volker policy mix in the
1980s reflected high deficits and high interest rates in the US. This is
point R (Republican) in Figure 8.9. When Bill Clinton ran for President
in 1992,[20] he promised to bring the deficit down in order to stimulate

growth and employment by lowering interest rates (Woodward 2000). Thus, the Democratic policy mix is somewhere near point E. Low interest rates will stimulate investment. Not surprisingly, the Clinton/Greenspan mix of the late 1990s was characterized by budget surpluses and low interest rates, high growth and macroeconomic stability.

Equilibrium positions on the policy mix trade-off curve reflect collective time preferences for intergenerational tax burden sharing. The choices can be represented by an indifference curve that picks an optimal policy mix out of the infinite possibilities assembled on the efficiency line. The public choice of a policy mix is the implicit result of electoral decisions and reflects the consensual preferences among a majority of citizens. These preferences emerge gradually from collective deliberation and political debates. These debates are intensified during electoral campaigns when competing parties bundle policies into specific programmes and voters have to make up their minds what to choose. Of course, citizens do not debate in abstract terms: 'What is our optimal policy mix?' But when parties and candidates propose a tax cut without saying where they intend to reduce expenditure, they implicitly suggest higher deficits and therefore higher interest rates. Choosing such a candidate implies choosing a policy mix. During the 1992 US elections, the budget deficit was widely discussed, due to the independent candidate Ross Perot. Clinton won because he captured the median voter. In 2000 Republicans promised to 'return' the budget surplus to tax payers, while Al Gore sought to use it for improving health care. The implicit choice of a policy mix within a broader bundle of policies is therefore at the core of any democratic society.

In Europe, the conduct of fiscal policy is more complicated and less democratic. From an economic point of view, what matters for the policy mix in the same currency area is the aggregate fiscal stance for the whole of euro-land that interacts with the single monetary stance of the ECB. Yet, in Europe's *governance without a European government*, fiscal policy is determined autonomously by twelve national governments. As discussed above, this creates collective action problems. Adhering to the Stability and Growth Pact would guarantee reasonably low equilibrium interest rates. But as we have seen, the SGP rule is not implemented.[21] We have explained the failure to implement the SGP (balanced structural budgets) by Europe's 'governance with many governments' that cannot deal efficiently with exclusive public goods. Fiscal policy is such a good. I will now show that euro-land's fiscal policy arrangement creates a bias for high equilibrium interest rates and therefore for lower steady state investment.

The SGP has often been criticized for being insufficiently flexible. However, it is not sufficiently understood that the Pact imposes effectively two forms of inflexibility:

1. It constrains effective stabilization policy in the short run, except for a limited range of automatic stabilizers.[22]
2. In the long run it impedes democratic choices regarding the intergenerational justice of tax burdens because it imposes a balanced structural deficit.

The SGP is therefore incompatible with *alternative* choices on the efficiency line, such as the implicit shift from Reagan/Volker to the Clinton/Greenspan policy mix in America. It imposes point E on the efficiency line once and for all for each member state. The question is which of these two inflexibilities dominates euro-land? Given that macroeconomic instability has disappeared, as we saw in the last section, short-term inflexibility does not seem to be a major issue. The main problem with euro-land's economy must be the equilibrium position of the policy mix.

Figures 8.10 and 8.11 show the interacting movements between fiscal and monetary policies for the USA and euro-land. The long-term trend line reflects a negative trade-off. This is what theory would lead us to expect.[23] The trend-line has a slope of −0.417 in the United States and −0.473 in euro-land. Thus, the two economies operate in a remarkably

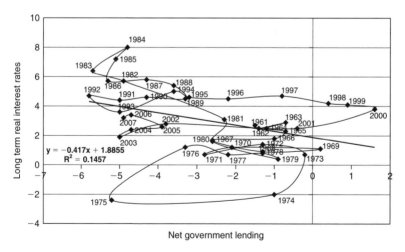

Figure 8.10 Policy mix USA

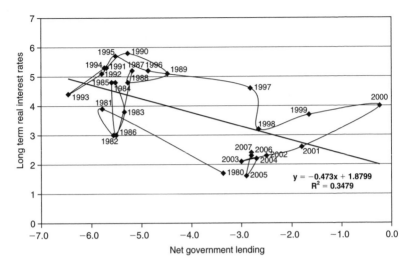

Figure 8.11   Euro-land policy mix

similar fashion. The structural improvement of the aggregate budget position by one percentage point of GDP will lower the equilibrium interest rate by 41.7 base points in the US and by 47.3 base-points in Europe. If euro-land stuck to the Stability and Growth Pact, the equilibrium interest rate in the capital market would be a full percentage point lower.[24]

Shifts along the optimal policy mix curve seem frequent in the US (Figure 8.10). The inflationary period (below the line) of the late 1960s and 1970s is clearly perceptible; the same applies for the Bush Jr. presidency of 2001–7. The late 1980s suffered from overly restrictive policy mixes and high deficits and high equilibrium interest rates. It is interesting that the fiscal consolidation of the Clinton years has reduced the equilibrium interest rate by nearly 200 base points, but took place in the context of a relatively restrictive macroeconomic environment. The overall message is clear: balancing budgets lowers equilibrium interest rates.

In euro-land a clear shift has taken place after the introduction of the euro. Figure 8.11 shows the cluster of excessively tight European policy mixes in the early 1990s. Deficits were high at that time, with an implicit maximum limit of 6 per cent. But monetary policy was excessively restrictive, when the Bundesbank dominated Europe, and repeated currency crises in the European monetary system caused high risk premiums in financial markets. Since the ECB has taken over, euro-land's policy mix has become more accommodating, even if the ECB at first needed to establish its reputation as an inflation fighter. However, fiscal consolidation fatigue after 2000 has pushed the steady state policy mix back to the left again. This move can be explained by the collective action problem in designing a coherent aggregate fiscal policy stance.

Here is why. Assume we start in equilibrium and one government decides to borrow at the low prevailing rates. This is a demand shock that pushes *the whole system* into an inflationary disequilibrium and requires monetary tightening. However, because the aggregate budget position is determined as the random outcome of each member state's policy, fiscal policy cannot be used as a stabilization policy instrument for the integrated euro-area. In other words, no other country will change its own policy stance and consolidate in order to keep the aggregate policy mix in equilibrium. Only monetary policy has the flexibility to respond at the European level. If uncoordinated national policies increase the aggregate deficit, euro interest rates need to go up. Thus, the apparent monetary tightness of the ECB is the product of Europe's 'governance with many governments'. The higher equilibrium interest rates may affect economic growth in all member states negatively, so that as a consequence of one member state's deviating behaviour, *all* national budgets are falling into deficits. A picture of fiscal indiscipline emerges, which may push the ECB to raise interest rates even further. These countries will now complain that interest rates are 'too high', although the ECB has simply restored macroeconomic equilibrium. *The new equilibrium, caused by the free-riding behaviour of one actor, reflects a higher aggregate structural deficit and higher interest rates for all.* Because euro-land's citizens cannot democratically determine the aggregate policy mix along a stable trade-off curve, the central bank has a persistent bias for conservatism.

Increasing the efficiency of the policy mix would require turning the aggregate budget stance into a policy tool for stabilization policy and at the same time imposing strict discipline on individual member states to stick to the defined policy. Thus, *the correct reform of the SGP would be more flexibility for the aggregate fiscal policy position and less discretion for individual member states.* The 'reform' of the SGP in 2005 has achieved exactly the opposite: individual countries now have more leeway to justify higher deficits, while the aggregate position is the random outcome of uncoordinated free-riding. The consequences are higher equilibrium interest rates, lower growth and more unemployment. Europe will remain the least dynamic region in the industrialized world economy.

One may object that after eliminating the exchange rate as an adjustment tool, national budgets must absorb asymmetric shocks in EMU.

However, the likelihood and intensity of asymmetric shocks has greatly fallen in euro-land and economic growth has become more uniform. The standard deviation of the twelve euro-member states' growth rates in 2005 is only one-third of what it was in 1999. Euro-land is converging – although to a low common growth rate. This fact highlights the increased importance of the policy mix for the whole of euro-land, while national discretion in fiscal policy has become counterproductive and damaging.

Moreover, there are some simple ideas in the public debate about how to design coherent, yet flexible, institutional arrangements for fiscal policy in euro-land (Casella 2001; Amato 2002; Collignon 2004b). For example, one may define the optimal aggregate fiscal stance at the euro-level by transforming the Broad Economic Policy Guidelines into a 'European DPEF'.[25] This would give flexibility in reacting to macroeconomic shocks. The aggregate stance would then need to be broken down into national (and even regional) deficit quotas for which each jurisdiction would obtain deficit permits. If one jurisdiction does not use its quota, it would be allowed to sell the permits to another authority that wishes to borrow more. This system, inspired by tradable pollution permits, would achieve vertical flexibility reflecting fundamental preferences for borrowing and taxes, and horizontal flexibility between different jurisdictions and overall coherence in the fiscal position.

3.3   The question of democracy

However, setting up the improved institutional framework for macroeconomic policy faces the same problem as the Lisbon supply-side agenda: potential benefits are huge, but national governments stand in the way of achieving them. The issue of improved policy co-ordination is ultimately dependent to the issue of democratic legitimacy. Therefore, Europe needs to tackle the core issue of its governance: democracy.

I have discussed the issue of fiscal policy and democratic legitimacy in separate papers (Collignon 2004b, 2007). The problem is the following. According to the classical definition, a democratic constitutional state is a political order 'created by the people themselves and legitimated by their opinion and will-formation, which allows the addressees of law to regard themselves at the same time as the authors of the law' (Habermas 2001: 99). Thus, voting for a government is the political act that allows citizens to regard themselves as the ultimate authors of laws, that is to say as the sovereign. But prior to the vote, political debate is the necessary condition for collective will-formation.

However, in the European Union, policy decisions are not democratic in this sense. Certainly, citizens are able to revoke national governments at national elections after a national debate has produced the collective will within this constituency. But, with respect to European public goods, national governments can never represent all European citizens; they act as the agent of a 'principal' that is only a faction of the European population. These national agents then decide policies at the European level that affect all European citizens, although they represent only the will of some European citizens. This is different from democracy in a national setting, where members of parliament are responsible to their constituency *and* for achieving the collective good.[26] The democratic will formation in one country has externalities for all other national constituencies. With respect to stabilization policy, this externality is a consequence of unifying the monetary system and having a single interest rate determined by the European Central Bank. In general, policy compromises negotiated at the European level are superimposed on a majority of citizens who were not involved in the process of collective will formation and therefore do not consider themselves as 'authors of law'. As this process is repeated for every individual country, European policy decisions will never command the same degree of democratic legitimacy as national decisions.

Moravcsik (2002) has denied the existence of a 'democratic deficit' in Europe, arguing that the EU simply operates like any 'advanced industrial democracy', because technical functions of low electoral salience are often delegated to specialized institutions. Thus, output legitimacy (good results) trumps input legitimacy (the right to choose). This view may have been justified when the scope of European integration was relatively narrow. It may be valid for inclusive public goods, which can be regulated by 'governance without government'. But when European policies such as monetary policy or the Lisbon agenda touch every European citizen's way of life, and when fiscal co-ordination reaches the sacrosanct domain of 'no taxation without representation', it is a matter of the normative coherence of modern society that European citizens must have a right to choose collectively. Yet, the only institutional channel through which they can express their choices is national and not European democracy. Hence, national interests dominate the European interest and collective action problems prevent efficient policies. The only logical solution to the dilemma is setting up a European government that is elected by all European citizens and responsible for the administration of the European exclusive goods, which affect them all. The coherence of input and output legitimacy is then restored, the co-operation failure is overcome and economic and political efficiencies are reduced.[27]

4   Conclusion

The prospects for Europe's future are bleak, but not hopeless. If Europe continues with the undemocratic intergovernmental approach of Lisbon, it takes little imagination to see that after fifty years of European unification, the European Union will die a slow death by gridlock, economic stagnation and unkept promises. Nor can we exclude a more violent crisis with extreme right-wing parties coming into power. The results of the constitutional referendum in France and the Netherlands gave an early taste of re-emerging nationalism. Alternatively, Europe could take a leap forward and create a proper democracy, where all European citizens choose their common government for the administration of European public goods. European policy choices would then be the outcome of democratic debates. I have called such a democratic system for the EU the *European Republic* (Collignon 2003a, 2004a); the Belgian Prime Minister Guy Verhofstadt (2006) has referred to the old idea of the *United States of Europe*. However, the fundamental dilemma remains: which national government will wish to set up a European democracy if it loses its own power? Perhaps the only way forward is for citizens to mobilize themselves and work through political parties in Europe. After the collective trans-European deliberation, which follows from party competition, a new democratic consensus might emerge and impose citizens' preferences for democracy on resistant national governments.

Annex

Euro-land quarterly

Dependent Variable: EURO_QUARTER

Method: ML – ARCH (Marquardt) – Normal distribution

Date: 06/04/06 Time: 13:26

Sample: 1980Q2 2005Q4

Included observations: 103

Convergence achieved after 23 iterations

Variance backcast: ON

GARCH = C(3) + C(4)*RESID(−1)^2 + C(5)*RESID(−2)^2

	Coefficient	Std. Error	z-Statistic	Prob.
@SQRT(GARCH)	−0.272058	0.371735	−0.731859	0.4643
C	0.007970	0.005570	1.430964	0.1524
Variance Equation				
C	0.000106	3.92E−05	2.690469	0.0071
RESID(−1)^2	0.438561	0.229310	1.912523	0.0558
RESID(−2)^2	0.326469	0.239623	1.362426	0.1731
R-squared	−0.040404	Mean dependent var		0.004731
Adjusted R-squared	−0.082870	S.D. dependent var		0.017706
S.E. of regression	0.018425	Akaike info criterion		−5.283531
Sum squared resid	0.033269	Schwarz criterion		−5.155631
Log likelihood	277.1018	Durbin-Watson stat		2.295435

US quarterly
Dependent Variable: GR_FI_US
Method: ML - ARCH
Date: 06/02/06 Time: 18:08
Sample (adjusted): 1947Q2 2006Q1
Included observations: 236 after adjustments
Convergence achieved after 39 iterations
Variance backcast: ON
GARCH = C(3) + C(4)*RESID(−1)^2 + C(5)*RESID(−2)^2 + C(6)*RESID
(−3)^2 + C(7)*GARCH(−1)

	Coefficient	Std. Error	z-Statistic	Prob.
@SQRT(GARCH)	−0.342548	0.209732	−1.633266	0.1024
C	0.019016	0.003665	5.188743	0.0000
Variance Equation				
C	−1.31E−07	4.04E−06	−0.032425	0.9741
RESID(−1)^2	0.281047	0.102087	2.753017	0.0059
RESID(−2)^2	−0.056367	0.119778	−0.470595	0.6379
RESID(−3)^2	−0.159850	0.069779	−2.290807	0.0220
GARCH(−1)	0.935525	0.033684	27.77359	0.0000
R-squared	−0.024989	Mean dependent var		0.010338
Adjusted R-squared	−0.051845	S.D. dependent var		0.022270
S.E. of regression	0.022840	Akaike info criterion		−4.868640
Sum squared resid	0.119458	Schwarz criterion		−4.765899
Log likelihood	581.4995	Durbin-Watson stat		1.264102

Notes

1. In the 1980s Japan and Germany were considered to be the superior model, given that these countries seemed to favour long-term relations, while the US system was seen as too short-term oriented. In the 1990s this view was inverted; now flexibility was thought to be the trump card.
2. This was the formulation frequently used by policy-makers. At the time, the author was an active participant in the Guterres ESP-group and in charge of the Lisbon inter-ministerial policy co-ordination in the German government. For the theoretical foundation of the macroeconomic strategy behind the Cologne process and Lisbon Strategy, see Collignon (1999).
3. Historically, the 'open method of co-ordination' (OMC) was an accident; it came about because several governments, and in particular the German chancellor, resisted having 'their hands tied', let alone delegating power to the Commission. Guterres therefore sought to enrol member states into an open intergovernmental process of policy co-ordination, where 'open' meant 'unconstrained'. In essence, the OMC is equivalent to respecting member states' veto power. Nevertheless, governments were urged to commit to specific common policy objectives, while implementation was left to them. To safeguard against uncooperative behaviour, multilateral surveillance by the Commission and peer pressure through 'naming and shaming' of non-performers were considered sufficient. The OMC is therefore a stronger form of policy co-ordination than simple voluntary action, but it suffers from the same dilemma as previous co-ordination attempts: incentives for free-riding hamper unified action necessary for the provision of exclusive European collective goods.
4. By partial interests, I mean collective preferences that dominate some groups, but are in contradiction with the general preferences of all European citizens. Partial interests are therefore welfare lowering. The general welfare could be optimized, if all citizens participated in the policy debate on issues that concern them as a whole.
5. See Federalist Papers 9 and 10 in Hamilton et al. (2001).
6. For monetary policy, for example, it took three decades.
7. For a more extensive discussion see Collignon (2003b). Jaquet and Pisani-Ferri (2001) and Buti et al. (1998) have argued that the answer to collective action problems in fiscal policy is the Stability and Growth Pact. However, this argument is based on the assumption that 'member states are at the same time willing to cooperate and reluctant to transfer further national sovereignty' (Jaquet and Pisani-Ferri, 2001: 4). Yet, the whole point of collective action problems is that nation-states are *not* willing to co-operate because they obtain higher benefits by not doing so.
8. Nevertheless, the recent Airbus difficulties show that a club may still encounter difficulties in the provision of collective goods if its management is bad.
9. The common resource goods are called exclusive because the members of the club will want to keep new members out, as this would reduce their benefits.
10. For a full elaboration of this argument and its underlying theory, see Collignon (2003a: Annex 2).

11. The Commission (2005a: 8) writes: 'In a number of Member States, key markets like telecoms, energy and transport are open only on paper – long after the expiry of the deadlines to which those Member States have signed up.'
12. A sufficient condition for this logic to be valid is the existence of increasing returns to scale as emphasized by the New Trade Theory.
13. All figures in this chapter come from the European Commission's AMECO database, unless otherwise specified.
14. The euro-land time series is without Belgium before 1985.
15. See for example Gros and Hobza (2001). A remarkable exception is Aghion and Howitt (2005).
16. Calculations from European Commission, AMECO, 2006, code CVGD.
17. I assume industry and 50 per cent of services to be tradables, and the other 50 per cent of services plus agriculture and construction industry to be nontradables. Data from European Commission, AMECO.
18. See also the technical annex.
19. In a stochastic setting the shocks are i.i.d, and the efficiency-line would reflect the co-integrating vector. We cannot pursue this line of reasoning in this chapter.
20. His motto was 'It's the economy, stupid!'
21. Figure 8.11 provides, however, some evidence that the excessive deficit procedure under the Maastricht Treaty, which is associated with penalties, has more binding power.
22. It is sometimes argued that there is an adjustment problem for countries which have started EMU with high debt and deficits, thereby constraining their automatic stabilizers. Nearly ten years after the EMU decision was taken, this line of argument seems daring. If France and Italy still have large budget deficits, it is a matter of political choice and not of business cycle.
23. The assimilation of the trend-line with the efficiency-line is justified if we assume that in the long run output gaps should balance out.
24. Thus balancing budgets would achieve the 'euthanasia of rentiers' so famously advocated by Keynes.
25. See Amato (2002). Documento di Programmazione Economico-Finanziaria (DPEF – Document of Economic and Financial Programming) is the Italian macroeconomic framework law, which gets voted before the finance minister can put forward his annual budget. France's Fifth Republic introduced a similar tool to overcome the budgetary inconsistencies of the Fourth Republic.
26. In representative democracies members of parliament are elected after a national debate, which is structured by the campaigns of political parties. The MP therefore has an interest to secure a majority for his or her party. In the EU, there is no constituency transcending institutions like parties. The campaigns are also constitutive elements of will formation. The Council operates more like an eternal parliament that replaces its members exclusively through by-elections, but no campaign takes place because none is accountable to the whole European constituency.
27. See Collignon (2003a) for a more extended analysis of the centralization/decentralization trade-off and the dilemma of what I call there type I and type II inefficiencies.

References

Aghion, P. and Howitt, P. (2005), 'Appropriate growth policy: a unifying framework', lecture given on 25 August at the 20th Congress of the European Economic Association, Amsterdam.

Amato, G. (2002), 'Verso un DPEF Europeo', *NENS No. 4* (Nuova Economia Nuova Società), July: 15–19.

Barroso, J. M. (2005), 'Debate on the preparation of the European Council', European Parliament, 9 March.

Buti, M. et al. (1998), 'Fiscal discipline and flexibility in EMU: the implementation of the Stability and Growth Pact', *Oxford Review of Economic Policy*, 14: 81–97.

Casella, A. (2001), 'Trade-able deficit permits', in A. Brumila, M. Buti and D. Franco (eds), *The Stability and Growth Pact: the Architecture of Fiscal Policy in EMU*, Basingstoke: Palgrave Macmillan.

Collignon, S. (1999), 'Unemployment, wage developments and the European policy mix in Europe', *Empirica*, 26: 259–69.

Collignon, S. (2002), *Monetary Stability in Europe*, London: Routledge.

Collignon, S. (2003a), *The European Republic*, London: The Federal Trust.

Collignon, S. (2003b), 'Is Europe going far enough? Reflections on the Stability and Growth Pact, the Lisbon Strategy and the EU's economic governance', *European Political Economy Review*, 1(2): 222–47.

Collignon, S. (2004a), *Vive la République européenne*, Paris: Éditions de La Martinière.

Collignon, S. (2004b), 'Fiscal policy and democracy', paper presented at Monetary Workshop, Österreichische Nationalbank, Vienna; published as ÖNB Discussion Paper no. 4, November (download: www.stefancollignon.eu).

Collignon, S. (2007), 'The three sources of legitimacy for European fiscal policy', *International Political Science Review*, 28(2): 155–84.

Council of the European Union (2005), *Presidency Conclusion*, 23 March, Brussels.

Enders, W. (2004), *Applied Econometric Time Series*, second edition, Hoboken, NJ: Wiley.

European Commission (2005a), *Communication to the Spring European Council. Working Together for Growth and Jobs: A New Start for the Lisbon Strategy* (http://europa.eu.int/growthandjobs/pdf/COM2005_024_en.pdf).

European Commission (2005b), *Staff Working Document, in Support of the Report from the Commission to the Spring European Council, 22–23 March 2005, on the Lisbon Strategy of Economic, Social and Environmental Renewal* (http://europa.eu.int/growthandjobs/pdf/SEC2005_160_en.pdf).

European Commission (2005c), 'Public finances in EMU', *The European Economy*, no. 3, Brussels.

European Commission (2006), Directorate General for Economic and Financial Affairs, *Quarterly Report on the Euro Area*, 5(4).

Feldstein, M. (1980), 'Fiscal policies, inflation, and capital formation', *American Economic Review*, 70(4) (September).

Gros, D. and Hobza, A. (2001), 'Fiscal policy spillovers in the euro area: where are they?', CEPS Working Document, no. 176, November.

Habermas, J. (2001), *The Postnational Constellation: Political Essays*, Oxford: Polity Press.

Hamilton, A., Jay, J. and Madison, J. (2001), *The Federalist Papers*, Indianapolis: Liberty Fund.

Hardin, G. (1968), 'The tragedy of the commons', *Science*, New Series, 162(3859): 1243–8.

Jaquet, P. and Pisani-Ferri, J. (2001), 'Economic policy coordination in the eurozone: what has been achieved? What should be done?' Sussex European Institute Working Paper, no. 40.

Kok, W. (2004), *Facing the Challenge: the Lisbon Strategy for Growth and Employment*; European Communities (http://europa.eu.int/comm/lisbon_strategy/index_en.html).

Kulahci, E. (2002), 'Theorizing party interaction within EPFs and their effects on the EU policy-making process', *European Integration On-line Papers*, 6(16) (http://eiop.or.at/texte/2002-016a.htm).

Moravcsik, A. (2002), 'In defence of the "democratic deficit": reassessing legitimacy in the European Union', *Journal of Common Market Studies*, 40(4): 603–24.

Olson, M. (1971), *The Logic of Collective Action: Public Goods and the Theory of Groups*, Cambridge, MA: Harvard University Press.

Putnam, R. (1988), 'Diplomacy and domestic politics: the logic of two-level games', *International Organisation* (Summer): 427–61.

Rhodes, R. A. W. (1996), 'The new governance: governing without government', *Political Studies*, 44(3): 652–67.

Rosenau, J. N. (1992), 'Governance, order and change in world politics', in J. N. Rosenau and E. O. Czempiel (eds), *Governance without Government: Order and Change in World Politics*, Cambridge: Cambridge University Press.

Talani, L. S. (2004), *European Political Economy: Political Science Perspectives*, Aldershot: Ashgate.

Verhofstadt, G. (2006), *The United States of Europe*, London: The Federal Trust.

Woodward, B. (2000), *Maestro: Greenspan's Fed and the American Boom*, New York: Simon and Schuster.

Conclusion: the Future of EMU

Leila Simona Talani

The main question this book has sought to answer is whether EMU can lead to the creation of a European supranational community or whether it is likely to collapse and thereby trigger the disruption of the EU project as a whole. The contributors to this volume have adopted various positions with respect to this question. Many chapters sketch scenarios for the future of EMU that are at odds with the conventional wisdom concerning the future trajectory of the euro-zone.

Asserting that the euro-system suffers from a serious problem of governance, De Grauwe (Chapter 1) foresees only two options: either a move forward to full political union in the EU, or the collapse of EMU which might provoke a more general crisis for the EU project as a whole. De Grauwe argues that tensions are bound to arise in the institutional, political and socio-economic spheres. At the institutional level, the discrepancy between the macroeconomic decisions taken by European institutions lacking political legitimacy and fully accountable national governments will produce an inevitable struggle between the member states and EU institutions. The suspension of the Stability and Growth Pact in 2003 was the first manifestation of this type of struggle. At the political level the lack of a redistributive mechanism between different euro-zone members will produce contradictory preferences in the event of asymmetric shocks and therefore trigger growing conflicts among the member states and a relaxation of the commitment to the EMU and to the EU. Finally, in the socio-economic context the absence of a common approach to social policy in general – and wage setting in particular – will widen the competitiveness gap among the member states, with the potential for great social and political instability within and among the member states.

The only solution is the construction of a deeper political union resting on three pillars: a strict system of accountability for the

European institutions responsible for the implementation of monetary and macroeconomic policy-making; a common budget to address the redistributive issues arising from asymmetric shocks; and the adoption of common EU approaches to social and structural policies. However, De Grauwe believes that the prospects for such a union are bleak and that therefore the future of the EMU and the EU are at best very uncertain.

Even worse is the scenario depicted by Collignon (Chapter 8). The failure to address the democratic deficit of the EU will lead to a profound malaise and, in his words 'the European Union will die a slow death by gridlock, economic stagnation and unkept promises' (p. 188). It is not possible to exclude an even more violent outcome of this situation if right-wing parties come into power. The alternative for Collignon is the creation of a democratic system, a 'European Republic', 'The United States of Europe', the supranational political community that neo-functionalists devised as the final outcome of the process of integration so many years ago. However, the likelihood of such a step being taken by the EU nation-states is low. Therefore, popular mobilization in favour of a more democratic EU provides the only feasible solution to the looming crisis.

That asymmetric shocks can happen and produce negative consequences on the EMU is confirmed by the analysis of Artis (Chapter 3). The object of his study was to see whether measures of business cycle synchronization or coherence support the view that there is a 'European business cycle' and, therefore, that asymmetric shocks are less and less likely to happen in the euro-zone. The results obtained seem to deny the occurrence of persistent business cycle groupings. In particular there does not seem to be a 'European' grouping. On the contrary, a distinct 'globalization effect' is overcoming the emergence of a 'Europeanization' process, with important implications for the reduction of economic convergence between the EU/EMU countries. The institutional consequences of such a discovery are not addressed by the author but seem rather evident and point again towards the need to increase political cohesiveness to avoid significant levels of political and economic instability. This is explicitly claimed by Torres (Chapter 4) when he underlines that asymmetric shocks may lead to disagreements over the EMU's macroeconomic framework and result in a change in commitments and policies.

The sustainability of monetary unions presupposes a certain degree of member state homogeneity, not only in economic terms, but also in terms of further political integration. Only if there is a political union will countries be able to endure the costs associated with pooling monetary policy together and resist the temptation to secede.

Verde (Chapter 6) adds that 'solidarity' is necessary if the old EMU member states are to close the gap between the costs and the benefits of belonging to a monetary union and avoid the prospect of a 'two-speed' EU as a consequence of enlargement. From his point of view the biggest threat to the cohesion of the euro-zone is indeed the opening of the EMU to new accession countries. After the enlargement a 'two-speed' EU will become a realistic prospect, as old member states fear migration from the new countries as well as the loss of competitiveness associated with lower wages and more relaxed social policies. Without solidarity, this outcome would be unavoidable, as extending EMU to 27 countries would push old states back to the previous (pre-enlargement) equilibrium and pave the way for a two-speed Union.

In Jones's opinion (Chapter 2) the challenge in Europe is to get the right balance between unity and diversity, solidarity and independence. His assessment of the EMU is more optimistic. Fixed exchange rates will help to achieve such a result, not so much because of the political symbolism of a common currency but because exchange rates were not floating freely in any event and they were imparting too many different shocks to different parts of the European economy. The common monetary policy is only a partial success, but it is a success and, although some measures to increase cohesion can be devised, this does not mean that there is a need for the adoption of a common budget with all that it means in terms of political integration. In the words of the author: 'the need to organize some sort of European fiscal stabilization in response to asymmetric shocks is a myth' (p. 51).

Fazio (Chapter 5) also stresses that the introduction of the European single currency represents an epochal event not only for its members, but also for neighbouring areas like the MENA region. Further trade integration is important to build peace and shared prosperity in the Euro-Mediterranean region.

Finally, according to Talani (Chapter 7), despite the recent crisis of the Stability and Growth Pact and the struggles over structural reforms, the future of EMU and of the EU is not at risk. Indeed, its sustainability at the political economy, structural level, is based on the consensus of the leading socio-economic actors in the euro member states, particularly Germany and France. These actors still support the set of anti-inflationary and supply-side policies which formed the basis for the consensus on the establishment of EMU. Similar policies are also vital to guarantee the competitiveness of the German and French manufacturing sectors. Indeed, it was precisely because the SGP had turned into an obstacle for the implementation of those same policies, that its stricter constraints were abandoned for the time being by Germany and France with the full support of their socio-economic constituencies. However, according to Talani the future of EMU has not been jeopardized by the latest developments of the SGP and the future of the EU is safe.

Index

NB: page numbers in **bold** refer to figures and tables